Chess Training for Budding Champions

Jesper Hall

Illustrations by Peter Jönsson

First published in the UK by Gambit Publications Ltd 2001

ISBN 1 901983 47 1

DISTRIBUTION:
Worldwide (except USA): Central Books Ltd, 99 Wallis Rd, London E9 5LN.
Tel +44 (0)20 8986 4854 Fax +44 (0)20 8533 5821. E-mail: orders@Centralbooks.com
USA: BHB International, Inc., 41 Monroe Turnpike, Trumbull, CT 06611, USA.

For all other enquiries (including a full list of all Gambit Chess titles) please contact the publishers, Gambit Publications Ltd, P.O. Box 32640, London W14 0JN.
E-mail Murray@gambitchess.freeserve.co.uk
Or visit the GAMBIT web site at http://www.gambitbooks.com

Edited by Graham Burgess and Helen Milligan
Typeset by Petra Nunn
Printed in Great Britain by The Cromwell Press, Wiltshire.

10 9 8 7 6 5 4 3 2 1

Gambit Publications Ltd
Managing Director: GM Murray Chandler
Chess Director: GM John Nunn
Editorial Director: FM Graham Burgess
German Editor: WFM Petra Nunn

Contents

Symbols

+	check
++	double check
#	checkmate
!!	brilliant move
!	good move
!?	interesting move
?!	dubious move
?	bad move
??	blunder
Ch	championship
1-0	the game ends in a win for White
½-½	the game ends in a draw
0-1	the game ends in a win for Black
(D)	see next diagram

Preface

When I was thirteen years old, Caspar Carleson called me and asked if I wanted to train with him. Carleson was by then the strongest player in my hometown Lund, with an Elo rating of about 2350. I agreed immediately. Once a week I went to his small student apartment and experienced for the first time how chess could be practised systematically. I was an untrained hacker with great gaps in my positional play, so Carleson had to roll up his sleeves and start with Rubinstein's instructive manoeuvres.

In addition to our training sessions, Carleson worked out what I needed to improve and gave tips on good books to read. The training was crucial for my development, and the most important reason for this was the element of structure. Beyond the beginner's level, I did not receive any proper help on how to train or advice on literature to read. Instead it was up to me to search, a search that wore on my motivation. Moreover, the few books I found lacked concrete advice about how to proceed with actual training.

Today, almost twenty years later, when I myself work as a trainer, I notice that plenty of chess-players still struggle with the same problems. It is just as frustrating to train someone who is not motivated as it is to meet someone with a burning interest who does not receive any proper training. With this as a background, I have tried to write an introductory book on how to train for those who have climbed above the beginner's level in chess – a book that offers advice first of all to players, but also to trainers of various playing strengths, which you can come back to when you need help at various stages of your career.

The book is best read chapter-by-chapter first, so that you get a grip on my perspective on training. You may then return to areas of specific interest. At the end of every chapter I give suggestions of various ways to train and advice on literature for further study. It is hard to say where the lower rating limit is for this book, but my ambition has been to provide something of interest to all players over 1600 standard. The book is structured so that it can easily be used in a series of training sessions. In that case, I recommend that the trainer should read the last chapter first.

The suggestions in the book of how to train have my own experiences as a starting point. With this I want to emphasize that the book should not be seen as a fixed formula. Instead, everyone must find his own method of training so that the impelling drive to play does not get lost. Maybe this insight sprang from what Grandmaster Tiger Hillarp Persson said when I told him that I wanted to write a guide to training: "Do not forget that the most important task for a trainer or a writer is to convey his own love for the game." The point is that you can never train on behalf of someone else; the students or readers must do the work for themselves and so discover their own reasons to love chess.

1   Grains of Gold Glitter Even in Darkness

On chess and inspiration

When I was seven years old I bought a white sealing-waxed writing book with Charlie Chaplin on the front.

Why Do We Play Chess?

The absolutely most important thing concerning training is to have fun. In the play of a child there is the joy that makes us develop and become better. Even when your ambitions have become greater and the training has become methodical, you have to stay in touch with what once made you start playing.

"It is not fun to play chess; it is fun to *win*!", International Master Stellan Brynell says with a smile on his face, refuting my theories. What he means is that the impelling reasons why he plays chess are his winning instinct and the pleasure of signing a scoresheet 1-0 after a game. This is an attitude that most strong players have.

The poet and chess-player Christer Niklasson is also an IM, but has a more philosophical approach to chess. Chess for him is more like a metaphor for life, but with a board that provides a more distinct framework. His fascination lies therefore in how to coordinate the pieces, seeing patterns and possibilities that together shape an inner world to be absorbed in. Maybe that is why Niklasson mainly enjoys chess in its analytical form, not as a game.

Personally I am somewhere in-between. I like the adrenaline kick that an exciting game can give, but a study where the pieces produce a magical dance can also captivate me.

Whatever the source of our motivation, it is essential to keep it alive and to recall it even when darkness shadows the board and we do not want to look at the dead pieces of wood.

A Personal Odyssey

When I was seven years old I bought a white sealing-waxed writing book with Charlie Chaplin on the front. When I open up the first page I see written in an unsteady hand: "My first game – 1 e4 e5 2 ♕h5." When I see this I recall that I first learned the basic mate, 1 e4 e5 2 ♗c4 ♘c6 3 ♕h5 ♘f6 4 ♕xf7#, but as Black learned the defence 3...g6 I had to learn new tricks. The game continued 2...♘h6 (the main point is of course that if 2...g6, then 3 ♕xe5+ wins the rook) 3 ♕xe5+ ♗e7. Now I did not dare to grab the g7-pawn as it looked too risky, even though you can all see that it would have won a piece. Instead I retreated the queen and lost quickly.

On the next page of my writing book there is another game with a special background story that I still remember clearly. I was nine years old and about to play one of my club's strongest juniors in a blitz game. He did not look especially inspired and snorted when he saw how small I was. What he did not know was that my trainer had taught me a new opening trick the week before.

NN – Jesper Hall
Norrköping 1980

1 e4 e5 2 ♘f3 ♘c6 3 ♗c4 ♘d4
My opponent looked up quickly, smiled, and played...
4 ♘xe5 ♕g5
Now the smile became almost a laugh as he saw how he could fork my queen and rook with his next move.

5 ♘xf7 ♕xg2
With some distress, he played...
6 ♖f1
Then his cheeks turned red as the finish was...
6...♕xe4+ 7 ♗e2 ♘f3# (0-1)
I remember how my opponent angrily reset the pieces, leaned forward and whispered "After the tournament we shall play ten blitz games to see who is really the best." I lost 10-0, but had a memory for life.

To play chess is something very personal. Everyone has his own moments of happiness, moments that must not be forgotten. My first piece of advice to any player is therefore to keep a little book, or as I do today, open a file in the computer, where personal experiences can be saved.

My little writing book continues with the following story. I developed an understanding that there were tricks in all parts of chess, and a love of endgame studies started to grow. With determined steps, I walked towards my chess idols at the time, three older juniors at my club (Hans Jonsson, Per Thorén and Niklas Ottenklev), and calmly set up this position.

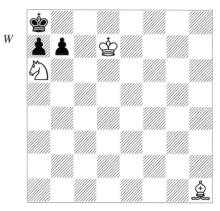

A little bit provocatively, I said "I have heard that there is mate in three here." With quite some effort three brains worked out the solution: **1 ♗c6 bxc6 2 ♔c8 c5 3 ♘c7#**. But before they in triumph delivered the final knight move, I said with a theatrical apology "Sorry, it is supposed be reversed", and presented the following parallel study.

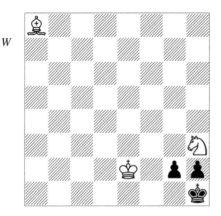

Again they found the solution after a while: **1 ♔f3 g1♕ 2 ♘f2+ ♕xf2+ 3 ♔xf2#**. Then it was the next person's turn to show a piece of chess magic.

Some experiences at the board have such importance that you can trace your whole career from a particular moment: a game, a combination, or an achievement. One day as I turned the pages in the *Anthology of Chess Combinations* (Šahovski Informator, 1995), I found this position (*see following diagram*):

1...♕h3!

There are other ways to win, but the queen sacrifice is the most aesthetically pleasing.

0-1

White resigned due to 2 gxh3 ♗f3 3 ♗d7 ♔xd7 with mate next move by ...♘xh3#.

Calle Erlandsson, who is the president of my club LASK (Lunds Akademiska Schack-klubb), told me that what I have just witnessed is the reason why he has spent so much time

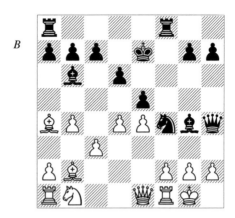

Lars-Gunnar Larsson – Calle Erlandsson
Correspondence game 1966

on correspondence chess through the years. The diagram is from the first game that he played and it is often included in books of combinations – a grain of gold that still glitters.

As with all aestheticism there is something personal about a beautiful game. The first time I saw the following position I got goosebumps on my arm as the final combination appeared on my inner board.

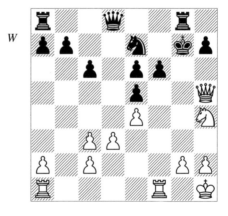

José Raúl Capablanca – Herman Steiner
Exhibition game, Los Angeles 1933

17 ♖xf6! ♔xf6 18 ♖f1+ ♘f5

18...♔g7 loses after 19 ♖f7+ ♔h8 20 ♕xh7#.

19 ♘xf5! exf5 20 ♖xf5+ ♔e7 21 ♕f7+ ♔d6 22 ♖f6+ ♔c5

22...♕xf6 is the best try, but gives Black a hopeless position after 23 ♕xf6+ ♔d7 24 ♕f7+ ♔d6 25 ♕xh7, when White has a decisive material advantage.

23 ♕xb7 ♕b6 24 ♖xc6+ ♕xc6 25 ♕b4# (1-0)

It is not only combinations and studies that make me shudder with delight. I have already declared my appreciation for Capablanca's immortal combination, but I also want to present another position that gave me as much joy.

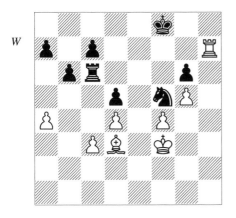

**José Raúl Capablanca –
Savielly Tartakower**
New York 1924

34 ♗xf5!

At first glance it appears that White has some problems, since his c3-pawn will be lost. However, in a rook ending, activity is paramount, and with this in mind White exchanges off the minor pieces.

34...gxf5 35 ♔g3!

The point of White's play is that a rook on the seventh rank, an active king and a passed pawn, all working in harmony, are more significant than Black's extra pawns on the queenside.

35...♖xc3+ 36 ♔h4 ♖f3

After 36...♖c1 37 ♔h5 White's king can creep in around its g-pawn. If Black plays 37...♖h1+ 38 ♔g6 ♖xh7 39 ♔xh7, then the g-pawn will promote.

37 g6 *(D)*

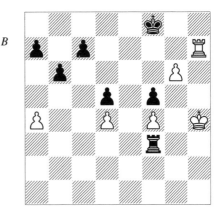

Opening a route for the king to its optimal square, f6, from where it will create mating threats.

37...♖xf4+ 38 ♔g5 ♖e4

After 38...♖d4 39 ♔f6 Black must give up his rook for the g-pawn in order to prevent mate.

39 ♔f6 ♔g8 40 ♖g7+ ♔h8 41 ♖xc7

White can win back the sacrificed material, while keeping all his positional advantages. Black's cause is hopeless.

41...♖e8 42 ♔xf5 ♖e4 43 ♔f6 ♖f4+ 44 ♔e5 ♖g4 45 g7+ ♔g8

After 45...♖xg7 46 ♖xg7 ♔xg7 47 ♔xd5 White can advance his d-pawn.

46 ♖xa7 ♖g1 47 ♔xd5 1-0

Exercises

Today, with my Chaplin book transformed into a computer file, it might be the following nuggets that I pick out to shine in the darkness when I have difficulties finding the motivation for chess. Try to find the best continuations yourself (solutions are given on pages 169-70).

My Favourite Combinations

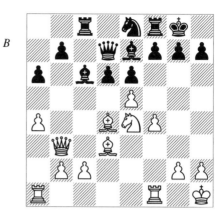

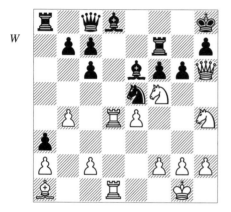

1)   Jesper Hall – Anders Kling
Swedish Ch, Norrköping 1988

White to play and win.

2)   Janis Klovans – Jesper Hall
2nd Bundesliga 1997/8

Black to play and win.

My Favourite Studies

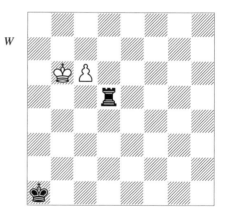

3)   Fernando Saavedra
(correcting Georges Barbier)
Glasgow Weekly Citizen, 1895

White to play and win.

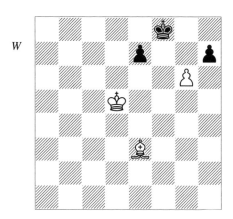

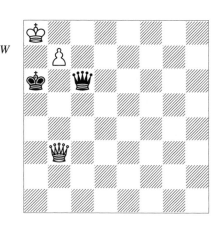

4)   **Aleksei Troitsky**
Novoe Vremia, 1895 (version, 1902)

White to play and win.

6)   **Louis van Vliet**
Deutsche Schachzeitung, 1888

White to play and win.

The Joy of Winning is the Same for Everyone

The source of motivation may be different, but I am sure that everyone enjoys winning an important game. In this respect there is no difference between a nine-year-old beginner and a mature international master. For me at least, the satisfaction was just as great in the following game as in the one at the beginning of this chapter.

Jesper Hall – Vladimir Chuchelov
2nd Bundesliga 1997/8

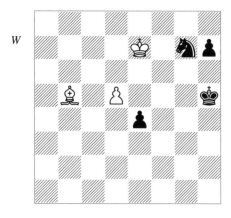

5)   **Ernest Pogosiants**
1st Pr. *Shakhmatnaya Moskva*, 1964

White to play and win.

This game was very important for two reasons. For the team, winning the division was at stake, and for me personally, my first grandmaster norm. If I won, I would have made the norm with a round to spare. During my preparation, I had found that Chuchelov played a home-made variation of the Kan

Sicilian. I thought that it looked dubious and wanted to give it a real test.

1 e4 c5 2 ♘f3 e6 3 d4 cxd4 4 ♘xd4 a6 5 ♗d3 ♘f6 6 ♘c3

I usually play 6 0-0 here to keep the possibility of c4, but I took a calculated risk. My psychological play in the opening meant that I was staring expressionlessly while begging inside "Please do not let him play another variation."

6...♕c7 7 f4 ♗b4?!

Chuchelov's patent.

8 ♗d2 d6 9 ♘b3!

It was a relief to be able to play this move, since my preparation had centred around it. Van der Plassche-Chuchelov, Belgian League 1996/7 went 9 ♕f3 ♘bd7 10 0-0 ♗c5 11 ♗e3 b5 and now White could not play 12 e5? because of 12...♗b7 13 exd6 ♕b6, winning, and so Black obtained a good game by playing ...♗b7 and ...0-0.

Players often choose to repeat a variation if they have won their last game with it, even if the variation itself is suspect. Because of that, it is often a good idea to search among your opponent's victories when you are trying to find improvements with which to surprise him.

9...♘bd7 10 a3 ♗xc3 11 ♗xc3 *(D)*

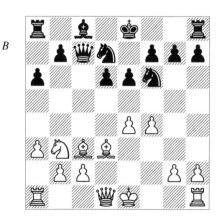

11...b6!?

Black already has problems. Where should the b-pawn be put? 11...b5 introduces new weaknesses on the queenside, of which White can take advantage by castling kingside and playing a4.

12 ♕e2

White prevents ...0-0-0 and prepares to play g4 and g5. Black's opening has given him a difficult game, while White has many attractive plans. He can either castle queenside and go for a pawn attack on the kingside, or vice versa.

12...♗b7 13 0-0-0 0-0 14 ♖he1!

There is no reason to play 14 g4, allowing 14...d5 15 e5 d4 16 ♗xd4 ♗xh1 17 exf6 ♕xf4+ 18 ♗e3 ♕f3, when Black seems to be OK.

14...♖fe8?!

The way the game develops, the rook has no function on e8. 14...♖fc8 is more logical.

15 g4 d5

Black is forced into a strategically worse position because of the threat of g5.

16 e5 ♘e4 17 ♗xe4 dxe4 *(D)*

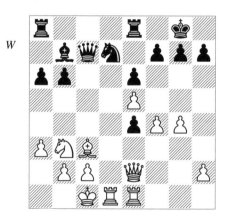

18 ♗b4!

In instructional chess books you often see games where one player shapes a plan right at the beginning that gives a straightforward victory. A good opponent puts up more resistance and disturbs the weave of the pattern you have chosen. It is then important to rethink and find a new plan that fits the position. Here I change focus from the kingside to the queenside, the d-file and especially the e4-pawn.

18...罝ac8 19 奧d6 圉c6 20 曾b1!

I wanted to play ♘d4 and 圉f2 without letting the black queen go to c4 and a2. With the king now on b1, the queen risks being trapped by b3 and 罝e3 if it goes to c4. Black also has problems because of his lack of coordination. The bishop is cut off by the e4-pawn and the best square for the knight would be d5, but this is unattainable. Therefore it is hard to find moves, because if the knight goes to c5 it will be exchanged for the white bishop. Then White has a pleasant choice between grabbing the e4-pawn or trying to penetrate on the d-file with the heavy artillery.

20...a5 21 ♘d4 圉c4 22 圉xc4!? 罝xc4 23 ♘b5! *(D)*

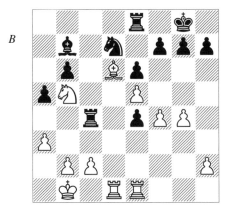

B

23...e3

Chuchelov thought for a long time before he made this desperate move. But what should he do? 23...罝ec8 is completely hopeless in view of 24 奧e7 奧d5 25 ♘d6 罝xc2 26 ♘xc8 罝xc8 27 罝c1, when White's rooks decide, while after 23...罝c6 24 ♘a7 罝c4 25 罝e3 it is not possible to defend against the threat of b3 winning an exchange.

24 奧c7! 罝xf4 25 罝xd7 e2

Chuchelov's last hope is the e-pawn. On 25...奧c6 there follows 26 罝d4, when White is winning.

26 罝d2!

If 26 罝xe2? then 26...奧c6 27 罝d4 罝f1+ is the problem.

26...奧a6 27 c4!?

White can win in many ways, such as 27 a4 or 27 ♘d6, but I saw that the e2-pawn would fall after the text-move.

27...罝c8 28 奧xb6 罝fxc4 29 ♘c3 a4 30 h3!

This safety move kills all Black's chances. The rest is technique, but it is instructive to see how well knight and bishop cooperate when there are opposite-coloured bishops.

30...h5 31 gxh5 罝f4 32 ♘xe2 罝e4 33 奧f2 罝xe5 34 ♘g3 罝xe1+ 35 奧xe1 f5 36 罝d6 奧c4 37 奧c3 罝c7 38 曾c1 曾h7 39 曾d2 f4 40 ♘e4 曾h6 41 奧e5 罝f7 42 罝d4 1-0

My Training Tips

My basic philosophy is that you train best when you enjoy yourself and are motivated. Consequently, you should not forget to enjoy chess even when your training is methodically structured. One way to reinforce your enjoyment of chess is to create a book or a database where you collect together your best games and combinations, together with any other chess gems that you are especially fond of.

If you are a trainer, give examples from your own games to demonstrate what chess means to you. Beauty is as personal as the source of motivation and students sense if you are involved in what you teach.

Let the students make their own books of their best games, where they write down or paste in their favourite combinations or something else that they find beautiful. For younger children, you can make a book for the entire group to keep at the club.

Always commend the students when they have done something good. Show the best of the students' games to the group and make a pamphlet of the group's best combinations. Help the students to annotate their own games and send them to newspapers and magazines. Seeing one's name and creative achievement in print can provide a great source of motivation.

Suggestions for Further Reading

Two books that inspire me more than others to play chess are *Kurzgeschichten um Schackfiguren* by Kurt Richter (1947). Here the beauty of chess is mixed with small poems, anecdotes and life's wisdom in a stimulating way. The first time I read it I was ten years old. Since then it has been placed on my bedside table.

A History of Chess by Jerzy Gizycki (1977) is a book that convinces me that all the time I have spent on chess has not been devoted just to a simple game. The book is about chess as a phenomenon in many different ways: its history, its occurrence in poetry and movies, its position as a metaphor for life. Fantastic pictures illustrate everything.

In terms of literature I can recommend *The Flanders Panel* by Arturo Pérez-Reverte (various editions). It is a detective story where chess is woven into the excitement in a skilful way, as opposed to most books in the genre that involve pieces set up wrongly and banal metaphors.

There are also other novels involving chess that are worth reading. The most famous is probably Nabokov's *The Luzhin Defence* (Penguin, 2000), which is also excellent.

On the subject of detective stories, I would like to mention a book that recently caught my attention: *The Chess Mysteries of Sherlock Holmes* by Raymond Smullyan (Times Books, 1979). This is a book of chess problems where the reader, like Sherlock Holmes, must discover what moves have been played in order to solve the problems. You gain new perspectives even though it is hard to think backwards.

In terms of studies, I very much like *Karpov's Endgame Arsenal* by Anatoly Karpov and Evgeny Gik (R&D Publishing, 1996). The book contains several endgame studies that by their simplicity increase my pleasure.

Finally, I should mention the practically oriented *Chess for Tigers* by Simon Webb (second edition, Maxwell Macmillan, 1990). To me, this book demonstrates that a book on chess can be both instructive and entertaining.

2 I Am Lucky to Have Made So Many Mistakes

On analysing your own games

In your own games you have all that you need to train with.

In Your Own Games There is Everything You Need to Improve

I look down into the shoebox that is filled with wrinkled scoresheets from twenty years of playing. I have just visited IM Johan Hellsten who told me that his only training in the last ten years has been to analyse all the games that he has played and to store them in his computer. "In your own games you have all that you need to train with," he explains.

Whew, what a job. I start with the games from 1986. After putting six games into the database, I start to think. I notice that it is the same type of mistake that I made in both the games I lost. It seems as if I had a tendency to overestimate my own attack and underestimate my opponent's. There was only one month between the two games and yet I do not seem to have given the mistakes of the first game a single thought; that is why I went down again to a similar blow. I shake my head and think about the proverb "A wise man is one who has learned from his mistakes." I threw the box into the wardrobe. I think to myself that I will give it another go tomorrow, and I open a different database in the computer. Here I have started to analyse my later games and I find, embarrassingly enough, a more or less direct parallel to the games in the shoebox.

Jesper Hall – Thomas Ernst
Swedish Ch, Ronneby 1998

1 d4

Ernst is known to be a strong theoretician who has slain many victims with the Dragon Variation of the Sicilian. In my preparation I saw that Ernst more or less always played 1...♘f6 against 1 d4. I had then planned the unorthodox Trompowsky Attack, 2 ♗g5. Ernst's hand was moving towards the knight, but suddenly it froze. Ernst looked up and played a confident...

1...d5

Hmm, what now? You probably won't believe me, but I had absolutely no idea what to do against 1...d5. I had never opened a theory book on the subject, and had never played it either, since I only play 1 d4 (intending the Trompowsky) when I am absolutely sure that my opponent will play 1...♘f6. Improvisation from move two, here we go. I wonder what the audience thought as an international master competing for the Swedish national title started to think for fifteen minutes on move two in one of the most common positions in the history of chess...

2 c4 c6 3 ♘c3 ♘f6 4 ♗g5

A rare move in this position, but I thought it looked playable and I wanted to get away from theory as soon as possible.

4...dxc4

This is considered best, though 4...♘e4 5 ♘xe4 dxe4 6 ♕d2 ♗f5 7 e3 ♘d7 also gives Black a playable game.

5 a4 ♕a5

5...♘a6 6 e4 ♘b4 7 ♘f3 ♗g4 8 e5 ♗xf3 9 gxf3 ♘fd5, with an equal game, is another possibility.

6 ♗d2 (D)

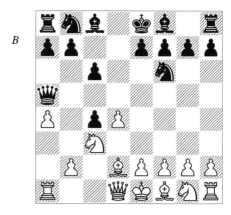

6...♕b6?!

Ernst could probably sense that I was on new ground, as I had already used loads of time, and he chose to go for a pawn. Instead he could have had a good game with 6...e5; for example, 7 e3 (7 dxe5 ♕xe5 8 ♘f3 ♕c5 9 e4 ♘g4 10 ♕e2 ♘a6 11 h3 ♘b4 12 hxg4 ♘d3+ 13 ♔d1 ♘xf2+ 14 ♔c2 ♘xh1 and Black is winning) 7...exd4 8 exd4 ♗e6 and it is not easy for White to get the pawn back. In the game, White's pieces will come to life, as the black queen has to sacrifice some tempi getting back.

7 e3 ♕xb2

White also has compensation after 7...♗f5 8 ♗xc4 ♕xb2 9 ♗b3 ♘e4 10 ♘xe4 ♗xe4 11 ♘f3 e6 12 0-0, when Black is forced to play 12...♗d5 to save the queen. After 13 ♗xd5 cxd5 14 ♖b1 ♕a2 15 ♖xb7 White is better.

8 ℤb1 ♕a3 9 ♗xc4 e6 10 e4 ♕d6

Black has to take care. After 10...♗e7? 11 e5 ♘d5 12 ♗xd5 cxd5 13 ℤb3 the black queen is trapped. Therefore Black must retreat his queen and his development is further delayed.

11 ♘f3

Not 11 e5? ♕xd4, when the c4-bishop is hanging.

11...♕c7 12 0-0 ♗e7

I have now got all my pieces on good squares and it is time to form a plan. Black has to castle kingside and as I have a lead in development I can try to transform my advantage into an attack on his king. I will therefore put queen and bishop on the b1-h7 diagonal in order to create dangerous threats when e5 is played. Black will be forced to defend with a knight on f8 or by making moves with the pawns in front of his king, creating new weaknesses that I can try to exploit.

13 ♕e2 0-0 14 ♗d3 ♘bd7 15 e5 ♘d5 16 ♘e4 h6?!

The position is already becoming critical. A small mistake from Black can have drastic consequences. White wants to proceed with ♗g5 or ♘eg5, forcing new black weaknesses. The question is what weakness to chose. 16...f5!? 17 exf6 gxf6 18 ♘c3 ℤf7 19 ♘xd5 exd5 20 ♘h4 gives White a dangerous initiative, but I think it would have been preferable to the game continuation.

17 ♘g3 f5 18 exf6 ♘7xf6

With 16...h6, the possibility of taking back with the pawn disappeared. White has therefore won control of the b1-h7 diagonal and has weaknesses on e6, h6 and g7 to harass. The next few steps are easy. All the pieces must join the attack and seek out their ideal squares.

19 ♘e5 ♗d6 20 ℤfe1 c5 21 ℤbc1 b6 22 ♗b1 ♗b7 23 ♕d3 ℤae8 24 ♘h5 ℤe7 25 ♕g6 ♔h8 26 ♕d3 ♔g8

Suddenly the manoeuvring is over. It is time to calculate exactly in order to find the correct continuation. This is a critical moment in the game. Black can only hope for a repetition of moves as the fork on g6 is devastating if the king is on h8, and ...♔h8 is the only move to avoid the threat of ♗xh6 when the white queen is on g6.

27 ♕g6 ♔h8 *(D)*

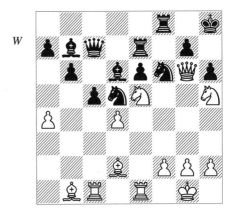

My intuition told me that White was winning. There just has to be a decisive continuation if you consider how active my pieces are and how weak Black's king-position is. The clock was ticking alongside my more and more desperate calculation and soon I had only three minutes left. My frustration grew and although I could not judge what was happening, I decided to throw the game into chaos, leading to a difficult ending.

28 ♗xh6?!

If I had taken a step back and thought about what Black could do I would have realized that it is difficult for him to find a constructive move. The only active possibility is to play ...♗c6 to try to reach e8, but then I can take on c6 followed by a capture on e6 with my rook. In analysis afterwards with Ernst I found 28 ♔h1, when after 28...a6 29

♕c2 ♔g8 30 ♘xf6+ ♘xf6 31 ♘g6 White wins the exchange with advantage. Observe that without ♔h1 Black would have had ...♗xh2+. That is the secret behind the king move. If Black tries to get his queen to e8 by playing 28...♕b8, the sacrifice on h6 works fine. However, there is also another more surprising continuation for White found by IM Ari Ziegler, the editor of the tournament bulletin: 28 ♘g4! ♘f4 29 ♗xf4 ♗xf4. I had also seen this far, but could not find any good way to continue. Ziegler's small electronic friend suggested 30 dxc5!. The idea is that White's minor pieces are as good as Black's rooks. Therefore White can give up the exchange with the hope of repayment when the attack breaks through; for example, 30...♗xc1? 31 ♖xc1 bxc5 32 ♘hxf6 gxf6 33 ♕xh6+ ♔g8 34 ♘xf6+ ♖xf6 (34...♔f7 35 ♕g6#) 35 ♕xf6 and White is winning.

28...gxh6 29 ♕xh6+ ♖h7

29...♔g8!? also seems to give Black the better chances after 30 ♕g6+ ♖g7 31 ♘xg7 ♕xg7 32 ♕xg7+ ♔xg7 33 dxc5 ♗xc5 34 ♘d3 ♗a3 35 ♖c4 ♖c8 36 ♖xc8 ♗xc8, when he has two pieces for a rook and two pawns, but far better coordination.

30 ♗xh7 ♕xh7 31 ♘g6+ ♔g8 32 ♕xh7+ ♘xh7 33 ♘xf8 ♘xf8 34 dxc5 bxc5 *(D)*

The game has reached a very interesting and unusual endgame. White has a nominal material advantage, but three minor pieces are often more efficient than two rooks. As Black also has a passed pawn on c5, I should have felt that Black had the easier game. However, in my eagerness to justify the feeling I had, I wanted so much for the endgame to be better for White that I lost my objectivity. I had planned to double my rooks on the c-file and sacrifice a rook for a piece and the pawn. I would then have had an advantage. With little time to think, this seemed possible to do, but I soon realized that my rooks

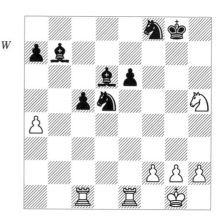

had been transformed into supernumeraries as the black bishops started to slice up the board.

35 ♘g3 ♘f6 36 f3 ♔f7 37 ♘e4 ♘xe4 38 fxe4 ♘g6 39 ♖c3 ♗e5 40 ♖f3+

Maybe I should have taken a slightly worse endgame with 40 ♖ec1 ♗xc3 41 ♖xc3 ♗xe4 42 ♖xc5, even though I would have had one pawn fewer than I had intended.

40...♔g7 41 ♖b3 ♗c6 42 ♔f2 ♗d4+ 43 ♔f3 c4 44 ♖a3 ♘e5+ 45 ♔e2 ♗xe4

The time-control was reached at move 40 and I started to become aware of how bad my position was. Since the e4-pawn has disappeared and Black is now well centralized, I started to realize my last hope lay in my only remaining plus – the kingside pawns. But I was of course too far behind.

46 ♖g3+ ♔f6 47 ♖f1+ ♔e7 48 h4 c3?!

48...♗d3+ 49 ♖xd3 cxd3+ 50 ♔d2 ♗b6 51 h5 ♗a5+ 52 ♔e3 d2 53 ♔e2 ♘c4 54 h6 ♘b2 55 h7 ♗c3 56 h8♕ ♗xh8 57 ♔xd2 ♘xa4 and Black is winning.

49 h5 c2 50 h6 ♘c4?

50...♔d6 51 ♖h1 ♗b2 wins as the h-pawn cannot move.

51 ♖g4?

Unexpectedly, White has chances to save the game, but I was too angry with myself to find the best defence 51 ♖h1!, with variations like:

a) 51...♔d6 52 ♖g4 ♔d5 53 ♖gh4 ♗b2 54 h7 ♗xh7 55 ♖xh7 a5 56 ♖d7+ ♔c6 57 ♖d2 ♘xd2 58 ♔xd2 c1♕+ 59 ♖xc1+ ♗xc1+ 60 ♔xc1 with a drawn pawn endgame.

b) 51...♗b2 52 h7 ♗xh7 53 ♖xh7+ ♔d6 54 ♖h1 ♔d5 55 ♖d3+ ♔c5 56 ♖d2, and now:

b1) 56...c1♕? 57 ♖xc1 ♗xc1 58 ♖c2 ♗g5 59 ♔d3 and White is even winning.

b2) 56...♘xd2 57 ♔xd2 c1♕+ 58 ♖xc1+ ♗xc1+ 59 ♔xc1 ♔d4 60 ♔d2 a5 61 ♔e2 ♔e4 is a draw.

51...♘e3 52 ♖g7+ ♔d6 53 ♖c1 ♗b2 54 ♖xc2 ♘xc2 55 ♖xa7

Despite the fact that White has two passed pawns, one on each flank, Black is winning easily. The rook cannot help the pawns to advance and the wonderful bishops in the centre demonstrate yet again their strength when there is play on both flanks. White fights until the last pawn is lost.

55...♗xg2 56 ♖a6+ ♔e7 57 ♔d2 ♘a3 58 ♖a7+ ♔f6 59 h7 ♔g6 60 a5 ♗g7 61 ♖c7 ♔xh7 62 a6 ♔g6 63 ♖e7 ♔f6 64 ♖e8 ♘b5 65 ♖b8 ♘c7 66 a7 ♗d5 67 ♔d3 ♔e7 0-1

Jesper Hall – Norbert Sommerbauer
Olympiad, Elista 1998

Sweden was paired against Austria in an early round of the Olympiad, and on the third board I was due to face an experienced international master. When I play chess as a member of a team, I want to get a firm grip on events early on with White so that my teammates can feel that Jesper is a guy to trust. Now it was a variation of the Sicilian that spooked me again. There is just so much theory on that opening... However, the computer affirmed that Sommerbauer played 1...♘f6 against 1 d4 in a very high percentage of

games. The case was clear; soon the Austrian would be suffering in my home-woven net in the Trompowsky, I thought cautiously. You all understand what lay in the future. Did I prepare myself for what was about to happen, wise from the experiences of the game with Ernst some months earlier? Is it difficult to see the parallels between the situations and the naïve thoughts in my preparations?

1 d4

As the gong sounded to start the round, my opponent was not at his place. Fifteen minutes later, he walked rapidly towards my 1 d4, ripped off his coat, and threw in...

1...d5

Uh-oh! I realized that he had come straight from his preparation. My cheeks flushed and a weariness spread throughout my body. I got a feeling that all the participants of the Olympiad were looking at my game, and I seemed to hear a whisper from the corridor: "Look at that guy from Sweden. He has been thinking for ten minutes after 1 d4 d5. Is this opening forbidden in Sweden or something? Surely it cannot be that he does not know the theory?" I felt like I was encapsulated in a big bubble and became totally fixated with remembering the theory, instead of thinking for myself.

2 c4 e6 3 ♘c3 c5 4 e3

Despite his late arrival, my opponent already had more time than me. I now realized that I sometimes have to play this position with reversed colours when my invitation to the Benoni is rejected after 1 d4 ♘f6 2 c4 e6 3 ♘f3 c5 4 e3 d5. Normally there will be some kind of isolani structure, I recalled. A glimmer of hope: a position-type to go for where understanding structures and ideas is more important than preparation.

4...♘f6 5 ♘f3 ♘c6 6 a3 a6 7 dxc5 ♗xc5 8 b4 ♗a7 9 ♗b2 0-0 *(D)*

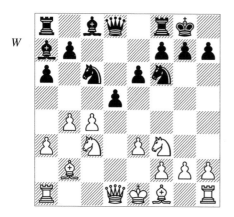

Up to this point I was pretty sure I was walking on known paths, but what now? The bishop and queen have to move out, of course, and then a rook to d1. But in what order? I just did not get it right. And what about the isolani structure? No, now you really have to pull yourself together, I thought, and quickly found an idea. I felt that it probably was not the recommendation of theory, but it seemed logical, given my desire to reach the isolani structure.

10 cxd5?!

10 &d3 (or 10 &e2) 10...♕e7 11 0-0 dxc4 12 &xc4 b5 13 &d3 &b7 leads to symmetrical positions that are approximately equal if Black knows how to play them.

10...exd5 11 b5

An isolani structure really has occurred. My idea, which I now put into effect, was that when Black took on b5, I would take back with the knight and get a firm grip of the key point d4. He would play ...&b6 and after &d3 he would reply ...&a5+ to hinder my development, but then my deep move ♔e2 with the idea of 'castling by hand' in three moves with ♖d1 and ♔f1 would come. Smart, logical and unusual. I felt as if I was on the right track and did not need to think so much now on each move.

11...axb5 12 ♘xb5 &b6 13 &d3

It was too late to change direction. For example, after 13 &e2? &a5+ 14 &c3 ♘e4 15 ♖c1 &xc3+ 16 ♘xc3 ♖xa3 17 ♘xd5? ♕a5+ 18 ♘d2 ♕xd5 Black wins a piece.

13...&a5+ 14 ♔e2 &g4 15 ♕b3 ♘e4

Black has developed his pieces to good squares. In an isolani structure the c4- and e4-squares are Black's key points as they are supported by the pawn. They can often be the springboards for an attack. However, I had my path clear ahead of me and moved quickly.

16 ♖hd1? *(D)*

16 h3 was absolutely essential, although it is not pleasant to have to weaken the future residence of one's king, and after 16...&h5 17 g4 &g6 Black has the better prospects.

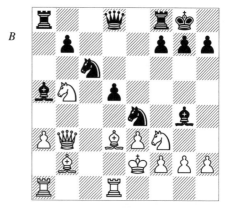

Now Black has a devastating move.

16...♕h4!

Just as my opponent grabbed his queen I understood where it was heading. The voice of the Swedish commentator from the match Sweden – Costa Rica in the 1990 Soccer World Cup started to ring in my ears. Sweden played miserably and lost the first two matches but miraculously had the chance to proceed if they could just beat the small country from Latin America. Sweden could still win the whole tournament, the newspapers screamed. As Costa Rica crushed Swedish pride by scoring 2-1 the commentator said "Good morning and good night" and I heard the voice keep on going: "In the match between Sweden and Austria the third board made a fool of himself after 16 moves, with White, and the rest of the heroic team did what they could but defeat was impossible to avoid." The only positive thing about the move was that it broke the spell. For the remainder of the game the only thing I could do was to make moves that did not lose immediately.

17 ♖f1

This is the only move, since 17 g3? ♕xh2 wins on the spot for Black.

17...♘d2 *(D)*

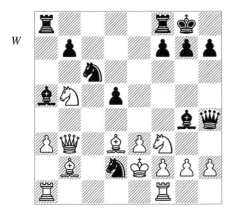

And here we have a fork on the queen and the rook. "This is not embarrassing; I am not afraid," I murmured to myself as I moved quickly without going too deeply into all the winning variations for my opponent.

18 ♕xd5 ♖ad8! 19 ♕c5 ♗xf3+ 20 gxf3 ♕h3!

Black will not let White get away with just the loss of an exchange. Instead he continues

the attack and waits for the right moment to grab material.

21 ♘c3 ♕xf3+?!

21...♘xf1! 22 ♖xf1 ♖xd3 wins a rook, and was the easiest way to finish the game.

22 ♔xd2 ♖d5 23 ♕c4 *(D)*

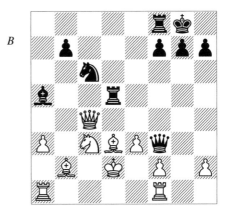

23...♖xd3+?

23...♘e5! is more or less a forced mate with 24 ♕f4 ♗xc3+ 25 ♗xc3 ♖xd3+ 26 ♔c2 ♕e2+ (the move Sommerbauer missed) 27 ♔b3 ♖xc3+ 28 ♗xc3 ♖c8+ 29 ♔b3 ♕c2+ 30 ♔b4 ♕b2+ 31 ♔a4 ♖a8#. This oversight also had unfortunate psychological consequences. Black played the rest of the game without enthusiasm, continuing to make small mistakes and grieving that he'd blown a nice winning game. On the contrary, White draws more hope and strength with each move.

24 ♕xd3 ♖d8 25 ♕xd8+ ♘xd8 26 ♖ad1 ♘e6 27 ♔c2

Black still has a clear advantage because White's king-position is weak and there is disharmony between White's pieces. Black's queen is good at f3, as it keeps White tied down. Sommerbauer therefore now advanced his h-pawn.

27...h5 28 ♔b1 h4 29 ♘d5 ♔h7 30 ♔a1 f6 31 ♖g1!

White's only chance is to go for a counter-attack against Black's king. I had to sacrifice some pawns for coordination among my pieces.

31...♘c5 32 ♘f4 *(D)*

32...♕xf2?

32...♗c7! still gave chances of obtaining the full point; for example, 33 ♖d5 ♘b3+ 34 ♔a2 ♗xf4 35 ♖d7 ♘c1+ 36 ♖xc1 ♗xh2 with a clear advantage for Black.

33 ♖g2!

White prepares to double the rooks on the g-file, which forces a repetition of moves.

33...♕xe3 34 ♖dg1 ♕xf4 35 ♖xg7+ ♔h6 36 ♖g8 ♔h7 37 ♖8g7+ ♔h6 38 ♖g8 ♔h7 39 ♖8g7+ ♔h6 40 ♖g8 ½-½

How Should You Analyse Your Games?

When you think about analysing your own games, it becomes clear how logical it is that this is the most important and natural way of training. You are personally involved, you have a deep understanding of the position as you have played the game yourself, you have

analysed it with your opponent afterwards and also gone through it a third time at home. This gives depth, but also an insight into the process of thinking during the playing situation. That insight is impossible to obtain when you study games by other players. I therefore recommend that you try to describe, with words, how you thought during the game, mixed with more objective analysis. Then it will be easier to see what you misjudged during the game. This is a perfect ground for your training as all aspects of chess are included, even your weaknesses. With the games as a starting point, you can plan your training and add the knowledge that you lack.

How thoroughly and well you analyse your games is correlated to ambition and time. GM Evgeny Agrest tells me that it takes him 12-14 hours to analyse a game if it is to be done properly. The best way is of course to keep going until you really feel finished, but if you do not have the time for that, I still think that there is a good plan to follow that makes the analysis methodical and effective. I used to compare it to what my mother says about ironing a shirt. You start with the collar and the cuffs, because these are the parts that catch the eye. If you do not have the time to finish the ironing, you have done the most important work. Just like analysing a game. This means that you should start by trying to find the critical position, the point where the course of the game turned and the mistakes were made. Was there a tactical oversight, a positional misjudgement, overconfidence in your own attack, a bad opening, or a lack of understanding in the ending?

After that I try, being as open-minded and creative as possible, to find improvements so that I will not make the same mistake next time the position arises. Then I analyse the other parts of the game, which are often easier to understand and explain once you know the turning points. I usually also put some extra time into the opening, as it is the first note struck which determines the course of the game. Who wants to start a journey with the wind against him from move one, as I started my games above? Again it is important to realize where the opening went wrong and where the mistakes were made that gave someone a grip on the game. I therefore add the recommendations of opening theory and try to find improvements.

In my own notes I made the following conclusions for the future:

- I shall analyse all my games as much as I can, so that I do not make the same mistake twice.
- I shall study variations and opening ideas after 1 d4 d5.
- I shall work on prophylactic and preparatory moves.
- I shall practise combinations and endgames.

A Scheme for Analysing Your Games

- Identify the critical moments.
- Think of the reasons for the mistakes.
- Try to find new possibilities and spot new critical moments.
- Draw your conclusions from the points above, so that you will not make the same mistake again in the future.
- If you realize that your knowledge of chess has defects, think of what you can do about it.
- Put some extra time into the opening.
- Do not use the computer until you have analysed the position thoroughly unaided.

To analyse is an important opportunity to practise. At the board you are not allowed to have a computer, so do not get used to having it as your partner at home.

Common Mistakes in Analysis

- You do not have the motivation to work at the position until there is nothing left to be unsure about.
- You justify your play and miss the possibilities that your opponent has to put up better resistance.
- You leave out unclear variations that you are not sure about when you annotate the game or show it to your friends, as you want to show off.
- You try to steer the analysis to make the result logical and therefore you miss possibilities.

My Training Tips

Try to make analysing your own games a routine. Even if you just manage the first steps in the analysing scheme it is worth a lot. Also think about the kinds of commentaries in books and magazines that help you develop your understanding. This gives you clues as to how you could find your way into the secrets of a game.

If you are a trainer, have your starting point in your own games when you teach. Explain how you have understood a weakness in your play and how you are going to get rid of it. Also, encourage your pupils to work on their own games by analysing together with them at tournaments, arranging analysis nights at the club or giving a prize to the student who has carried out the best analysis of his game.

Suggestions for Further Reading

Learn from the masters. There are a lot of nice collections of games where strong players analyse their own games. Your personality and playing style determines what attracts you most. A classic in this field is *Zurich International Chess Tournament 1953* by David Bronstein (Dover, 1979). The great value of this book is that the plans and ideas are described primarily in words. By almost philosophical arguments, Bronstein succeeds in finding a way into the core of each position and explains the strategy of getting there. I recommend it warmly.

Another fascinating book, but with a completely different angle on the game, is *My 60 Memorable Games* by Bobby Fischer (various editions). The games are interwoven with variation after variation, which can easily terrify a beginner, but which can be read as an example of Fischer's concrete style of chess.

There are three other titles that I wish to mention: *Larsen's Selected Games of Chess 1948-69* by Bent Larsen (Bell, 1970), *The Life and Games of Mikhail Tal*, by Mikhail Tal (reissued by Cadogan, 1997), and *Chess Praxis* by Aron Nimzowitsch (various editions). Larsen is Scandinavia's greatest chess writer and I am fond of his style of commentary. The book by Tal is packed with tactical masterpieces but the aspect that makes it stand out is Tal's 'interviews' with himself. I have chosen the book by Nimzowitsch as I admire his effort to explain the mystery of chess not only theoretically but also by using himself as an experimental guinea-pig.

For students wanting to know more about how to annotate their own games, I recommend the chapter 'Analysing Your Own Games' in *Training for the Tournament Player* by Mark Dvoretsky and Artur Yusupov (Batsford, 1993).

3 Rationality Has an Older Sister; Her Name is Intuition

On calculating in chess

Instead of analysing all the moves in a position, we use our experience,
our intuition, to decide which are worth calculating.

You do not mean that you have doubts concerning intuition? Personally, I trust it blindly; I simply believe that it is knowledge that has jumped over a couple of steps ...

After all, we receive enormous amounts of information each second ... all is stowed away, but only a fraction gets to the active mind. The rest lurks in the subconscious, sending signals ...

Translated from *Kommissarien och Tystnaden* (The Commissioner and the Silence) by HÅKAN NESSER, Bonniers 1999.

Introduction

The most fundamental skill in chess is the ability to calculate the next few moves. The brilliant and masterful plans you ought to have are irrelevant if you lose your queen in two moves or fall into a one-move checkmate. You can say that chess thought begins with calculation and ends with it.

First you check if danger is lurking in a forced variation. When that is under control you try to understand the structure of the position. You form a plan from the conclusions you make. Then you calculate again to work out the small details that make it possible to execute the plan correctly.

People are not computers. Instead of analysing all the moves in a position, we use our experience, our intuition, to decide which are worth calculating. This means that training in how to calculate in chess is divided into two parts: *technical* and *thematic*.

I would like to compare this with music. A musician practises scales every day so that he can play quickly and precisely over the whole register without losing a clean, clear tone. He wants technical control over his instrument. In chess this correlates to long exact calculation. However, a musician is not a musician if he cannot put the notes together to form melodies and even a musician who improvises usually has frames of reference shaped by a chord or a basic melody. It is the same with combinative play. With the position as a starting point, we remind ourselves subconsciously of the combinative themes that we have seen before, and this helps us to find the right continuation.

Technical Calculation – Long and Exact

The first thing that strikes you when you see the best players in the world is how often they turn their heads away from the board. Instead, they fix their gaze somewhere unascertainable beyond their opponent. Suddenly they wake up and deliver a brilliant combination. They must have been analysing the position's tactical possibilities without looking at the board. For some of them it almost seems as if the real board hinders more than it helps. It was even the case that when Shirov

was interviewed in his home and the photographer asked for a chessboard for the picture, Shirov at first could not find one, as he never uses one when he is training!

To calculate deeply and correctly you must be able to visualize the forthcoming moves in your head. Often the first moves of the calculation work fine, but soon the chaos spreads and you forget where the pieces stand or miss obvious possibilities. The ability to make the moves on the chessboard of your inner mind, certain that you have the right position, is fundamental.

Stepping-Stone Diagrams – A Technique For More Advanced Players

Jonathan Tisdall has given currency to the idea of the stepping-stone diagram. The basis of this is that he separates the visualization of where the pieces stand from the calculation itself. He believes that when you calculate, you tend mainly to look at the part of the board where the calculation is happening, especially when the moves are forced. When they are at an end and there are many possibilities to consider, you need to stop and ascertain where the pieces stand, before you start to calculate again. I think that this process can develop one's ability to calculate deeply and precisely. You can compare the technique with an establishing shot and a close shot in film. First you see the entirety and then the details. Switching between shots is important so that the audience does not lose its understanding of the situation during close-ups.

Stepping-Stone Diagrams in Practice

You start to calculate. You move forward easily as the first moves are forced. Then there is a position where there are many replies. At this point you take a step back and for about thirty seconds you concentrate only on where all the pieces stand. When you have the right position visualized on your inner board you can once again continue to calculate.

This sounds simple, but it is easy to lose the big picture when you calculate details. If you create a stepping-stone diagram from which you can take off, I believe the calculation will be easier and will become more efficient. Let me give an example.

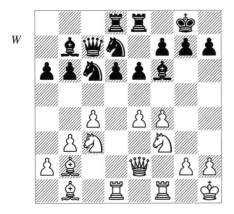

Jesper Hall – Krzysztof Gratka
Usedom 1999

Calculation is a combination of intuition and logic. In particular, when you sacrifice, everything is on a knife-edge and exact calculation is needed. If the sacrifice works, you win; if not, you lose. In the following game I had to use the technique of stepping-stone diagrams many times.

1 e5!

Before I made this move I calculated for about forty minutes. The move forces the play and I had to calculate quite a bit in several different variations. My intuition told me that Black's king was insecure with so many of his pieces on the queenside.

1...dxe5 2 ♘e4 ♗e7

I soon rejected 2...exf4 as I thought that 3 ♖xd7 ♖xd7 4 ♘xf6+ gxf6 5 ♗xf6 must give White a winning attack, and I did not continue with the variation. A possible continuation would have been 5...♘e7 6 ♘g5 f3 7 ♗xh7+ ♔f8 8 ♘xf3 ♖ed8 9 ♗g5 ♗xf3 10 ♕xf3 with a decisive advantage for White.

3 fxe5 ♘dxe5 4 ♘eg5 ♗xg5 5 ♗xh7+

It was this possibility that made me play 1 e5 and it was the reason why I used so much time in the starting position. The sacrifice is forced because if White had to play 5 ♘xg5? then Black would be better after 5...f5.

5...♔xh7 6 ♘xg5+ *(D)*

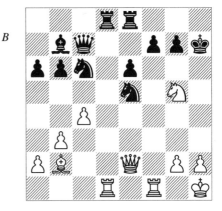

Here I had to shape a stepping-stone diagram in my head to calculate the two moves 6...♔g6 and 6...♔g8.

6...♔g6

After 6...♔g8 7 ♕h5 ♖xd1 8 ♖xd1 I felt that White had a good position in view of the killing ♗a3. However, I continued to calculate a bit further with 8...b5 9 ♕h7+ ♔f8 10 ♕h8+ ♔e7 11 ♕xg7 ♖d8 12 ♖f1 and here I stopped as Black is going to lose the f7-pawn.

7 ♕c2+ *(D)*

A second stepping-stone diagram was shaped to study the defensive possibilities 7...f5, 7...♔xg5, 7...♘d3 and 7...♖d3.

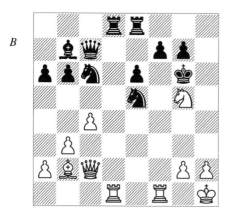

B

7...f5
Or:

a) 7...♔xg5 8 ♗c1+ ♔h4 9 ♕h7+ ♔g4 10 ♕h3#.

b) After 7...♖d3 8 ♖xd3 ♘b4 9 ♖g3+ ♘xc2 10 ♘xe6+ White is winning.

c) 7...♘d3 8 ♖xd3 ♘b4 9 ♕c3 ♖xd3 10 ♕xg7+ ♔h5 11 ♕h7+ ♔g4 (D) (11...♔xg5 12 ♗f6+ ♔g4 13 ♕h4#).

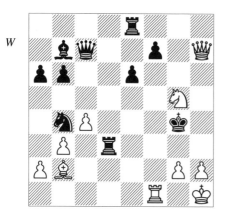

W

I had calculated this far before playing 1 e5 but when I tried to shape a stepping-stone diagram I could not get a clear view. However, with the king on g4, I refused to believe that Black could survive. If the game had

continued along this path I hope that I would have found 12 h3+ ♔g3 13 ♘e4+ ♗xe4 14 ♕xe4, when Black cannot prevent both the mate on g4 and the one on e1 with the white queen.

8 ♘xe6 ♕f7 9 ♘xd8 ♘xd8 10 ♗xe5 ♗e4 11 ♕c3 ♘e6 12 ♖d6

and White won eventually.

My Training Tips

The most important method of learning how to calculate is to stop making the moves on the board all the time as you go through a game. Try to analyse the variations without moving the pieces. Just overcoming this laziness will help you a lot. Besides this, the most efficient training is to take a tactically complicated position from a book, set the clock on 15 minutes, and then calculate as much as you can in that time. Compare with the analysis in the book. Good supplementary exercises are to play blindfold chess, to go through a game directly from the book, to solve blindfold small opening traps that are given with annotations but without diagrams. More advanced players can try to play two blindfold simultaneous games against one and the same opponent.

For those unaccustomed to blindfold chess, 'move-after' chess is an excellent initiation. You play a game where White announces his first move, but does not make it on the board. Black announces his first move, but does not make it either. White announces his second move and plays his first on the board, and Black does the same. Thus a complete game is played where the position on the board is always a move behind.

To develop your ability to create a stepping-stone diagram, you can try to frame an establishing shot whenever you go through a combination. If you analyse together with someone you can test each other by asking where the various pieces stand.

Thematic Calculation – Learning What to Calculate

A chess-player's fundamental training is to analyse combinations. Just like in music, daily practice is needed. However, to build up intuition, it is a good idea to study thematic combinations. The Dutch grandmaster Jan Timman has stated that there is no combinative theme that he has not seen before. With that kind of knowledge-base, he is very likely to calculate the continuation correctly, as he knows what to look for. Your intuition sends signals about the position to your brain and indicates which themes are of current interest.

I believe in the method of going from the simple to the difficult. Therefore it is important to pick out the basic theme that can then be adapted to more advanced tasks. Consider the basic theme of smothered mate (*see following diagram*):

This is a classical motif where the queen is sacrificed so that the knight can give checkmate.

1 ♘f7+ ♚g8 2 ♘h6++ ♚h8 3 ♕g8+ ♖xg8 4 ♘f7#

The combination works, as the black king has no holes to escape to in his pawn-structure. The king will be walled in by its own

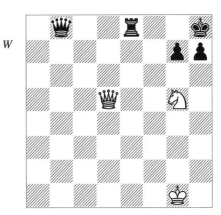

pieces after the sacrifice. With this as a fundamental theme, you can build a new position by putting the rook on f8 and the queen on a8:

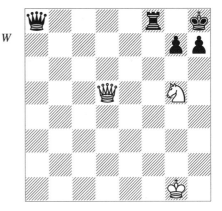

In this example there are two combinative themes, the smothered mate and mate on the back rank.

1 ♘f7+ ♚g8

1...♖xf7 2 ♕xa8+ ♖f8 3 ♕xf8#.

2 ♘h6++ ♚h8 3 ♕g8+ ♖xg8 4 ♘f7#

To understand what makes these themes possible, you can list the following criteria.

1) Shared criteria: the king has no way to escape.

2) Mate on the back rank: there is no piece that can usefully interpose after the queen's check.

3) Smothered mate: inflicted by a knight when the king is walled in by its own pieces.

A tip when you solve combinations is to formulate in words how the combination is constructed, just as above. There is then a greater chance that small bells will ring when the criteria appear in a game situation. It can also help you to find preparatory moves that will make a combination work later on. Therefore it is important during your whole chess career to work with combinations, even when you have learned the basic themes. When the various combinative themes come together in a game situation, the 'double threat' is the most important form. The simplest form is when two pieces are threatened at once and the more advanced form is when two different themes are threatened. It is in this case, when themes are combined, that even a grandmaster of Timman's calibre can be surprised.

More Examples of Smothered Mate

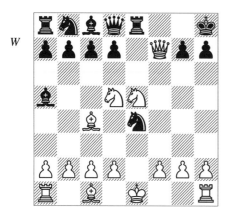

1 ♕g8+ ♔xg8

1...♖xg8 2 ♘f7#.
2 ♘e7++ ♔f8
2...♔h8 3 ♘f7#.
3 ♘7g6+ hxg6 4 ♘xg6#

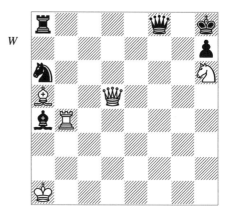

Josef Kling
circa 1850

1 ♖b8 ♖xb8 2 ♗c3+ ♕g7 3 ♕g8+ ♖xg8 4 ♘f7#

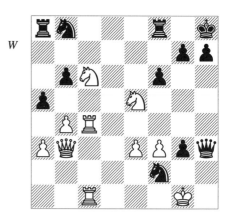

Phillip Stamma
Essai sur le jeu des échecs, 1737

1 罩h4 營xh4

Well done if you saw 1...fxe5! 2 罩xh3 ♘xh3+ 3 ♔g2 ♘xc6 4 ♔xh3 ♘e7 5 bxa5 bxa5 6 營b5, when White is only slightly better.

2 營g8+ ♔xg8 3 ♘e7+ ♔h8 4 ♘f7+ 罩xf7 5 罩c8+ 罩f8 6 罩xf8#

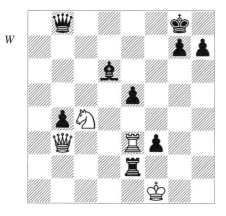

1 ♘xe5+ ♔h8 2 ♘f7+ ♔g8 3 ♘d8+!

If you have understood the criteria needed to make a smothered mate work, you will realize that White needs to entice the black rook down to the back rank before the theme can be delivered.

3...♔h8 4 罩e8+ 罩xe8 5 ♘f7+ ♔g8 6 ♘h6++ ♔h8 7 營g8+ 罩xg8 8 ♘f7#

Building Up a Combination

When you solve combinations from a diagram in a newspaper or a magazine you know that there is something to be found. In a game the problem is to get to a position where a combination can be played. By studying thematic combinations you build up a feeling for which themes are relevant in various positions. As an aid to building up a combination, the following three questions can be used:

1) Where should I put my pieces to make a theme possible? The best square for a piece often activates many themes.

2) If I were allowed to make several moves in a row, which moves would they be? If you can answer this, you can more easily pick out the weaknesses that your opponent has, and that will prompt suitable combinative themes.

3) Which of my opponent's pieces are unguarded or exposed? You then understand which pieces to target with your combination.

A trick for assessing the possibility of breaking through with an attack is to count the pieces that are attacking and the ones that are defending. If you have a majority of attacking pieces, there is a good chance of success.

A method of training yourself in how to build up an attack is to play 'progressive chess'. It works like this: White starts with one move, Black continues with two in a row, White makes three in a row, Black four, and so on. Soon you will realize that you have to be very aware of mating themes. Note that you are only allowed to give check on the last move of a sequence.

Instead of playing, you can try to find as many mating patterns as possible in a certain position. As a trainer I usually stop the play after a couple of games when I see an interesting position and let the players compete over who can find the most mating variations in it.

How to Calculate in a Game Situation

Very seldom is a variation single-lined. Often there are variations and themes mixed together. An important method is therefore to isolate the *candidate moves*, meaning the moves worth calculating. It has been said that Tigran Petrosian never calculated more than three moves, but that within these three moves he never missed a candidate move or a combination. It is certainly not completely true, but the story shows the importance of calculating the right lines. It is important to be creative and open to finding the difficult candidate moves. If you have problems with this it could be a good idea to solve studies that are constructed in such a way that they are likely to appear in a real game. You then develop a feeling for spectacular candidate moves.

The next step is to calculate from the candidate moves. The grandmaster and chess writer Alexander Kotov suggested that you scientifically and methodically analyse all the candidate moves that you have chosen, to see which is the best. However, there is a big difference between a game and a training situation. During training it is important to pick out all the candidate moves and to do thorough research. In a game situation, on the contrary, you choose intuitively the variation that seems most promising and start to analyse it immediately. This becomes the main variation. This assumes that you have been working up a feeling for the candidate moves, like Petrosian. Often you benefit from taking a step back and using thirty seconds to find alternative candidate moves in the position. Otherwise you risk missing something.

During a game you often jump back and forth between several variations. Uncertainty easily sneaks in, generally about whether you have calculated correctly. This is often due to lack of practice or confidence. Before a tournament it is therefore good to solve some combinations so that the brain starts working and you can trust your analysis. In all kinds of chess training it is also important to want to see or calculate a bit further. Otherwise, the all-too-common thought "It looks good" easily sneaks in. In a game situation

you normally see a lot more of the important variations during the first five minutes than you see in the next five minutes, and so on. John Nunn therefore says that if you can't decide between two moves after twenty minutes, then you might as well choose between them at random. This is perhaps too drastic, but I think it is most often a sign of problems with your ability to concentrate if you think for more than twenty minutes without a very good reason.

Exercises

There follow a number of exercises to provide practice in how to calculate. Solutions are given on pages 170-1.

Theme: Pins and Skewers

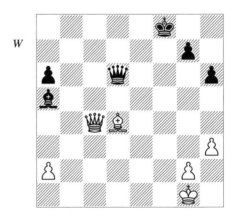

1) White to play and win.

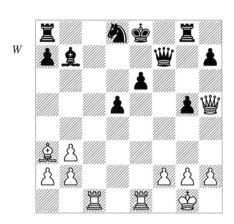

2) White to play and win.

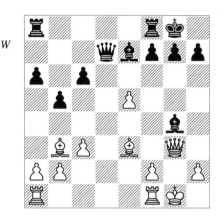

4) White to play and win.

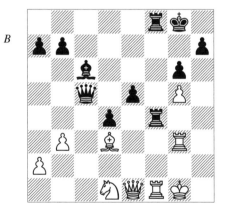

3) Black to play and win.

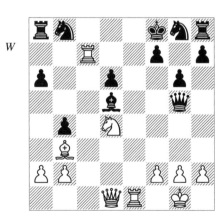

5) White to play and win.

Two Studies

Two Progressive Chess Problems

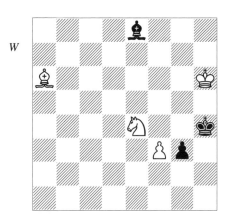

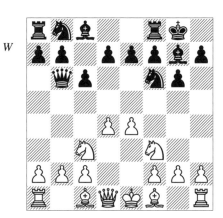

6)   **Ernest Pogosiants**
Shakhmaty Moskva, 1961

White to play and win.

8) White has five moves in a row. Who can find the most ways to deliver mate?

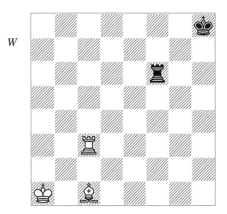

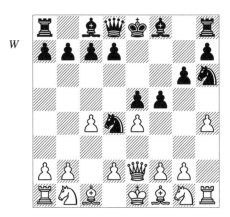

7)   **Rinaldo Bianchetti**
L'Italia Scacchistica, 1925

White to play and win.

9) White has five moves in a row. Can you find a mate?

Opening Traps to Solve Blindfold

How should Black proceed in the following positions? (Do not set up the position on a board; try to visualize it in your mind.)

10) 1 e4 e5 2 ♘f3 ♘c6 3 d4 exd4 4 ♘xd4 ♘f6 5 ♗g5 ♗e7 6 ♘f5 d5 7 exd5 ♘e5 8 ♘xe7 ♕xe7 9 ♗xf6.

11) 1 e4 e5 2 ♘f3 d5 3 exd5 ♕xd5 4 ♘c3 ♕a5 5 ♕e2 ♘c6 6 d3 ♗g4 7 ♗d2 ♘d4 8 ♕xe5+.

12) 1 e4 e5 2 f4 exf4 3 ♘f3 ♗e7 4 ♗c4 ♗h4+ 5 ♔f1 d5 6 ♗xd5 ♘f6 7 ♘xh4 ♘xd5 8 ♘f3.

13) 1 e4 e6 2 d4 d5 3 ♘d2 ♘c6 4 ♘gf3 ♘f6 5 e5 ♘d7 6 c3 f6 7 exf6 ♕xf6 8 ♗b5 a6 9 ♕a4.

In the next example, what is White's best move?

14) 1 e4 ♘f6 2 ♘c3 d5 3 e5 ♘e4 4 ♘ce2 d4 5 c3 dxc3.

Practice in Finding Candidate Moves

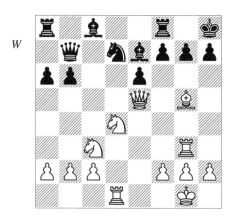

15) David Bronstein – Alexander Kotov
Moscow Ch 1946

How should White proceed? Which moves are worth taking a closer look at?

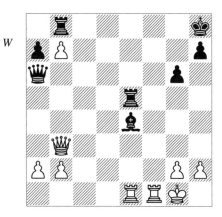

16) How should White proceed? Which moves are worth taking a closer look at?

Suggestions for Further Reading

There are loads of combination books with problems to solve. Most of them are certainly useful, but I prefer those with a systematic arrangement. *1001 Ways to Checkmate* by Fred Reinfeld (Barnes & Noble, 1955) is a good book for those who have just left the beginner's level.

Then it is time to move to *Test Your Chess IQ* (three volumes) by Avgust Livshits (Pergamon/Cadogan, various years). This is an excellent series of books that inspires by giving points for solving within a certain time.

The real bible is the *Anthology of Chess Combinations* (Šahovski Informator, 1995), which will keep you occupied for many hours with its 2001 problems.

John Nunn's Chess Puzzle Book by John Nunn (Gambit, 1999) is a book where the reader is put into a real game situation, with few hints as to the theme or aim, though clues are available if needed.

As for books on how to calculate, I first of all recommend the readable and inspiring book *The Art of Sacrifice in Chess* by Rudolf Spielmann (1935).

For more advanced players, there are *Secrets of Chess Tactics* by Mark Dvoretsky (Batsford, 1992) and *Schachtaktik für Fortgeschrittene* by Yuri Averbakh (Sportverlag Berlin, 1979). Both deal with various types of combinations and give explanations of how to think in order to find them. *Improve Your Chess Now* by Jonathan Tisdall (Cadogan, 1997) has recently given me new angles on calculation and is in a way a pioneering work.

4 And Larsen Spoke: You Must Have a Plan!

On the method of eight questions

The task of finding a plan was like monsters under my bed:
something unknown, huge and dangerous.

All children have idols and role models. What separated me from the other children in the school playground was that my idols, Wedberg, Cramling, Andersson, Fischer and Larsen, never appeared on any picture cards. The one that was at the top of my list changed from week to week, depending on who had won any tournaments lately or if I was about to read a book or an article he (or she) had written. For the latter reason, Larsen was at the top for a long time. He was, and is, a brilliant writer who can explain how a grandmaster

thinks, and I had discovered his series of titles such as *Du Kan Kombinera* (You Can Combine) and *Du Måste Ha en Plan* (You Must Have a Plan).

I thought that I understood roughly how to set up a combination, but the task of finding a plan was like monsters under my bed: something unknown, huge and dangerous. Before I read the slim volume *Du Måste Ha en Plan*, good players had fascinated me when they annotated their games as they saw so far and could perceive the game's contours even into the endings. I could not understand how I would ever be able to learn that. But the number one on my chess list now switched on a torch and I bent over the bed and peered into the unknown.

A Demystification

Forming a plan is not something inexplicable or mystical that grandmasters do without some basis in logic. Indeed, a plan takes its shape from the position on the board. I believe that in most of their games even grandmasters do not have the thought "Now I am going to create a huge, overall plan." Instead, they conceive a mini-operation and seek to regroup towards a position that is slightly better than the one they had. The reason is that they already know the overall plans: that you should seek a breakthrough on the side where you have a pawn-majority, or go for an attack on your opponent's king if he has a piece stuck on the queenside. They devote their energy to the key positions, where various positional elements and strategies interact, as here chess is about exact calculation. The game is therefore woven from a series of mini-operations by both sides.

With regard to planning, I believe in a training method which leads from the simple to the difficult, from clear examples to unclear. What matters is to understand which basic plan should follow from each type of central pawn-structure, and to learn to recognize the various types of advantages and disadvantages that you can have. The next step is to learn how to weigh the elements and advantages against each other in order to appreciate when one is more important than another. You also need to have a balance between single-mindedness and flexibility in your planning. In hindering one plan, your opponent might create other weaknesses that can be exploited by a new plan. Do not forget that chess is a fight where it is always important to put up as much resistance as possible. It is only when the difference in playing strength is very large or if one player has a great advantage that a complete overall plan can be carried out without any resistance.

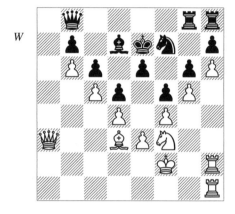

José Raúl Capablanca – Karel Treybal
Karlsbad 1929

This is a position where we have both an uneven relationship in strength between the players and a superior position for White. Capablanca was at the time one of the strongest players in the world and a quick glance at the position is enough to appreciate that White is better. All White's pieces are active and he has taken possession of the only open file: the a-file. As the kingside and the centre are closed we understand that it is on the queenside that a breakthrough must be made. Logically, the pieces should be located there. As we continue to identify our opponent's problems, we find the weak link in the black pawn-chain at b7. How should the white pieces be positioned in order to attack it as efficiently as possible? Yes, a rook on a7 and the knight on a5. Maybe also the move ♗a6 might be of interest, to increase the pressure even more.

40 ♖a1 ♖c8 41 ♕b4 ♖hd8 42 ♖a7 ♔f8 43 ♖h1 ♗e8 44 ♖ha1 ♔g8 *(D)*

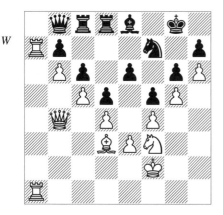

Black has no activity and therefore can only wait and hope that his defence on the queenside does not crack or that he might be able to counterattack if White overpresses. This demonstrates an important aspect of planning: it must take into account your opponent's possibilities.

45 ♖1a4 ♔f8 46 ♕a3 ♔g8 47 ♔g3

Playing the knight towards a5 immediately with 47 ♘d2 gives Black an opportunity to counterattack by 47...♘xg5 and after 48 fxg5 the black queen penetrates to h2 and creates trouble. But why should White hurry? Black can do nothing. Therefore Capablanca first finds his king the right square before moving the knight.

47...♗d7 48 ♔h4 ♔h8 49 ♕a1 ♔g8 50 ♔g3 ♔f8 51 ♔g2

After a little walk the king has finally found its rightful place.

51...♗e8 52 ♘d2 ♗d7 53 ♘b3 ♖e8

After 53...♗e8, there is 54 ♘a5 ♖d7 55 ♘xb7 ♖xb7 56 ♖a8 winning the queen.

54 ♘a5 ♘d8 55 ♗a6 bxa6 56 ♖xd7 ♖e7 57 ♖xd8+ ♖xd8 58 ♘xc6

White regains the exchange and then wins with his two connected passed pawns.

1-0

"So, Mr Hall, What is Your Position Like Now?", Asked the Knight

I was playing against the 1996 Swedish Champion Robert Åström in a small tournament in Iceland. Suddenly I saw my opponent's lips moving. I leant forward and heard him mumble "I put my queen on b3 and bind his queen to the defence of the b-pawn. Then I bring my knight to the super square b6 where it restricts the whole black queenside." I could hardly resist the impulse to start whispering myself "I put my pawn on c4, take his queen on b3 and when his knight comes to b6 he is a queen down and I can simply take the knight."

Åström is an honest player who would never do anything to disturb his opponent; he was just following one of the most important principles for learning how to create a plan: *talking to yourself.* In the Russian school this motto is more familiar as "Talk with your pieces," but the idea is the same. With the help of words you give your analysis new depth; through the medium of the inner monologue you find a way to improve your position. (Naturally, this should be done silently!)

Most philosophers of language say that if you do not put words to a thought, it does not exist. I do not know if I agree with that, but if we formulate with our own words what the position is about and what we want to do, then we have structured all the calculation and found a direction for our play. The best way to train the inner monologue and the planning is to try to answer a few questions.

The Method of Eight Questions

1) What type of pawn-structure is it?
The central pawn-structure is the skeleton of the position. A plan is often related to how the pawns are placed. If there are no pawns, play with the pieces becomes more important. If the centre is blocked, what matters is to break through on the flanks, and so on. You should learn the basic principles for the various formations in the centre and relate the position in the game to this knowledge.

2) What is good and what is bad about my position?
Here it is important to identify the elements that speak for and against you. Then you try to weigh these against each other and make a conclusion about who stands better. With this as a starting point, you can often form a plan to neutralize your opponent's advantages or to profit from your own.

3) Which pieces do I want to exchange, and which to keep?
This is often connected with the question above. If your opponent has a strong piece and you have a weak one, then you do not mind an exchange, and vice versa. Often this can result in a plan.

4) Which side of the board should I play on?
It is obvious that your opponent's weakest spot should be attacked, but it is also important that you play where you have most pieces to use. A simple trick such as thinking about which side of the board the pieces are on and where they have best chances to do something can lead to enlightenment.

5) What is my dream position?
You have to have a vision to strive towards. Maybe the most important technique in planning is therefore to think: "If I were allowed to make several moves in a row, which would they be?" You can of course easily think up a quick mate by this method, which very seldom will come to pass. The real point is to find the weak spots of your opponent, in addition to his insecure king, and with the 'several-moves-in-a-row' method, you are prompted where the pieces should go to be most useful.

6) What does my opponent want to do?
If your opponent has an obvious plan or idea at his disposal, it is often good to hinder it. In the world of chess this is called prophylaxis. You could say that you take the sting out of the attack before it has even started. Clearly, it is a very effective way to defend.

7) Can I take a step in the right direction?
When you find an overall plan it is important to identify the partial goals on the way. Here the planning becomes more concrete. The routes to the partial goals are what I call the mini-operations. These are small manoeuvres that improve your position a little bit. In a game it is often here that you use most of your energy. The overall plan is mainly the result of intuition, but achievement of the aims demands concrete thinking. You have an opponent who will do all that he can to hinder you from reaching your dream position.

8) Which moves are worth taking a closer look at?
Identify the moves you consider worth taking a closer look at. These are the candidate moves. Analyse them more deeply and select the one you think is the best.

Questions 1 and 2 are the basis for planning. Questions 3-6 pursue and develop the plan and make it more specific, while questions 7 and 8 are about how to carry out the plan. In a practical game situation, you do not sit and mumble all these questions to yourself all the time, as the answers will come intuitively. Naturally, playing style and personality decide how the inner conversation should work. For building up your intuition so that you can trust it during important parts of the game, the questions are important tools.

Standard Positions

Players often strive towards an advantageous standard position, which means a position where they know who is better and why. If you are under pressure, you can play towards a standard position that is known to be equal. With these positions as your goals, it becomes easier to answer the questions and to guide yourself through the process of thinking.

Practice in judging who is better and why is fundamental for planning. The more standard positions that you know, the better your assessment of the position will be. The beginner learns that rook + king against king will win, that king + knight against king is a draw and that a huge material advantage is decisive. The grandmaster is able to make more subtle judgements of structures and positioning of the pieces. To memorize a standard position, not one where there is a material advantage, it is important to recognize the components that the questions above try to identify. You will soon realize that the better you become, the more difficult it will be to add a new standard position, but the method is the same whatever your strength. It is only the tools and the process that have been refined.

Important keywords

- *Inner monologue*: talking with yourself/your pieces.
- *Standard positions*: positions where you know who is better and why.
- *Candidate moves*: the moves that are worth considering in a position.

My Training Tips

The method of eight questions is mainly a training tool. In a game our intuition steers our process of thinking. However, it is important to formulate your own method of using the inner monologue, just like Åström. Try to be aware of which questions you intuitively answer and which you must always try to work out. When you train, you can be more methodical than when you are in a game with time-pressure. Therefore, make a habit of checking off the questions when you analyse a game or a position.

Suggestions for Further Reading

I have never seen this type of structured questioning myself, but as the idea is not new it might have been published without my knowledge. My sources of inspiration are mainly *Du Måste Ha en Plan* (You Must Have a Plan) by Bent Larsen (originally published in Danish by Samlerens Forlag in the Skak Skole series; they formed chapters of *Bent Larsen's Good Move Guide*, published by Oxford University Press in 1982), which by means of examples gives a good guide to how to plan, *The Art of the Middlegame in Chess* by Paul Keres and Alexander Kotov (Penguin, 1964) and a number of other books by Kotov, including the classic *Play Like a Grandmaster* (Batsford, 1978). These fine authors demonstrate the importance of words and questions when they write about a position. Mark Dvoretsky and Artur Yusupov are leading modern writers; their *Training for the Tournament Player* (Batsford, 1993) corresponds best to the theme of this chapter.

5 Pawns are the Soul of Chess

On central pawn-structures

The pawns form the skeleton of the position, as they give the framework within which the other pieces should be deployed.

I stand in front of my bookshelves with all my chess books. My eyes are drawn to a well-thumbed volume without a spine: *The Art of the Middlegame in Chess* by Paul Keres and Alexander Kotov (Penguin, 1964). In the book there is a chapter that has been etched into my brain because I have read it so often: 'Various Pawn Positions in the Centre'. This chapter, and the other chapters in this book, continued the development of my thinking processes that Larsen began. The moves I had formerly played intuitively now acquired words and explanations and I found tools to separate the various positional factors. I devoured all the facts, such as when the centre has no pawns the coordination between the pieces becomes more important. Or that an attack on the flank is best answered by a counterattack in the centre, even if the centre is closed. The reason why the chapter has been read so many times is that it is useful no matter which level you may be on.

We usually say that pawns are the soul of chess, as they are fundamental to the assessment of the position, and as the pawn is the only piece that can be transformed into another. Maybe it is a better metaphor to call them the skeleton of the position, as they give the framework within which the other pieces should be deployed. Therefore the pawn-structure determines the plan. The players' strategy must always be related to how the pawns stand. Often the players either try to

occupy the centre with pawns in order to gain space to manoeuvre, or to exert pressure on the centre with the pieces, for example by fianchettoing the bishops. Kotov's classic division of the various centres is as shown below.

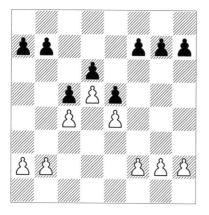

Closed centre
White's and Black's pawns form an interlocked chain in the centre.

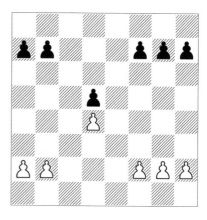

Fixed centre
Two opposing pawns are nailed to each other.

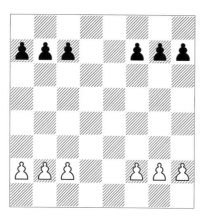

Open centre
There are no pawns in the centre.

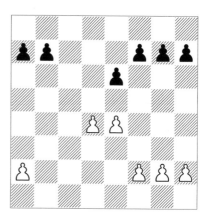

Mobile centre
One of the players has two or more pawns that are capable of advancing in the centre.

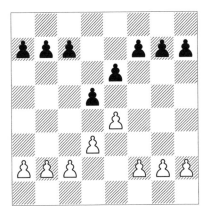

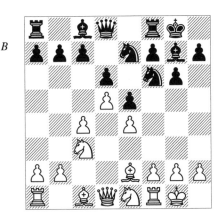

Fluid centre

The structure of the centre is not yet decided.

Closed Centre

With the pawns in the centre wedged against each other, it is on the flanks that breakthroughs are usually made. Often the players take one flank each and then try to be first to break through. However, the rule "An attack on the flank is best answered by a counterattack in the centre" can be relevant even with a closed centre, as it may be possible to disintegrate the centre by sacrificing a piece.

Ari Ziegler – Mikael Johansson
Åstorp 1990

1 d4 ♘f6 2 c4 g6 3 ♘c3 ♗g7 4 e4 d6 5 ♘f3 0-0 6 ♗e2 e5 7 0-0 ♘c6 8 d5 ♘e7 9 ♘e1 *(D)*

This is a common variation of the King's Indian Defence. The centre is closed so play is shifted to the flanks. Black's pieces are placed to act on the kingside. The key move is ...f5 followed by ...f4 and then the g-pawn will advance to open up files towards White's king. White wants to make his key move, c5,

and penetrate on the c-file with the major pieces.

9...♘d7 10 ♘d3 f5 11 ♗d2 c5

A radical way to prevent White's key move, but White now has a new way to break up Black's pawn-structure, with the advance b4. More common than the move played is 11...♘f6 12 f3 ♔h8 with the idea ...♘eg8 and ...♗h6.

12 ♖b1 ♘f6 13 f3 f4 14 g4!? *(D)*

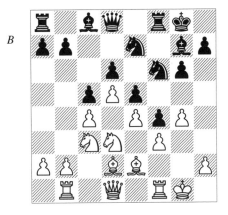

This move looks crazy at first, as you seldom want to advance the pawns in front of your own king. However, in the race to break through first, White wants to create a blockade on the kingside. The move g4 is similar to Black's ...c5, directed against the opponent's natural key move.

14...h5

After 14...fxg3 15 hxg3 White intends to proceed with ♖f2 and ♖h2, when it is hard for Black to make progress.

15 h3 ♔h8

Black already has problems in organizing his pieces for the attack. The move played frees the g8-square for the e7-knight. He then wants to play ...♘h7 to make it possible for the queen or the bishop to reach the dark squares g5, h4 and g3.

16 ♗e1 ♘h7 17 ♖f2 ♘g8 18 ♖g2

It is instructive to see how calmly White plays. Before his own breakthrough, he suppresses Black's counterplay. Closed positions are seldom as sensitive to tempi as open ones; instead it is the placing of the pieces that is important.

18...♗f6

After 18...♘g5 19 ♖h2 the black knight will make no use of the pseudo-active square g5.

19 b4 b6

19...cxb4 seems to be a better attempt to start an attack. In the game it takes too long before Black is able to play ...♗h4 and ...♘g5, and White remains ahead in the race. For example, 20 ♖xb4 ♗h4 21 c5 ♘g5 22 ♔h2 ♗xe1 23 ♕xe1 hxg4 24 hxg4 ♖f7 25 cxd6 ♖h7+ 26 ♔g1 ♕xd6 leads to an unclear game.

20 bxc5 bxc5

After 20...dxc5 White can proceed with 21 a4 followed by 22 a5. If Black tries to stop White's breakthrough with 21...a5 he will have a backward pawn on b6.

21 ♕a4!

Threatening ♕c6, as the reply ...♗d7 is not possible because the d6-pawn is hanging.

21...a5 22 ♘b5

Again a strange move at first sight, but the explanation will come soon.

22...♖a6 23 ♕a3! *(D)*

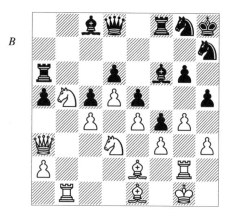

White knows the basic rule that an attack on a flank is best answered by a counterattack in the centre. Therefore he prepares a knight sacrifice on d6 or c5. If the two pawns disappear, the black spine will disappear. White gets two dangerous passed pawns, but also the possibility of winning the e5-pawn. This will allow an attack on the a1-h8 diagonal.

23...♗h4 24 ♗c3

White does not want to exchange bishops and points it towards the black king.

24...♘g5?!

Black stakes everything on one card, but goes down quickly. Better was 24...♗f6 to try to mitigate the effects of the sacrifice. However, the defence is difficult after 25 ♘xd6 ♕xd6 26 ♕xc5 ♕xc5+ 27 ♘xc5 ♖a8 28 ♘d3 ♖e8 29 c5 with an advantage for White, as the passed pawns will soon cost Black material.

25 ♘xd6 ♘xh3+ 26 ♔f1 ♖xd6 27 ♕xc5 ♗g3

After 27...hxg4 28 ♘xe5 ♔h7 29 ♘xg4 White has a decisive advantage.

28 ♘xe5 ♔h7 29 ♕a7+ ♔h6 30 ♖b8

White activates one more piece in the attack and threatens to play c5 or to move the knight to give his queen greater activity. Black cannot resist all the threats and has some way to go before his own attack becomes really dangerous.

30...♕e8

To attack the white king via a4.

31 c5 ♕a4 32 ♖xg3 ♗a6 *(D)*

32...fxg3 was probably the best chance, but even then White has a decisive attack. You can, for example, have some fun finding 33 cxd6 g2+ 34 ♔xg2 ♘f4+ 35 ♔h1 ♘xe2 36 ♕e3+ ♔h7 37 ♖xc8 ♕d1+ 38 ♔h2 ♖xc8 39 ♕a7+ ♔h6 40 ♘f7+ ♔h7 41 ♘d8+ ♔h6 42 g5+ ♔xg5 43 ♘e6+ ♔h4 44 ♕e7+ ♘xe7 45 ♗f6+ g5 46 ♗xg5#.

In the game Ziegler finds as beautiful a finish.

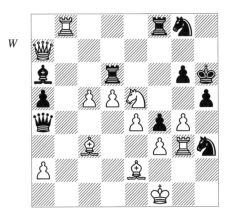

33 g5+! ♘xg5 34 ♘g4+ hxg4 35 ♕g7+ ♔h5 36 ♕h8+ ♘h6

If Black plays 36...♘h7 we can conjure up the finish 37 ♕xh7+ ♘h6 38 fxg4+ ♔g5 39 ♕xh6+! ♔xh6 40 g5+ ♔h7 41 ♖h3+ ♔g8 42 ♖h8+ ♔f7 43 ♖h7+ ♔g8 44 ♖g7+ ♔h8 45 ♖xf8#.

37 fxg4+ ♔h4 38 ♕xh6+ 1-0

Miguel Najdorf – Robert Hübner
Wijk aan Zee 1971

1 d4 ♘f6 2 c4 e6 3 ♘c3 ♗b4 4 e3 c5 5 ♗d3 ♘c6 6 ♘f3 ♗xc3+ 7 bxc3 d6 8 e4 e5 9 d5 ♘e7 10 g3 *(D)*

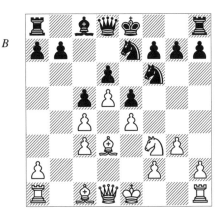

Hübner has played the variation of the Nimzo-Indian that is now named after him. It gives rise to a blocked structure, directing the weight of the struggle towards the wings. Therefore both players are preparing to seize space and important squares on the kingside.

10...h6!

Better than 10...♘g6 11 h4 ♕a5 12 ♕b3 ♗g4 13 ♘h2 ♗d7 14 ♗g5 0-0 15 ♗xf6 gxf6 16 0-0 with a big advantage for White, Gligorić-Korchnoi, Wijk aan Zee 1971.

11 ♘h4 g5

Black takes the chance to gain space on the kingside. Already you can understand that it is here that the decisive battle will be. The doubled pawns on the c-file mean that White has lost the breakthrough possibility b4, which otherwise would have been the natural plan.

12 ♘g2 ♕a5 13 ♕b3 ♗h3

Black has to distract White so that he cannot play f4.

14 0-0 0-0-0 15 ♖b1 ♕c7 16 f3 ♔b8 17 ♖f2 ♖hg8 18 ♘e3 ♗c8 19 ♔f1

White cannot break through on the queenside and therefore brings the king to the centre, intending to try to open files on the kingside.

19...♖df8 20 ♔e1 ♘e8

Threatening to play ...f5.

21 ♘f5 (D)

A sign that White has problems. Now it is only Black who can open files on the kingside. Maybe White should have tried 21 ♖fb2 with the idea of preventing Black from playing ...f5 by building up pressure against b7. Black can then manoeuvre around, forcing White to make concessions in return. Manoeuvring around is a central concept in closed positions and in endgames. It means that you work alternately against two weaknesses, oscillating your attention between the two flanks. The game could then have continued 21...♖g7 22 ♕b5 f6 23 ♗c2 ♖gf7 24 h3 ♘g7 25 ♘g4 ♖h8 26 ♘f2 f5 with an advantage for Black.

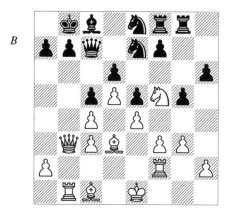

21...♘xf5 22 exf5 f6 23 g4

Forced sooner or later, since Black can threaten the pawn with ...♕h7 or ...♘g7.

23...♖h8

Black is the one to decide when the h-file will be opened.

24 ♗e3 h5 25 ♗f1 ♖f7 26 h3

White has given up his own plans on the kingside and has to direct his energy into restraining Black.

26...♕d7

Preparing a beautiful manoeuvre. Observe that the question "If I could make several moves in a row, which would they be?" is a good guide for finding a plan in closed positions, as they are not as sensitive to tempi as open ones.

27 ♔d2 ♘c7! (D)

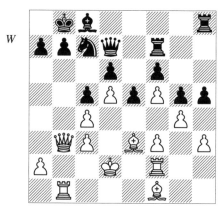

Black follows one of the most important rules: the principle of the two weaknesses. He can conquer the h-file, but needs another weakness to work against to be able to win. Black's knight therefore moves towards the queenside.

28 a4?!

White should stay passive and not give Black new targets.

28...♖e7 29 ♖e1 ♘a8 30 a5 ♕d8 31 ♕a3 ♖hh7!

Black plays splendidly. Before the h-file is opened all the pieces should be at maximum readiness. The rook move makes the h8-square available for the queen and prepares the transfer of the rook to the queenside.

32 ♖b1 b6 33 ♗d3 ♖b7 34 axb6

If 34 a6?, then 34...♗be7 followed by ...♘c7 and the pawn is lost.

34...♘xb6 35 ♖a1 ♕h8 36 ♔c2 hxg4

The black pieces are finally ready to open up the position.

37 hxg4 ♗d7 38 ♕a2 ♖h2 39 ♔d2 ♖xf2+ 40 ♗xf2 ♕h2 41 ♔e2 ♘a4 42 ♕d2 ♗e8

Maybe Black did not want to go in for 42...♖b2 43 ♕xb2+ ♘xb2 44 ♖b1 a5 45 ♖xb2+ ♔c7 with some technical problems to overcome even though it should be winning fairly easily.

43 ♖b1 ♖xb1 44 ♗xb1 (D)

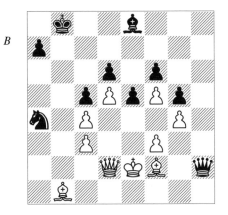

B

44...♕f4!

Liquidating into a winning endgame. The bishop-pair is totally paralysed in the blocked position and together with the weakness on c4 this decides the game.

45 ♗d3 ♕xd2+ 46 ♔xd2 ♘b6 47 ♔c1 ♗a4 48 ♗c2 ♗d7

48...♗xc2 49 ♔xc2 ♘xc4 50 ♔d3 ♘a5 51 ♗e3 is not completely clear as White has ♗xg5 if the black king advances on the queenside.

49 ♗d3 ♔c7 50 ♔b2 ♗c8 51 ♔b3 ♗a6 52 ♗e3

If 52 ♔c2, then 52...♘xc4 53 ♔c1 ♔b7 threatens ...♘b6 and the d5-pawn is lost. Therefore White cannot reach the endgame with knight against White's dark-squared bishop, given in the variation above.

52...♘xd5 0-1

After 53 cxd5 ♗xd3 Black's bishop will mop up the pawns on the light squares.

Open Centre

When the centre lacks pawns the positions of the pieces grow in importance. Active piece play is the key to success. A common plan is to coordinate your troops to create weaknesses in the pawn-structure on either flank. The rooks usually play an important role as they have good prospects on the open files, striving towards the seventh rank.

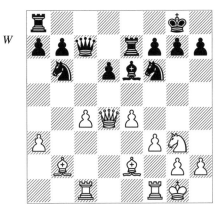

W

Mikhail Botvinnik – Paul Keres
World Ch, The Hague/Moscow 1948

Black has gone wrong in a variation of the Nimzo-Indian Defence and Botvinnik therefore takes the opportunity to open up the position. In an open game the bishops are effective as they have lengthy diagonals to work on. If they can also take aim at the opponent's king, an attack will be well-supported.

17 c5

This advance opens the position up for White's b2-bishop and gives the white rook the chance to join the attack against the weak spot g7.

17...dxc5 18 ♖xc5 ♕f4?!

18...♕d8 19 ♕e3 (19 ♕xd8+ ♖xd8 20 ♗xf6 gxf6 21 ♘h5 f5 is not clear) 19...♖d7 is a better chance for Black, even though after 20 ♖fc1 White has a grip on the events.

19 ♗c1! ♕b8 20 ♖g5 ♘bd7 (D)

Black can do nothing as 20...♘e8 21 ♘h5 f5 22 exf5 ♗xf5 23 ♖e1 ♗e6 24 ♗b5 gives White a decisive advantage.

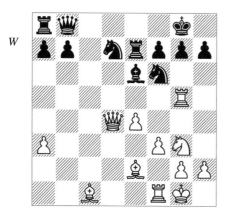

21 ♖xg7+

White finishes with a logical combination against the black king.

21...♔xg7 22 ♘h5+ ♔g6

22...♔g8 23 ♘xf6+ ♘xf6 24 ♕xf6 followed by ♗b2 or ♗h6 with mate.

23 ♕e3

With unavoidable mate on g5 or h6 to follow.

1-0

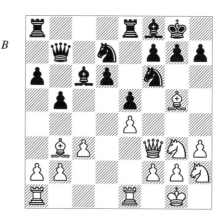

Nigel Short – Alexander Beliavsky
FIDE KO World Ch, Groningen 1997

We throw ourselves into an exciting moment in a Spanish Game. This is an opening that can generate more or less any type of structure in the centre, so it is difficult to play. With his next move Black shows his intention to open up the position.

18...d5?!

Given the consequences of this advance, 18...h6 was a better try; for example, 19 ♗xf6 ♘xf6 20 ♖ad1 ♖ac8 21 ♘g4 and White has an advantage as he controls the d5-square.

19 ♘g4

White's pieces are ready to attack the black king, a common plan for the side that is ahead in development. Again it is a bishop that plays the main role. From b3 it points towards the weak f7-square, which ties Black down. As you will notice, there are many tactical motifs, most of which are connected to the bishop. Short probably did not see more than half of all the variations that I give, but he knew where to put his pieces in this position-type to make tactical opportunities come to life. Then they arose spontaneously.

19...dxe4

19...♘xg4 does not work because of 20 exd5 ♘xf2 21 dxc6 ♘xh3+ 22 gxh3 ♕a7+ 23 ♗e3 ♘c5 24 ♖f1 ♖e7 25 ♕d5 followed by ♘e4 and White is winning.

20 ♕f5

White has heavy pressure against f7 that increases with each move.

20...♘d5

There was no alternative; for example, 20...e3 21 ♖xe3 ♗c5 22 ♖d3 ♗xg2? 23 ♘xf6+ ♘xf6 24 ♗xf6 gxf6 25 ♘h5 with a winning attack, while after 20...♗e7 21 ♘h5! ♘d5 22 ♗xe7 ♖xe7 23 ♕g5 f6 24 ♘hxf6+ ♘7xf6 25 ♘xf6+ ♔f7 26 ♘xe4 Black's position falls apart.

21 ♘xe4 ♖e6

21...h6 loses for tactical reasons: 22 ♗xh6 gxh6 23 ♗xd5 ♗xd5 24 ♘ef6+ ♘xf6 25 ♘xf6+ ♔g7 26 ♖e3 ♗d6 27 ♖g3+ ♔f8 28 ♖d1 ♗e6 29 ♘h7+ ♔e7 30 ♕f6+ ♔d7 31 ♖gd3 and White gets the piece back with a winning position.

22 ♖ad1 *(D)*

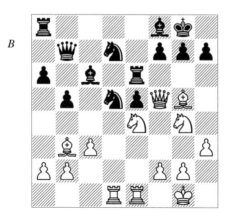

White activates the last piece in his attack. Every move, Black risks being felled by a tactical blow.

22...h5?!

A novelty. Otherwise:

a) 22...♖ae8 was played in A.Kovačević-Gligorić, Yugoslav Ch, Nikšić 1997, which ended badly for Black: 23 ♖d3 h5 24 ♗xd5! ♗xd5 25 ♘gf6+! ♘xf6 26 ♘xf6+ gxf6 27 ♗xf6 ♗h6 28 ♖xe5 ♗e4 29 ♖xe6 ♗xf5 30 ♖xe8+ ♔h7 31 ♖g3 ♗g4 32 hxg4 ♗f4 33 gxh5 1-0. Mate is unavoidable.

b) 22...♘7b6 is the only chance. White's best idea then seems to be to put pressure on the e5-pawn with 23 ♗h4 followed by ♗g3.

23 ♘e3!

White steps up the pressure against the d5-knight.

23...♘f4

Black is lost and can only choose between horrors:

a) 23...♘e7 24 ♕xf7+! ♔xf7 25 ♘d6+ ♔g6 26 ♘xb7 ♖xb7 27 ♗xe6 and White is winning.

b) 23...♘xe3 24 ♖xe3 g6 25 ♕f3 ♘c5 26 ♗xe6 ♘xe4 27 ♗d7! ♗xd7 28 ♕xe4 and White can cash in his material advantage.

c) 23...♘7b6 24 ♘xd5 ♗xd5 25 ♗xd5 ♘xd5 26 ♕f3 and there is no good defence against ♖xd5 and ♘f6+.

24 ♗xf4 ♗xe4

Or:

a) 24...exf4 25 ♗xe6 fxe6 26 ♕xe6+ ♔h8 27 ♘f5 gives White a decisive attack.

b) 24...g6 25 ♕g5 ♗e7 26 ♗xe6 ♗xg5 27 ♗xf7+ ♔g7 28 ♘d6 exf4 (28...♕b6 29 ♗xg5 gives White a rook and two pieces for the queen) 29 ♘xb7 fxe3 30 ♘a5 exf2+ 31 ♔xf2 and White is winning.

25 ♖xd7 ♗xf5

25...♕xd7 26 ♕xe4 exf4 27 ♗xe6 ♕xe6 28 ♕xa8 is totally lost for Black.

26 ♖xb7 exf4 *(D)*

After 27 ♗xe6 ♗xe6 28 ♘c2 ♗xa2 White still has some technical problems to overcome. However, Short found a beautiful finish.

27 ♖xf7 1-0

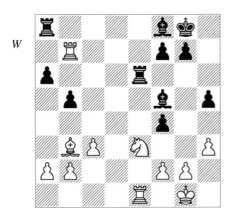

27...♔xf7 (27...fxe3 28 ♖xf5 and the e6-rook is doomed) 28 ♘xf5 ♔f6 (28...♖ae8 29 ♘d4 is also winning for White) 29 ♗xe6 ♖e8 30 ♘d4 ♗c5 31 ♖d1 ♗xd4 32 ♗d7 and White ends up with a piece more.

Fixed Centre

With a fixed structure in the centre there are various types of plans, but often it is important to get a grip on the centre and to reinforce it with pieces. After that, the attacker tries to create weaknesses in his opponent's position, infiltrating with his pieces or starting an attack on the flank.

Mikhail Botvinnik – Alexander Alekhine
AVRO tournament, Amsterdam 1938

1 ♘f3 d5 2 d4 ♘f6 3 c4 e6 4 ♘c3 c5 5 cxd5 ♘xd5 6 e3 ♘c6 7 ♗c4 cxd4

7...♘f6 is a major alternative.

8 exd4 ♗e7 9 0-0 0-0 10 ♖e1

White waits to see where Black will develop his light-squared bishop. If White had taken on d5 immediately, the bishop could have reached natural developing squares such as f5 or g4.

10...b6? *(D)*

After seeing the course of this game you get the feeling that this move is more or less the decisive mistake. If Black wants to fianchetto the bishop he must take on c3 before playing ...b6. Other possibilities are 10...♘f6 and 10...♗f6.

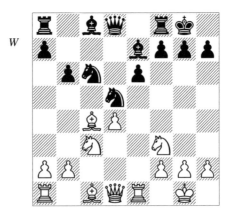

11 ♘xd5! exd5 12 ♗b5

White has chosen to go into a middlegame with a fixed centre. The reason why White now gets pressure is the weakness on the light squares created by 10...b6.

12...♗d7?!

When the light-squared bishops disappear, the weaknesses on the queenside will be even more obvious. Black must therefore try 12...♘a5, but then also White has natural developing moves, while Black's pieces desperately try to coordinate; for example, 13 ♘e5 a6 14 ♗d3 ♗b4 15 ♖e3 with a dangerous attack looming.

13 ♕a4 ♘b8

Or 13...♖c8, and now:

a) Note that 14 ♗xc6? is not good because after 14...♗xc6 15 ♕xa7, 15...♗b4! is a great intermezzo which forces White to sacrifice his queen with 16 ♗d2 ♖a8 17 ♕xa8 ♕xa8 18 ♗xb4, when the position is about equal.

b) 14 ♗d2 threatens to grab the a7-pawn and forces Black to accept new weaknesses through 14...a5.

14 ♗f4 ♗xb5 15 ♕xb5 a6 16 ♕a4

If Black's knight were placed on the ideal square e4, his position would be OK. Now instead, the knight is forced to the back rank and has desperate problems getting out.

16...♗d6

Maybe 16...b5 was a better try, despite the risk of incurring new weaknesses: 17 ♕c2 ♖e8 18 ♘e5 ♗b4 19 ♖e3 ♖a7 20 a4 bxa4 21 ♕xa4 and White's pressure continues.

17 ♗xd6 ♕xd6 18 ♖ac1 ♖a7 (D)

White has reached an ideal position. His rooks control the open c- and e-files, while his queen supports the rooks and his knight has access to the natural square, e5. Black also has problems with the pawns on a6 and b6: one of the pawns risks falling when Black tries to activate his passive rooks and his stranded knight. For example, 18...♘d7 19 ♖c6 ♕f4 20 ♕b3 ♕f5 21 ♖d6 ♖ae8 22 ♖f1 ♘f6 23 ♖xb6 and White is winning.

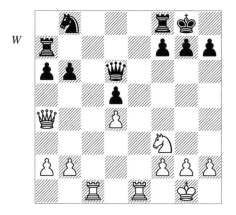

19 ♕c2 ♖e7

19...f6 loses to 20 ♕f5, when White will exchange queens on e6 to reach a winning endgame.

20 ♖xe7 ♕xe7 21 ♕c7 ♕xc7 22 ♖xc7

White takes no risks. Normally the side with the initiative tries to avoid exchanges, but Botvinnik sees that the advantage does not disappear. The whole game centres around the problem Black has extricating the knight. This is a problem Black has to struggle with even in the endgame.

22...f6 23 ♔f1 ♖f7 24 ♖c8+ ♖f8 25 ♖c3

Black has managed to chase the white rook away from the seventh rank, but how should he proceed? Whichever move he chooses allows the rook to take hold again. Therefore he decides to remove the pawns from the seventh rank, so that they cannot be attacked. However, in an endgame every pawn move risks generating new weaknesses.

25...g5 26 ♘e1 h5

After 26...h6 White will get an advantage by securing the f5-square with 27 ♘c2 ♔f7 28 ♘e3 ♔e6 29 g4.

27 h4

A thematic move worth remembering. However Black reacts, the pawns are weakened. If he takes on h4 his pawns are split into more pawn-islands and if he passes he allows White an ideal square for the knight on f4. Instead Black chooses to let the formation stay and finally brings out the unfortunate knight.

27...♘d7 28 ♖c7 ♖f7 29 ♘f3

Forcing a decision.

29...g4 30 ♘e1 f5 31 ♘d3 f4

The only chance. After 31...a5 32 ♘f4 ♘f6 33 ♖c6 White dominates and will soon win a pawn on the queenside.

32 f3!

Nailing down the f4-pawn. Botvinnik has played very instructively, gaining control of the queenside pawns and trying to create new weaknesses on the kingside. The knight in particular has been effective and has found outposts that tie the black rook to defence.

32 ♘b4 would have won a pawn, but in the endgame control can often be more important than material.

32...gxf3 33 gxf3 a5 34 a4 ♚f8 35 ♖c6 ♚e7 36 ♚f2 ♖f5 37 b3 ♚d8 38 ♚e2 ♘b8!

The best chance.

39 ♖g6!

After 39 ♖xb6 Black will get his knight into play with 39...♚c7 followed by ...♘c6. However, Botvinnik again chooses to keep the initiative and push back the black pieces rather than win a pawn.

39...♚c7 40 ♘e5 ♘a6 (D)

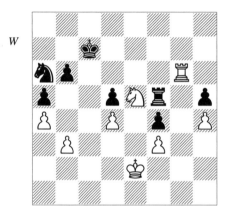

Here the game was adjourned. According to Botvinnik, Alekhine said that he would have resigned immediately if Botvinnik's sealed move had been 41 ♖g5. This move wins the h5-pawn as the g-pawn queens after 41...♖xg5 42 hxg5. Botvinnik chose another move, but the outcome of the game was the same.

41 ♖g7+ ♚c8

If 41...♚d6, then 42 ♖b7 wins the b6-pawn.

42 ♘c6 ♖f6 43 ♘e7+ ♚b8 44 ♘xd5 ♖d6 45 ♖g5 ♘b4

The knight finally becomes active but it is far too late.

46 ♘xb4 axb4 47 ♖xh5 ♖c6

47...♖xd4 48 ♖f5 and again the black rook is tied to defence and the white h-pawn can decide the game.

48 ♖b5 ♚c7 49 ♖xb4 ♖h6 50 ♖b5 ♖xh4 51 ♚d3

With the white king moving towards e4, Alekhine had had enough.

1-0

Erik Malmstig – Jesper Hall
Swedish Ch, Lidköping 1996

At the start of the 1996 Swedish Championship I was paired against a lower-rated opponent. I had prepared some openings, but the question was whether I wanted to reveal my variations to my main opponents so early. Why not play a solid variation in the Nimzo-Indian? I had played this opening before, although with other set-ups. If I just think logically and play solid moves I will get through the opening and then I will win in the middlegame. You probably realize my mistake: underestimation. My opponent understood the middlegame that arose much better as he was used to the opening.

1 d4 ♘f6 2 c4 e6 3 ♘c3 ♗b4 4 e3 0-0 5 ♗d3 d5 6 cxd5 exd5?!

This natural-looking move is the root of Black's problems. The best move is to take back with the knight so that it will not be stranded on f6, as in the game. This move indicates not only that Black has misunderstood the opening but also that he does not understand the structure that will arise.

7 ♘e2!

White has a natural formation, with ideas of f3, ♗c2, ♕d3 and perhaps g4 with an attack. The text-move is much better than 7 ♘f3, which justifies Black's move 6...exd5 as the e4-square will then be available for the black knight to use.

7...♖e8 8 f3 c5

Black wants to create counterplay in the centre as White has weakened his pawn-structure on the kingside, but the main question is whether f3 is a weakness at all in this middlegame structure.

9 0-0 ♘c6 10 a3 cxd4 11 exd4! *(D)*

11 axb4 dxc3 12 bxc3 ♘e5 gives Black satisfactory play on the c-file and a strong square at c4. Instead White chooses a pawn-structure with a fixed centre. The reason why Black has problems in this type of centre is paradoxically the f6-knight. It is perfectly placed to reach the ideal e4-square, but once f3 has been played, it has no prospects. One could say that White's strategy is prophylactic. The ideal square for the white knight is e5, but if White had gone for it, he would have allowed Black's knight to reach e4. Therefore White accepts a slightly worse position for his knight, in return for crippling Black's.

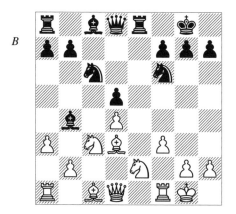

B

11...♗e7 12 ♗c2

White can calmly and methodically develop his pieces, as Black has no counterplay. He can either attack the king or put pressure on d5 with ♗b3 and ♘f4. Black's only natural plan is to put pressure on d4

with the knight on e6 and the bishop on f6, but this is not possible to achieve in practice, as the d5-pawn is too weak. I now used up a lot of time without finding any decent plan. In the end I decided to expand on the queenside, despite the risk of new weaknesses.

12...a6 13 ♗g5 b5 14 ♕d3 g6 15 ♕d2!

The queen heads for the dark squares, as weaknesses have been created there.

15...b4

Desperation, but what should Black do?

16 axb4 ♘xb4 17 ♗b3 ♖b8 18 ♘f4 ♕b6

After 18...♕d6, White has the decisive plan of doubling rooks on the e-file; for example, 19 ♖fe1 ♗b7 (19...♗e6 does not work because of 20 ♘xe6 fxe6 21 ♗f4, when White wins the exchange) 20 ♖e2 ♘e4 21 ♗xe7 ♘xd2 22 ♗xd6 ♖xe2 23 ♘fxe2 ♘xb3 24 ♖a3 and White wins at least a piece.

19 ♖fe1 ♗e6 20 ♘a4

Moving towards the key point c5.

20...♕b5 21 ♘c5?!

I do not remember what I had planned on 21 ♘xe6. White wins easily after 21...fxe6 22 ♖xe6 ♔f7 23 ♘c5 h6 24 ♗a4, when he is an exchange up.

21...♗xc5 22 ♗xf6!?

22 ♗a4 ♕b6 23 ♗xf6 ♗e7 transposes to the game.

22...♗e7 23 ♗a4 ♕b6 *(D)*

24 ♘h5!

White takes the chance to bring another piece into the attack on the dark squares. Malmstig has no intention of letting Black get away with a simple loss of the exchange. Other moves are less incisive:

a) 24 ♗xe8 ♗xf6 gives Black counterplay.

b) After 24 ♗e5 ♗g5 25 ♗xe8 ♖xe8 26 ♖ac1 ♘c6 White should win, but Black has some compensation in the form of the bishop-pair, with gives him a spark of hope.

24...♘c6 25 ♕f4

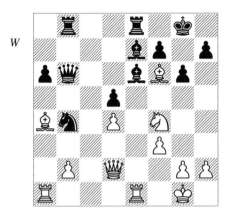

W

White continues to press, threatening ♗xc6, followed by ♗xe7 and the b8-rook is hanging.

25...♖bc8

After 25...♗b4 26 ♗xc6 ♕xc6 27 ♗e5 the threats of ♕h6 and ♗xb8 will decide the game.

26 ♗xc6 ♖xc6 27 ♗xe7 ♖xe7 28 ♕f6

A minor imprecision. After 28 ♘f6+ ♔g7 29 ♕e5! Black cannot do anything against the double check. For example, 29...♗h3 (29...♔h6 30 ♘g8#; 29...♕c7 30 ♘e8++ and White wins the queen) 30 ♘e8++ ♔h6 31 ♕xe7 and White is winning. In the game White wins easily as the split black pawns on the kingside cannot form a fortress that can stand against the extra white rook.

28...gxh5 29 ♕xe7 ♕xd4+ 30 ♔h1 ♖b6 31 ♕g5+ ♔f8 32 b3 ♖xb3 33 ♖xa6 ♖b8 34 ♕h6+ ♕g7?

This loses immediately, but even after the better 34...♔g8, 35 ♕g5+ ♔h8 36 ♕xh5 ♕f4 37 ♖a4 ♕xa4 38 ♕e5+ ♔g8 39 ♕xb8+ is winning for White.

35 ♖axe6 fxe6 36 ♕f4+ 1-0

After the game I felt like a schoolboy. Malmstig explained the various ideas and plans in the position. There was no doubt about who had played on home ground.

During the analysis it was embarrassingly obvious that the basic problem with the game was that I did not understand how to play with a fixed centre.

Mobile Centre

The side that has a mobile centre often wants to advance the pawns to create a passed pawn. However, if the opponent prevents this, an attack on the king might become possible, as the opponent's troops are focused on controlling the centre.

The side that plays against a mobile centre wants to control and blockade the pawns, and later to undermine them and destroy the centre.

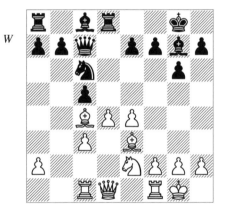

W

Svetozar Gligorić – Vasily Smyslov
USSR-Yugoslavia match, Kiev 1959

The Grünfeld has a mobile centre as its basic structure. The middlegames usually revolve around Black's attempts to attack the white centre. On the other hand, White can use his strong centre to create a passed pawn or launch an attack on the king.

12 h3?!

A waste of time. 12 ♕d2 seems more natural.

12...b6

Black points his second bishop towards White's centre.

13 f4 e6 14 ♕e1 ♗b7

14...♘a5 is another possibility; for example, 15 ♗d3 f5 16 g4 fxe4 17 ♗xe4 ♗b7 18 ♘g3 ♘c4 19 ♗xb7 ♕xb7 20 ♕f2 ♕c6 and Black had a slight advantage in Spassky-Fischer, Olympiad, Siegen 1970, as his minor pieces have better prospects.

15 ♕f2?

To avoid the terrible blockade that Black sets up in the game, White should have taken the chance to play 15 f5. Black seems to have somewhat better chances in the following variations, but it is far from clear: 15...♘a5 16 ♗d3 exf5 17 exf5 ♖e8 18 ♗g5 ♕c6 and now:

a) 19 ♕f2 cxd4 20 fxg6 fxg6 21 cxd4 (21 ♗c2? loses to 21...♕g2+) 21...♕d5 22 ♖c7 ♖f8 23 ♕g3 ♖xf1+ 24 ♔xf1 ♗xd4 and White's king is more exposed than Black's.

b) 19 ♖f2 cxd4 20 cxd4 ♕d5 with an advantage for Black as his pieces are better coordinated.

15...♘a5 16 ♗d3 f5!

A typical move for this type of central pawn-structure. It destroys White's attacking idea f5 and also clears the way for the b7-bishop.

17 e5

Not a fun move to make, but after 17 ♘g3 ♕d7 White has great problems holding the centre.

17...c4! 18 ♗c2 *(D)*

Black has a dream position against the mobile centre. Black actually has such complete control that White's centre has totally lost its mobility. The b7-bishop dominates the board and now, as White's central pawns are immobile, he has to find a new plan. First

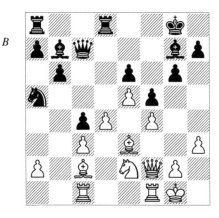

B

of all he wants to occupy the long a8-h1 diagonal, followed by a breakthrough on the queenside. Therefore the queen should be on c6 and the knight on d5, so the queenside pawns can start their march forward.

18...♘c6! 19 g4

The last attempt at activity, but White cannot break up Black's kingside. The rest of the game is therefore a fruitless wait for Black to go wrong. Another line is 19 ♖cd1 ♘e7 20 ♗c1 ♘d5 21 ♗a3 ♕c6, with the threat of ...♘e3.

19...♘e7 20 ♔h2 ♕c6 21 ♘g3 b5 22 a4 a6 23 ♖b1 ♖ab8 24 ♗d2 bxa4 25 ♖a1 ♗a8 26 ♗xa4 ♕c7 27 ♖a2 ♖b6 28 gxf5 exf5

Black does not need to be afraid of the two passed pawns in the centre as they are tied up. Observe that Black should not play 28...gxf5 as 29 ♘h5 suddenly gives White chances for an attack.

29 ♗c1 ♘d5 30 ♘e2 a5 31 ♗c2?!

31 ♗a3!?, trying to activate White's bad bishop, is certainly better, even though Black still keeps a clear advantage with 31...♕b7.

31...♖b3!

A very strong sacrifice. Note that Black's light-squared bishop is stronger than a rook, as there are no open files for rooks to use.

32 ♗xb3

After 32 ♗d2 ♖db8 33 ♖fa1 ♖b2 Black establishes a firm grip on White's second rank.

32...cxb3 33 ♖a4 ♗f8

33...♘xc3? is a big mistake as White's pieces come to life after 34 ♘xc3 ♕xc3 35 ♗d2. The game continuation just keeps them dead.

34 ♗b2

After 34 ♕g3 ♖b8 35 c4 b2 Black is winning.

34...♘e3!

On the way to the ideal c4-square.

35 ♖fa1

35 ♕xe3 ♕c6 36 d5 and now:

a) 36...♕xa4 37 d6 gives White unnecessary counterplay.

b) 36...♖xd5 gives Black gets an irresistible attack: 37 ♖aa1 ♖d2 38 ♖f2 ♖xb2 39 ♖xa5 ♖b1.

35...♘c4 36 ♘g3

36 ♖xc4 ♕xc4 37 ♖xa5 is answered by 37...♗e7 with the idea ...♗h4.

36...♗e7 37 ♘f1

After 37 ♘xf5 gxf5 38 ♕g3+ ♔f8! 39 ♖g1 ♗d5 White's attack is parried.

37...♕c6 38 ♖xc4 (D)

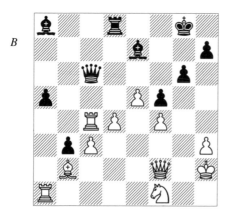

38...♕h1+! 39 ♔g3 h5 0-1

Mate is inevitable; for example, 40 ♕h2 ♕f3#, 40 ♕e3 ♕g2# or 40 ♕e2 ♕g1+ 41 ♕g2 ♕xg2#.

In this game Black managed to halt the advance of White's pawn-centre, and was able to set up a firm blockade and establish a grip on the long a8-h1 diagonal, leading to the white king's residence. Black invested an exchange in a queenside breakthrough, and this saddled White with one weakness too many. Black rounded off the game with a crisp mating attack.

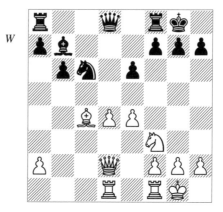

Boris Spassky – Tigran Petrosian
World Ch match (game 5), Moscow 1969

White has a mobile centre. The plan is again to advance the pawns to create a passed pawn or to point the pieces at the black king. Black wants to attack the white centre as in the previous game, but must take note of White's two ideas and neutralize them.

14 ♖fe1

When two different strategies meet, the fight often turns concrete and tactical. A variation like 14 d5!? ♘a5 15 dxe6!? ♘xc4 16 exf7+ ♔h8 17 ♕xd8 ♖axd8 18 ♖xd8 ♖xd8 19 e5 ♖c8 20 e6 ♗d5 21 ♘g5 ♘e5 22 f4 ♘g6 23 f5 ♘e7, with an interesting endgame, is typical for the structure.

14...♖c8 15 d5! exd5?

White gets a good game whichever way Black chooses to take back. 15...♘a5 is better, challenging White's centre:

a) If 16 dxe6, then 16...♕xd2 (and not 16...♘xc4 17 exf7+ ♔h8 18 ♕xd8 ♖cxd8 19 ♖xd8 ♖xd8 20 e5, when White's e-pawn is unstoppable) 17 exf7+ ♔h8 18 ♘xd2 ♘xc4 19 ♘xc4 ♖xc4 20 e5 ♗c8 21 e6 ♗xe6 22 ♖xe6 g6 23 ♖e7 ♖a4 24 ♖dd7 a6 leads to a draw as White cannot keep both his a-pawn and his f-pawn.

b) 16 ♗d3 exd5 and now:

b1) 17 exd5 ♕xd5 18 ♗xh7+ ♔xh7 19 ♕xd5 ♗xd5 20 ♖xd5 ♖fd8 with a level ending.

b2) 17 e5!? is a thematic move worth remembering, which gives White good attacking chances. Polugaevsky-Tal, USSR Ch, Moscow 1969 continued 17...♘c4 18 ♕f4 ♘b2 19 ♗xh7+ ♔xh7 20 ♘g5+ ♔g6 21 h4, and after 21...♖c4? 22 h5+ Polugaevsky won a beautiful game. 21...♕e7 is a better chance, when I cannot find anything decisive for White.

16 ♗xd5

White opts for an open centre, since his pieces are more active than his opponent's. The problem for Black is that if he wants to get rid of the strong bishop on d5 he has to allow White a strong passed pawn on the d-file. However, the question is whether 16 exd5 is stronger. After 16...♘a5 17 ♗f1 ♕d6 18 ♘g5 we see that White is now ready to push the passed pawn with the help of the e4-knight: 18...h6 19 ♘e4 ♕g6 20 ♕f4. White has the advantage as the pawn is ready to move forward.

16...♘a5?!

I do not like this move as it takes the knight away from the centre. 16...♕e7, to

bring the f8-rook into play, feels better, even though White has some pressure after 17 ♕f4 ♖c7 18 ♖d2 ♖fc8 19 ♖ed1.

17 ♕f4 ♕c7 18 ♕f5 ♗xd5

White was threatening to start an attack with ♘g5, so Black is forced to exchange on d5.

19 exd5

Now we are back in a position that is typical for the mobile centre. White has managed to get a passed pawn that is causing Black great difficulty.

19...♕c2

Or:

a) After 19...♘c4 20 ♘g5 g6 21 ♕h3 h5 22 ♘e4, White threatens both to start an attack on the weak dark squares around the black king and to advance the pawn.

b) 19...♕d6 20 ♘g5 ♕g6 21 ♕xg6 hxg6 22 d6 ♘b7 23 d7 ♖cd8 24 ♖e7 ♘c5 25 ♖d6 and Black is totally squeezed.

20 ♕f4!

20 ♕xc2 ♖xc2 21 ♖e7! also gives White a large advantage.

20...♕xa2 *(D)*

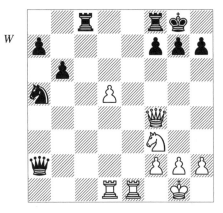

21 d6!

You could say that the passed pawn negates normal positional rules. The reason is that its promotion would lead to a decisive material advantage. In this respect the a2-pawn is not worth very much. Such pawns are commonly used as bait, to distract defenders from the advance of the passed pawn. Also note that Black's own passed queenside pawns are too far from reaching their goals to be really dangerous.

21...Rcd8 22 d7 Qc4 23 Qf5 h6

After 23...Qc6 24 Ne5 Qe6 25 Qc2 Ra8 26 Qc7 Qf6 27 Re3 White has strong pressure and should win, since Black has no counterplay.

24 Rc1 Qa6 25 Rc7 b5 (D)

White maintains the upper hand after 25...Nb3 26 Qd5 Nc5 27 Ne5.

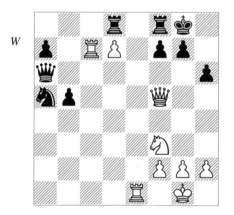

26 Nd4

26 Re8!, with the idea of Ne5, is even stronger; for example, 26...Qd6 27 Rc8 Nb7 28 Qxb5 Qd1+ 29 Ne1 Kh7 30 Rcxd8 Nxd8 31 Qa5 Nc6 32 Qf5+ Kg8 33 Qc5 and White is winning.

26...Qb6

Black could have prolonged his suffering with 26...Qd6 27 Nxb5 Qd2 28 Rf1 Nb3 29 Rxa7, though it is only a matter of time until the d-pawn will cost Black more material.

27 Rc8! Nb7 (D)

This allows a nice finish, but the alternatives also give White the opportunity to decide the game tactically:

a) 27...b4 28 Re8 Qxd4 29 Rxf8+ Rxf8 30 Rxf8+ Kxf8 31 Qc5+! Qxc5 32 d8Q#.

b) 27...g6 28 Rxd8 Qxd8 29 Qxb5.

c) 27...Qxd4 28 Rxd8 Rxd8 29 Re8+ Rxe8 30 dxe8Q#.

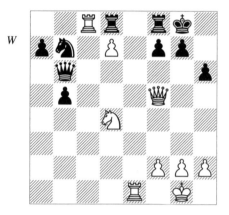

28 Nc6! Nd6 29 Nxd8!

The point. The fight to promote the passed pawn justifies big sacrifices.

29...Nxf5 30 Nc6 1-0

Fluid Centre

In a fluid centre the structure in the centre has not yet been decided; the centre is still under tension. Both players therefore must strive toward the structures that suit them best.

Jesper Hall – Marinus Kuijf
2nd Bundesliga 1996/7

1 e4 e6 2 d3

Those who play the French often like the closed position that arises after 2 d4 d5 3 e5.

However, with 2 d3, the character of the game is completely different and many other types of structure can appear.

2...d5 3 ♘d2 c5 4 ♘gf3 ♘c6 5 g3 g6 *(D)*

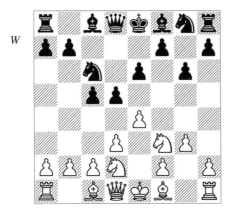

W

This opening is called the King's Indian Attack. White's idea is to delay any decision in the centre until he knows where Black is developing his pieces. If Black puts his king on the kingside, White wants to close the centre with e5, followed by ♗g2, 0-0, ♖e1, h4, ♘f1, ♘h2, ♘g4, ♗f4 or ♗g5 with an attack. If Black puts his king on the queenside, White wants to open the centre in combination with a queenside attack beginning with a3, c3, and b4. In summary, if Black castles kingside, White closes the centre, and if Black castles queenside, White opens it. Black's ideas are to go for ...b5, ...a5, and ...a4, and if possible ...a3, in combination with castling kingside, or to castle queenside and attack the white king with ...h6 and ...g5. An important finesse is that after ...e5 Black is two tempi behind in a common variation of the King's Indian. That is at least one tempo too many. All in all this means that the position becomes a kind of trench warfare where both players conceal their strategies. The main question is where the black king should hide.

6 h4!? h6

After 6...♗g7, 7 h5 is unpleasant.

7 ♗g2

On 7 h5 Black could now play 7...g5.

7...♗g7 8 0-0 ♘ge7 9 ♖e1 b6 10 ♕e2 ♗b7 11 c3 ♕c7 12 a3

Black has developed his pieces on natural squares and it is time to select a plan. However, before he does that, he tries to force a decision from White about the centre by putting pressure on the d3-pawn.

12...♗a6

Here I was satisfied. I did not think that Black's last move could be the best, since I learned as a beginner that you should not move the same piece twice in the opening. The question is how should White proceed. I had a similar position in an earlier game where ...a5 had been played and with this in mind I found an idea.

13 ♖b1 dxe4 14 ♘xe4 ♖d8 15 c4! *(D)*

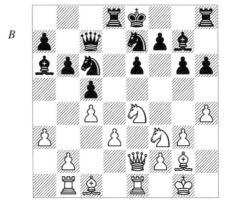

B

A difficult move to play. As part of our investigation into central pawn-structures, you should really ask yourself what White is doing. I freely accept a backward pawn on d3 and also give Black's knight access to the great square d4. However, I gain some advantages too. Most importantly, I have a dominating bishop on the h1-a8 diagonal, as its black counterpart cannot challenge the diagonal once the b-file is opened. With a fluid centre the players must always be ready to handle various central formations, even the unorthodox.

15...♘f5 16 b4 ♘cd4 17 ♘xd4 ♘xd4 18 ♕d1 ♗c8 19 bxc5 bxc5 20 ♗f4 *(D)*

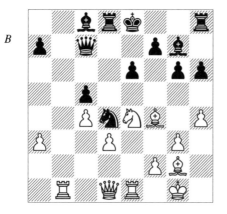

To entice ...e5, which gives my knight d5.
20...e5 21 ♗d2 f5 22 ♘c3 0-0 23 ♘d5 ♕d6 24 f4 ♘e6 25 ♕e2

White wants to exchange knights. After that the light-squared bishop can dominate the board and the rooks can occupy the open files. The move also sets a trap.

25...exf4?

It is better to return the knight to d4. I had then planned to retreat the queen to d1 with the idea of trying to find the correct path through the messy variations after taking on e5. For example, 25...♘d4 26 ♕d1 ♘e6 27 fxe5 ♗xe5 28 ♗xh6 ♖f7 29 h5 ♖h7 30 ♕d2 ♗d4+ 31 ♗e3 ♖xh5 32 ♗xd4 ♘xd4 33 ♕f4 and White has a small advantage.

26 ♘xf4 ♘xf4 27 ♗xf4 ♕xd3 *(D)*
28 ♕xd3!

Black had missed this move. Kuijf only calculated 28 ♗d5+ ♖xd5 29 cxd5 ♕xd5,

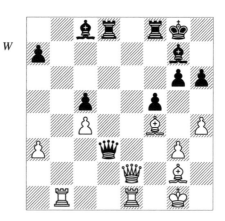

which gives Black good play on the open diagonals towards the white king.

28...♖xd3 29 ♗d5+ ♔h8 30 ♗d6 ♖d8 31 ♗c7 ♖f8 32 ♗d6 ♖d8 33 ♗e7 ♖8xd5?!

33...♖e8 34 ♗xc5 ♖xe1+ 35 ♖xe1 should be winning for White, but there are more technical difficulties. Observe how passive the black light-squared bishop has been throughout the game.

34 cxd5 ♗d7

White has a brutal and simple plan at his disposal: to double the rooks on the seventh rank. Black can do nothing.

35 ♗xc5 ♖xg3+ 36 ♔h2 ♖d3 37 ♖b8+ ♔h7 38 ♖e7 ♖d2+ 39 ♔g1 ♖d1+ 40 ♔f2 ♖d2+ 41 ♔e3 ♖xd5 42 ♖b7 f4+ 43 ♔f2

In the end White will be a rook up.
1-0

As your experience grows, planning the centre will come very naturally. Soon it will be instinctive. However, I still think that it is important that, once or twice during a game, you remind yourself of the basic rules. Otherwise it is easy to focus so much on variations that you forget the bigger picture. Therefore, clear your mind of variations once in a while and check whether your plan is in line with the demands of the pawn-structure.

Is your plan in accordance with classical principles? This is a question that suggests how you should proceed. Then you can focus again on the exact calculations.

Kotov's scheme gives the basis of the pawn-centre, but nearly all openings have their own structure. What matters is to find what is unique about the structure on the board and what part of it resembles the basic positions above. We then reach what I call position-types, which have a chapter of their own but are also mentioned in Chapter 9.

My Training Tips

Pawn-structures in the centre can be studied as position-types. For those who want to extend their knowledge I refer to Chapter 8.

Suggestions for Further Reading

In this area there are two real classics. I have already mentioned the chapter 'Various Pawn Positions in the Centre' in *The Art of the Middlegame in Chess* by Paul Keres and Alexander Kotov (Penguin, 1964). The other book is *My System* by Aron Nimzowitsch (various editions in many languages; there is an English-language algebraic edition published by Hays/Batsford), which explains the pawn's function. In these books I think that you will find what you need to understand the dynamic pawn. Moreover, all these books will amply repay re-reading at various stages of your chess career, as you will gain additional insights each time.

6 How to Find Your Way Through the Terrain of Chess

On various kinds of positional advantage

We have to learn how to recognize an advantageous position in order to decide what to search for and what to strive towards.

In a game of chess there is a myriad of possibilities. Computers might soon be able to calculate chess down to mate, but you as a human being have to learn how to recognize an advantageous position in order to decide what to search for and what to strive towards. It is therefore critical that you learn how to detect the various advantages and weaknesses in the position. In the training situation it is important to start with examples which have clearly defined advantages. When you have learnt what each advantage consists of, you can gradually go on to positions containing several different advantages. Then, of course, it is a matter of finding and understanding the most important advantage.

Various Kinds of Advantage

Here are examples of the advantages that you can encounter in a position:

1) The opponent has a vulnerable king-position.

2) Material advantage.

3) Better pawn-structure.

4) Control of a key file, key rank or key square.

5) Better-placed pieces.

6) Space advantage.

7) Development advantage.

8) The initiative.

The first three categories are rather obviously advantageous, while the others demand quite a bit of experience for you to make them part of your subconscious understanding. You will continue learning to recognize advantages for the rest of your chess career. This knowledge is linked to relevant standard positions. Your judgement will gradually become subtler as your understanding deepens.

1) The Opponent Has a Weak King-Position

If your opponent has a weak king-position, you have an obvious advantage. Not even a huge material advantage can save a player who is confronted with mate. This is what happens in the following study where David beats Goliath.

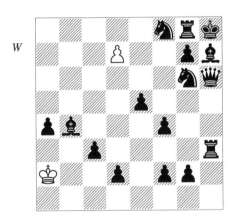

Cyril Stanley Kipping
1936

1 d8♘
Mate follows on f7 next move.

The weakness of the opponent's king is not always as obvious as this. Often it is a question of seeing the advantage long before the final mating combination is delivered. A good tip is to count how many pieces are attacking and how many are defending. The next step is to identify the weaknesses around your opponent's king and to find active and favourable outposts for your own pieces, targeting the weaknesses.

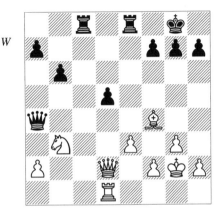

José Raúl Capablanca – Alexander Alekhine
World Ch match (game 3), Buenos Aires 1927

The position is roughly level on material, but White has a slight edge as the d5-pawn is weak and White's knight has a good outpost on d4. However, White chooses to change the character of the position, as Capablanca has spotted another type of advantage.

23 ♕xd5! ♖c2

23...♕xa2 24 ♖a1 ♕c2 25 ♖xa7 gives White a clear advantage.

24 ♖d2 ♖xa2?!

Maybe 24...♕xa2 was a better attempt, trying to get the queen back to defend. Even then, Black has great problems as White forces the black queen to protect the a-pawn with 25 ♕d7 ♖f8 26 ♖xc2 ♕xc2 27 ♘d4 ♕e4+ (after 27...♕a2 we are more or less back in the game continuation) 28 f3 ♕a8 29

♕g4 g6 30 ♗h6, and White can start a dangerous attack on the weak dark squares.

25 ♖xa2 ♕xa2 26 ♕c6 *(D)*

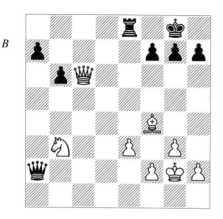

White has allowed Black two connected passed pawns on the queenside. In the event of a queen exchange, Black would probably win the position as White would have difficulties blockading the pawns. However, there is another element that is critical: White's minor pieces form a strong attacking team together with the queen against the black king. The rook is not a good defensive piece and therefore the queen is needed on, e.g., g6 for a successful defence. The rest of the game is very instructive. All White's pieces will be directed towards the weak spot g7. That means the knight on f5 or e6 and the bishop on d4.

26...♖f8 27 ♘d4 ♔h8 28 ♗e5 f6 29 ♘e6 ♖g8 30 ♗d4

White threatens 31 ♘xg7 ♖xg7 32 ♕xf6 ♕g8 33 h4 with the idea of moving the pawn to h6. If Black then plays 33...h5, there follows 34 ♕h6+ ♕h7 35 ♗xg7+ and White is a piece up.

30...h6 31 h4

Before White sacrifices on g7, he gives his king some space to avoid perpetual check.

31...♕b1 32 ♘xg7 ♕g6

32...♖xg7 33 ♕xf6 ♕e4+ (33...♕h7 34 ♕f8+ ♕g8 35 ♗xg7+ and White is winning) 34 ♔g1 ♕g4 (34...♕b1+ 35 ♔h2) 35 ♕xh6+ ♔g8 36 ♕xg7+ ♕xg7 37 ♗xg7 ♔xg7 38 ♔f1 and White is winning the pawn ending.

33 h5 ♕f7 34 ♘f5

With its backbone removed, the black position falls apart. Note that the black queenside pawns do not have the time to move a single step during the final phase of the game.

34...♔h7 35 ♕e4 ♖e8 36 ♕f4 ♕f8 37 ♘d6 ♖e7 38 ♗xf6 ♕a8+ 39 e4 ♖g7 40 ♗xg7 ♔xg7 41 ♘f5+ ♔f7 42 ♕c7+ 1-0

2) Material Advantage

When you have won material the normal plan is to try to exchange pieces to obtain an endgame. A practical idea is also to break through where you have your extra piece or pawn. You should consolidate and centralize your pieces so that you have control over a possible counterattack, before you force the play. Time is on your side.

Duncan Suttles – Vasily Smyslov
Venice 1974

As we have observed, with a material advantage the most common strategy is to exchange pieces and head for a won endgame. Good endgame technique makes it possible to use this strategy even more subtly. Here, Smyslov is a pawn up, but his opponent has some initiative. Time to look for liquidations.

29...♘f7! 30 ♖d1

30 ♘xf7 provides better chances, but even then Black seems able to achieve an endgame in which he has a large advantage by 30...♔xf7 31 ♘d4 ♘e3 32 ♖b1 ♕g4 33 ♖b7+ ♔g8 34 ♕e6+ ♔h8 35 ♕xg4 ♘xg4 36 ♘e6 ♖e8.

30...♘xd6 31 ♘xd6 ♕xd6 32 ♕xd6 ♖xd6 33 ♖xd2 ♖b6!

Smyslov must have seen this key move in advance.

34 ♗d4

After 34 ♖d1 ♘e3 35 ♖c1 ♘xc2 White cannot take the knight because of the back-rank mate.

34...♖b1+ 35 ♗g1 ♘c3! *(D)*

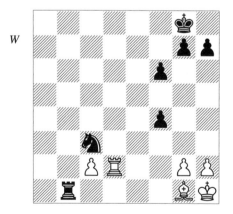

This wonderful move ties up White's pieces. If the rook leaves the second rank, ...♘e2 wins the bishop, and if White plays g3, then ...f3 followed by ...♘e2 has the same effect. The only remaining option for White is to play h3, which incurs new weaknesses.

36 h3 ♔f7 37 ♔h2 g5 38 ♖d7+ ♔g6 39 ♖c7 ♘e2

Now we see the drawback of 36 h3. Black can get a dangerous attack either by putting the knight on g3 or with a pawn-storm.

40 ♗f2 ♖f1 41 ♗a7 h5

There is no defence against the threat of weaving a mating-net with ...g4. White becomes desperate.

42 g4 fxg3+ 43 ♔g2 ♖e1

Black plans to continue ...h4 and ...♘f4+, with a decisive advantage.

0-1

3) Better Pawn-Structure

Doubled pawns, backward pawns, pawn-islands and passed pawns are examples of topics on pawns which lie beyond Chapter 5. Generally speaking, doubled pawns are a slight weakness as two pawns on the same file are not as dynamic as two beside each other. Exceptions do exist, when, e.g., the doubled pawns cover important squares in the centre, give extra support to a pawn-chain, strengthen a defensive barricade or are compensated for by a strong rook on an open file.

A backward pawn is not something to strive for. It is a pawn that, while not necessarily isolated, has a weak square in front of it, and has no real hope of advancing. Here you have to watch out. It is easy to assume a pawn is backward even when it can move forward or when it is compensated for by other advantages.

'Pawn-islands' is a chess term that refers to the number of groups of connected pawns in your position which are isolated from each other. Often it is best to have as few islands as possible, since pawns can guard each other and tend to be weaker in smaller groups.

There is an old saying that a passed pawn outweighs all other types of advantage. The possibility of promotion often decides games.

Therefore you should always take a passed pawn seriously. Nimzowitsch said that the passed pawn was "a criminal that should be kept under lock and key". This idea is worth remembering.

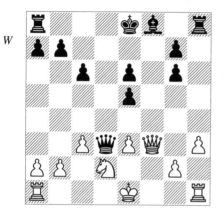

W

David Bronstein – Savielly Tartakower
Interzonal tournament, Saltsjöbaden 1948

Doubled pawns can be dynamic if they are linked to other pawns, but if they are isolated they are almost always bad. In this example Black has an extra pawn but also two pairs of isolated doubled pawns. The fundamental principle is that doubled pawns are weaker the further the game proceeds. White can therefore exchange queens despite his material inferiority.

17 ♕e4 ♕xe4 18 ♘xe4

The reason why Black has real problems in this position is that the white knight has better prospects than the black bishop.

18...♗e7 19 ♔e2 ♖d8 20 ♖ad1 0-0 21 ♖xd8 ♖xd8 22 ♖f1

To cut off the black king.

22...b6

This is forced, as after 22...♖f8 23 ♖d1 ♖d8 24 ♖xd8+ ♗xd8 25 ♘c5 White wins a pawn.

23 ♘f2

White has reached an ideal position where all his pieces are perfectly positioned. However, although the white knight looks beautiful on e4, this does not enable White to make further progress. Time to go for the e5-pawn with ♘d3.

23...♖d5 24 ♘d3 ♗f6 25 ♘b4 *(D)*

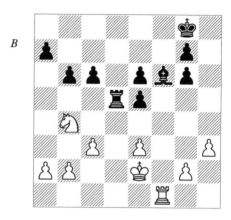

B

25...♖b5?

25...♖d6 offers Black more hope, even though the endgame arising after 26 ♖d1 ♖xd1 27 ♔xd1 is very promising for White. The knight can force the black pawns on the queenside to squares the same colour as the bishop, and then the king can penetrate on the light squares d3, c4, b5, and a6. It is not completely clear that White is winning but I have found the following promising variation: 27...c5 28 ♘c6 a5 29 e4 ♔f7 30 b3 ♔e8 31 ♔c2 ♔d7 32 ♘a7 ♗h4 33 ♔d3 ♗e1 34 ♔c4 ♔c7 35 a4 ♔b7 36 ♘b5 ♔c6 (Black has succeeded in keeping the white king away, but with precise manoeuvring White can put Black into zugzwang and force a way in) 37 ♘a3 ♗d2 38 ♘c2 ♗f4 39 ♘e1 g5 40 ♘f3 g6 41 g4 ♔d6 42 ♔b5 ♔c7 43 c4 ♔b7 44 h4 ♔c7 45 hxg5 ♗g3 (otherwise White will play ♘h4) 46 ♔a6 ♔c6 47 ♔a7 ♔c7 48 ♘d2

♗f4 49 ♘b1 ♗xg5 50 ♘c3 ♗e3 51 ♘b5+ ♔c6 52 ♔b8 and White wins.

26 a4!

Black's rook now risks becoming totally passive and it takes considerable difficulty to save it.

26...♖c5 27 e4 b5 28 a5 ♗d8 29 ♖a1 ♖c4 30 ♔d3 ♗e7 31 ♘a6

Stronger than 31 b3 ♖xb4 32 cxb4 ♗xb4, when White still has some technical problems to overcome.

31...♖a4 32 ♖xa4 bxa4 *(D)*

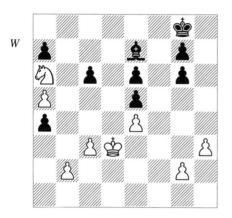

Black now has three pairs of doubled pawns and when the c6-pawn disappears the doubled pawns will be the only ones left. Therefore White wins easily by means of a king-march to a6.

33 ♘b8 a3 34 bxa3 ♗xa3 35 ♘xc6 ♗c5 36 ♔c4 ♗g1 37 ♔b5 ♔f7 38 ♔a6 ♔f6 39 ♘xa7 ♔g5 40 g3 ♗f2 41 c4 ♔f6 42 ♘c8 ♗xg3 43 c5 1-0

4) Control of a Key File, Rank or Square

Key file and key rank

The rooks and queen are the only pieces that can control a key file or rank. All files can be key files, but normally it is only the seventh and the second ranks that are key ranks, as most of the opponent's pawns are located there and can be attacked from the side. Often you try to get control of a key file in order to obtain control of a key rank.

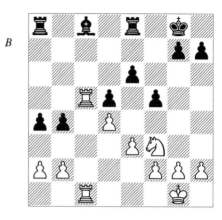

Alexander Alekhine – Frederick Yates
London 1922

White has a superior position with a better minor piece which has access to the key e5-square. Above all, White controls the only open file. White can take it easy and put his king and knight on the best squares before the decisive attack is delivered, because an exchange of rooks on the c-file would give White a won endgame with a strong knight against a bad bishop.

20...♗a6 21 ♘e5 ♖eb8

After 21...♖ec8 22 ♖xc8+ ♖xc8 23 ♖xc8+ ♗xc8 24 ♘c6 White wins a pawn or the bishop.

22 f3 b3

If 22...a3 then 23 b3, so as not to give Black's rooks any open file to operate on.

23 a3 h6

White would win a pawn after 23...♖c8 24 ♖xc8+ ♖xc8 25 ♖xc8+ ♗xc8 26 ♘d3 and 27 ♘c5.

24 ♔f2 ♔h7 25 h4 ♖f8 26 ♔g3 ♖fb8 27 ♖c7 ♗b5 28 ♖1c5 ♗a6 29 ♖5c6 ♖e8 30 ♔f4 ♔g8 31 h5 ♗f1 32 g3 ♗a6 *(D)*

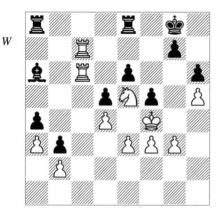

White's position is perfect, but he needs to find the knockout blow. A common plan for the player who possesses a file is to transform the vertical control to horizontal control of the seventh rank. You can see that the weak point is g7. With a beautiful finish, Alekhine takes advantage of this.

33 ♖f7 ♔h7 34 ♖cc7 ♖g8 35 ♘d7 ♔h8 36 ♘f6 ♖gf8

36...gxf6 37 ♖h7#.

37 ♖xg7 ♖xf6 38 ♔e5! *(D)*

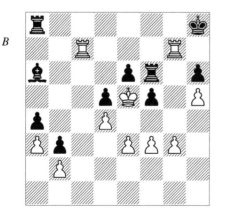

Winning a rook, as any rook move to f8 is answered by ♖h7+ followed by ♖cg7#.

1-0

Key squares

If you have access to a key square then you have a good outpost for a piece. These squares do not appear by themselves: you must force your opponent to concede them. The first step is to learn to recognize a key square and to know what to strive for.

Anatoly Karpov – Walter Browne
San Antonio 1972

This game made a strong impression on me as a young junior. The clear positional theme that runs through the game starts as early as move four. It made me realize that the strength of the two bishops can be more than balanced by a weak square.

1 c4 c5 2 b3 ♘f6 3 ♗b2 g6 4 ♗xf6 *(D)*

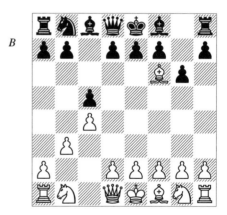

White gives Black the bishop-pair but obtains the important d5-square. Black is also given a backward pawn on d7 and doubled f-pawns. All in all, this guarantees that the exchange is to White's advantage. Look how Karpov subsequently exploits his advantage.

4...exf6 5 ♘c3 ♗g7 6 g3

The bishop will support the knight on d5, using the nice h1-a8 diagonal.

6...♘c6 7 ♗g2 f5 8 e3 0-0 9 ♘ge2

The g1-knight also heads for the key square via c3 or f4.

9...a6 10 ♖c1 b5 11 d3 ♗b7 12 0-0 d6 13 ♕d2 ♕a5 *(D)*

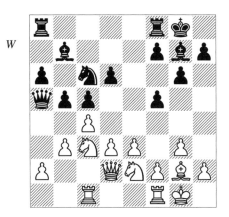

It is hard for Black to find a plan because a white knight will dominate the position from d5. In order to defend, Black has to exchange pieces and wait for chances that might appear when White tries to break through. White plans to play d4 followed by dxc5 with the idea of penetrating with the rooks on the d-file.

14 ♖fd1 ♖ab8 15 ♘d5 ♕xd2 16 ♖xd2 b4

White threatened 17 cxb5 axb5 18 d4.

17 d4 ♖fd8 18 ♖cd1

According to Karpov, White should prefer 18 dxc5 dxc5 19 ♖cd1, threatening 20 ♘e7+, although Black could continue the fight with 19...♔f8.

18...cxd4 19 exd4 ♔f8 20 c5

Black has succeeded in keeping the d-file closed, forcing White to find a new plan for a breakthrough. White therefore chooses to transform his advantage into a passed pawn

on the queenside. This is a dubious plan that gives the black pieces better opportunities. Instead White should proceed with 20 ♘e3 to continue manoeuvring without forcing the play.

20...♘a7!

The knight suddenly has access to the excellent b5-square.

21 ♘e3

21 cxd6 ♗xd5 22 ♗xd5 ♖xd6 23 ♗g2 ♘b5 and Black even has the better prospects.

21...♗xg2 22 ♔xg2 dxc5 23 dxc5 ♖xd2 24 ♖xd2 ♖c8

White still has the advantage of an extra pawn on the queenside, but the black pieces now have good squares, diagonals and files to work on. Therefore, exact planning is necessary.

25 ♘d5!

After 25 ♖c2 ♘b5 the black pieces are active. White must act quickly.

25...♖xc5 26 ♘xb4 a5 27 ♘d5 *(D)*

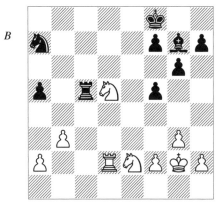

27...♖c6?!

27...♘c6 would have made it much harder for White to take advantage of the extra pawn. Now White can move forward and force some exchanges. Remember my comments from previous chapters: if you have an extra pawn, then you should desire to exchange pieces.

28 ♘e3 ♖c5 29 ♘f4 ♗h6 30 ♖d5 ♖xd5 31 ♘fxd5 ♗xe3?

Now White has excellent winning prospects. If Black had played 31...♘c6 instead it is far from clear that White would have been able to push the extra pawn.

32 ♘xe3

Knight endings usually correspond to pawn endings. White therefore has a more or less decisive advantage. Black's only chance is to block the queenside and not allow the exchange of knights.

32...♔e7 33 ♘c4 ♘c6 34 ♔f3 ♔e6 35 ♔e3 ♔d5 36 a3

Preparing ♔d3.

36...♔e6 37 ♔d3 ♔d5 38 f3 h6 39 ♔c3 h5 40 ♔d3 f6 *(D)*

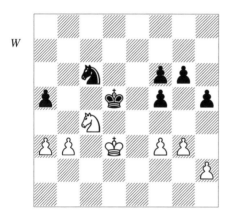

41 f4!

Black is in zugzwang.

41...g5

Or:

a) 41...♔c5 42 ♘xa5 ♔xa5 43 b4+ ♔b5 44 bxa5 ♔xa5 45 ♔c4 and White's king will pick off Black's kingside pawns.

b) 41...♔e6 42 ♘b6 ♔d6 43 ♔c4 and White's king comes in on the queenside.

42 ♘e3+ ♔e6

Black is forced to leave the way free for the white king to penetrate the queenside and is bound to lose. The only chance is to create counterplay on the kingside.

43 h4!

Preventing all counterplay and fixing the weak black pawns.

43...gxh4 44 gxh4 ♘e7 45 ♔c4 ♘g6 46 ♘g2 ♔d6 47 ♔b5 ♔d5 48 ♔xa5 ♔e4 49 b4 ♔f3 50 b5 ♔xg2 51 b6 ♘f8 52 ♔b5 ♘d7 53 a4 ♘xb6 54 ♔xb6 ♔f3 55 a5 ♔xf4 56 a6 ♔e3 57 a7 f4 58 a8♕ f3 59 ♕e8+

White picks up the h- and f-pawns, sacrifices on f3, and advances the h4-pawn.

1-0

5) Better-Placed Pieces

Active pieces are pieces which have influence over many squares and are in positions that restrain your opponent. Therefore it is important to understand exactly what makes a piece well-placed with good prospects. To have an advantage, your own pieces should be more active than your opponent's.

William Winter – José Raúl Capablanca
Hastings 1919

1 e4 e5 2 ♘f3 ♘c6 3 ♘c3 ♘f6 4 ♗b5 ♗b4 5 0-0 0-0 6 ♗xc6 dxc6 7 d3 ♗d6 8 ♗g5 h6 9 ♗h4 c5

Capablanca was not an opening specialist, but the longer the game lasted, the more his strengths appeared. By the middlegame he had normally equalized and in the endgame he won. He was one of greatest positional players of all time. Now he prepares a pawn advance on the kingside, but he knows that you must then watch out for a counterattack in the centre. Therefore he plays ...c5 first.

10 ♘d5?

10 ♘d2 seems to be more logical, to avoid the continuation in the game and to place the knight on the ideal e3-square. White can then hope for a small advantage.

10...g5 11 ♘xf6+

Not a fun move to make, but the only alternative is 11 ♗g3, which gives Black the chance to storm the kingside by 11...♘xd5 12 exd5 ♗g4 13 ♖e1 ♖e8 14 c4 f5 15 h3 ♗h5, with a clear advantage to Black.

11...♕xf6 12 ♗g3 (D)

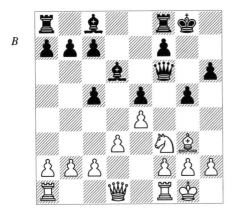

This position has become a 'classic'. The plan that Capablanca executes is so logical and simple that when I am White I hardly dare to retreat a bishop to h4 after ...h6.

12...♗g4 13 h3 ♗xf3 14 ♕xf3 ♕xf3 15 gxf3 f6! (D)

When I saw this position for the first time my gaze fixed on the black pawns and bishop, standing on squares of the same colour. White must surely be better. However, with ...f6 Capablanca demonstrates that there is another positional element that weighs much more heavily – the g3-bishop is dead. If you appreciate that, then Black's plan appears natural. Which flank should Black play on? The queenside! Where should the king stand to prevent a break in the centre, the only

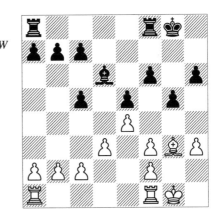

possible way to free the bishop? On e6! The continuation is grim for White.

16 ♔g2?!

If White had understood what was about to happen, he would have tried to bring the king to the queenside, either here or on move 21.

16...a5 17 a4 ♔f7 18 ♖h1 ♔e6 19 h4 ♖fb8

A breakthrough on the queenside is unavoidable, because it will always be possible to support ...b5 with a pawn on c6.

20 hxg5 hxg5 21 b3 c6 22 ♖a2

White tries to create counterplay against Black's a-pawn, but it becomes clear that Black has finesses he can use.

22...b5 23 ♖ha1 c4! 24 axb5

24 bxc4 bxc4 25 dxc4 ♖b4 and Black is winning.

24...cxb3 25 cxb3 ♖xb5 26 ♖a4 ♖xb3 27 d4 ♖b5 28 ♖c4

28 dxe5 must, for reasons of chess aesthetics, be met with 28...fxe5.

28...♖b4 29 ♖xc6 ♖xd4 0-1

A game that feels clean, neat and logical.

In the following position, White is a pawn up but has a bad bishop that is penned in by its own pawns. If Black could transfer his knight to e5 it would dominate the position

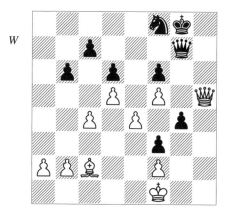

Alexander Alekhine – Hans Johner
Zurich 1934

and he would have a considerable advantage. Alekhine finds a way to transform the bad bishop into a good one. Surprisingly, the game only lasts for four more moves.

44 e5! dxe5

After 44...fxe5 45 f6 ♕xf6 46 ♕xg4+ ♔f7 47 ♗e4 White regains the sacrificed pawns with a more or less winning position, a pawn up with a bishop that has good prospects.

45 d6! c5

45...cxd6 allows the logical finesse 46 c5!, a new pawn sacrifice that prepares the decisive ♗b3+ and threatens to create a passed pawn.

46 ♗e4

From the point where we joined the game, where Black had a lovely key square for his knight on e5, things have changed; it is now White who has one on d5 for his bishop.

46...♕d7 47 ♕h6 1-0

Black resigned as 47...♔f7 48 ♗d5+ ♔e8 49 ♕xf6 ♕h7 50 ♗c6+ ♘d7 51 ♕g6+ wins for White. A game where the pawns were not worth much compared with the importance of bringing the pieces to life.

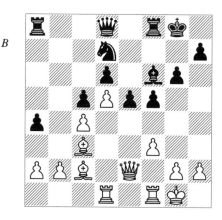

Herman Pilnik – Efim Geller
Interzonal tournament, Gothenburg 1955

White has problems finding diagonals for the pair of bishops. Therefore Black has the advantage. But how to proceed? Where to put the pieces? The continuation is a classic: once you have seen it you will always look for it in this position-type.

22...e4! 23 ♗xf6

Maybe 23 fxe4 ♗xc3 24 bxc3 f4 25 ♖b1 was to be preferred, to obtain a file for the rooks to work on. In the game White is totally squeezed with no counterplay at all.

23...♕xf6 24 fxe4 f4! *(D)*

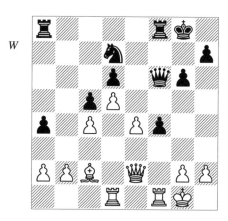

This is Black's thematic idea. For the price of a pawn, White's bishop is walled in and the black knight is given access to a great outpost on e5. As the centre is closed, the knight dominates the position. In closed positions play proceeds on the flanks, so Black's next step is to prepare to attack on the kingside.

25 ♖f2 ♘e5 26 ♖df1 ♕h4 27 ♗d1

The threat of ...♘g4 forces White to put all his pieces into the defence.

27...♖f7

Black wants to play ...g5 to attack the white king, but as there is no counterplay in sight he can slowly put his pieces on the best squares before advancing the pawns.

28 ♕c2 g5 29 ♕c3 ♖af8 30 h3 h5 31 ♗e2 g4 32 ♖xf4 ♖xf4 33 ♖xf4 ♖xf4 34 g3 ♘f3+ 35 ♔f2

35 ♗xf3 ♕xg3+ 36 ♔g2 ♖f3 is hopeless for White.

35...♕xh3 36 gxf4 g3+ 37 ♔xf3 g2+ 38 ♔f2 ♕h2 0-1

Black's g-pawn will promote.

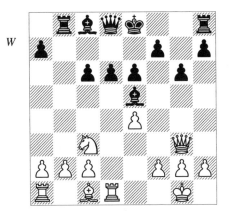

Elizbar Ubilava – Gennadi Timoshchenko
Cheliabinsk 1974

I have always thought that it is a bit dangerous to say that a rook is worth five pawns and the knight and bishop are worth three each. Many players forget that pieces are worth different amounts depending on the position. It is especially easy to miss exchange sacrifices if you only judge the position on these criteria. Here a very convincing example where the minor pieces are worth more than the rooks.

14 ♕xe5!

A beautiful move with the idea of achieving an endgame where Black's h8-rook is bricked in. White has seen that he can reach a position where his minor pieces will totally dominate the board from excellent outposts.

14...dxe5 15 ♖xd8+ ♔xd8 16 ♗g5+ ♔e8

Black cannot clear the way for the h8-rook since 16...♔c7 17 ♗f6 ♖e8 18 ♗xe5+ is winning for White.

17 ♗f6 ♖g8 18 ♖d1 ♗d7 19 ♘a4!

The white pieces have great squares to head for. With the knight on c5, the black king and the g8-rook will not be able to get out. This is much more important than grabbing the e5-pawn.

19...♖b4

The problem for Black is that after 19...♖b5 20 h4 ♖a5 21 b3 c5 he is not threatening to take on a4 as it is mate on d8.

20 ♘c5 ♖d4

Black tries to reduce the pressure by exchanging a pair of rooks, but his real problem, the g8-rook's predicament, remains.

21 ♖xd4 exd4 *(D)*

22 h4!

A move that decides the destiny of the rook, by preventing ...g5 and its only hope of liberation.

22...e5

Or:

a) 22...g5 23 hxg5 ♖g6 24 e5 h6 25 f4 hxg5 26 fxg5 and the rook cannot come out.

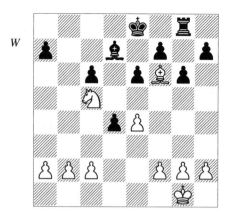

b) 22...h6 23 g4 g5 (23...e5 24 f3 makes no difference) 24 h5 and Black is all tied up on the kingside.

23 f3 ♗e6

After 23...g5 24 hxg5 ♖g6 25 ♘d3 White is winning.

24 b3

With the black pieces stuck on the king-side, White has a winning plan in advancing on the queenside.

24...a5 25 g4 h5 26 g5 ♗h3 27 ♔f2 ♖f8 28 ♔e2 ♖g8 29 a4

The a-pawn will win the game for White.

Important guidelines for pieces
- The bishop is often stronger than the knight when the centre is open and there is play on both flanks.
- The knight is often stronger than the bishop in closed positions.
- For the knight to be good in a game with play on both flanks, it needs a supported outpost in the centre.
- Pawns should usually stand on squares of the opposite colour to that of their bishop.
- Knights often complement the queen well in an attack.
- Bishop and rook work together well in the endgame.

- The rook prefers open files.
- The queen needs to be active.
- The king is a very powerful piece in the endgame.

6) Space Advantage

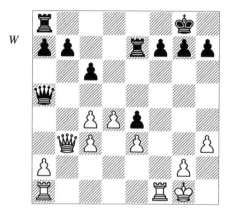

Vladimir Epishin – Jesper Hall
Bundesliga 1998/9

You are about to see a real Russian bear-hug, courtesy of Vladimir Epishin. All the minor pieces have been exchanged and it is important to get the major pieces moving. White has access to two semi-open files and has more space in the centre. Therefore, he has a small but clear advantage. If you examine the black position for weaknesses you find the squares b7, f7 and e4. The natural plan that first comes to mind is therefore to play c5, ♖f4 and ♖af1 or ♖b1. Black on the contrary has problems in finding counter-play as active moves might easily concede new weaknesses. Nevertheless, I should have tried to break up the queenside with ...b6 and accepted new weaknesses in exchange for more activity and space. In the game I chose to wait passively.

17 c5 ♖ae8 18 ♖f4 ♕c7 19 ♖b1 ♕d7 20 a4 h6 21 ♖bf1 ♖f8 *(D)*

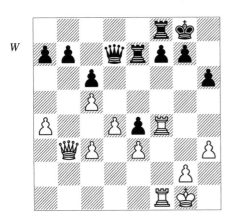

White's partial plan has been carried out and it is time to move the goalposts a bit further. Soon you realize that a breakthrough must come on the kingside or in the centre, since Black can meet trebling on the b-file by ...f6, with the idea of defending the b-pawn along his second rank. If you break through by rolling the g- and h-pawns, you do not want Black to get a counterattack with ...b6. White therefore wants to lock up the queenside before the breakthrough comes. Here we have a fundamental rule for positions with a space advantage: it is important to suppress all counterplay and gradually and methodically squeeze your opponent to death.

22 ♖f5 ♕c7 23 ♖1f4

The rooks are now ideally placed.

23...♕d7 24 c4 ♖fe8 25 a5!

The idea is to play a6, which would split Black's pawns and give targets on c6 and a7. It would also deny the c6-pawn support against the pawns moving forward in the centre. The move played is therefore forced.

25...a6

White has suppressed Black's only chance for active play and has more space all over the board. Now he can start advancing on the kingside.

26 h4 f6 27 h5!? ♔h8 28 ♕c2 ♕c7 29 ♕c3 ♕d7 30 g4 ♕c8 *(D)*

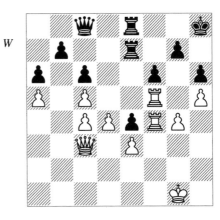

White has only one weakness, the a5-pawn. The problem is that all the major pieces are needed on the kingside for the breakthrough. By putting his king on b4, White solves the problem. Observe that White has all time in the world as Black totally lacks counterplay. An opponent who just plays around with his pieces, demonstrating his superiority, is hard to face. Often the passive party does something drastic and desperate to avoid the squeeze.

31 ♔g2 ♕d7 32 ♖f1 ♖e6 33 ♖b1 ♖6e7 34 ♕e1 ♕e6 35 ♖c1 ♕d7 36 ♕g3 ♕d8 37 ♖a1 ♖d7 38 ♕f4 ♔g8 39 ♔f1 ♔h8 40 ♔e1 ♔g8 41 ♖a2 ♔h8 42 ♔f2 ♔g8 43 ♔g2 ♔h8 44 ♕g3 ♔g8 45 ♕e1 ♔h8 46 ♖af2 ♔g8 47 ♕c3 ♖de7 48 ♔f1 ♕d7 49 ♔e1 ♔h8 50 ♖2f4 ♔g8 51 ♔d1 ♔h8 52 ♔c2 ♔g8 53 ♔b3 ♖c8 54 ♔b4 *(D)*

Finally the king is in position. Now comes the finish. A good way of thinking when it comes to planning is: where do I want my pieces? Which pieces do I want to exchange? White wants to put his queen on g6 with the

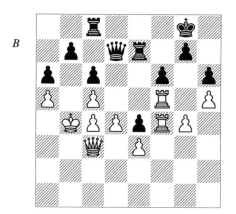

idea of playing g5 at the right moment, allowing the rooks to penetrate via the f-file after ...fxg5, or to play h6 after ...hxg5. Why does Black allow the white queen to reach the g6-square? I came to the conclusion that after an exchange of queens White could win the double rook ending by playing d5, putting the king on d4, and putting the rooks on f4 and b1. Whatever Black then chooses, White can play d6 and he will win the b7-pawn or the one on e4. Despite that, it was the best chance.

54...♕e8 55 ♖f1 ♕d7 56 ♕e1 ♕c7 57 ♕f2 ♕d8 58 ♕g3 ♕e8 59 ♖5f2 ♖d7 60 ♕f4 ♕e7 61 ♕f5!

The point. There is no defence against White's threat to double rooks on the h-file, creating ideas like ♖h8 or ♖h6 and ♖g6.

61...♖e8 62 ♕g6 ♔h8 63 g5 hxg5 64 h6 ♖f8 65 ♖h2 ♔g8 66 hxg7 ♕xg7 67 ♕f5 ♖e8 68 ♖fh1 1-0

7) Development Advantage
He who gets his pieces out quicker and is thus ahead in development can employ two techniques: either to break through directly by an attack on the king or to try to transform the lead in development into some of the other types of advantages we have discussed.

Heinz Lehmann – P. Müller
Germany-Switzerland, Lucerne 1952

1 e4 e5 2 ♘f3 ♘c6 3 ♗c4 ♗c5 4 b4!?

In the 19th century, players strove for a lead in development and an attack whether they were White or Black. Pawns were just the little guys who were sacrificed in the interests of the attack. The Evans Gambit is an opening which dates from this period, but was more or less forgotten until Kasparov came up with new ideas and showed that even this opening may have a future.

4...♗xb4 5 c3 ♗a5 6 d4 exd4 7 0-0 ♗b6?!

White's plan is brutal and simple. For the price of some pawns he wants to play his bishop to a3, cage the black king in the centre, activate his knights and put his rooks on the d- and e-files. Then it will be time to break through. Black must try to get his pieces out, so it is not a good idea for him to break the golden rule of not moving the same piece twice in the opening. Instead, theory suggests, e.g., 7...♘ge7 with the idea ...d5.

8 cxd4 d6 9 ♘c3 ♘f6? (D)

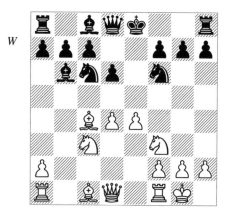

10 e5!

Winning a tempo as the knight is threatened.

10...dxe5 11 &a3! &a5

After 11...&xd4 12 ♕b3 ♕d7 13 ♘g5 ♘d8 14 ♖ad1 ♘e6 15 ♘f3 White has strong pressure against the black position. Therefore Black tries to exchange the strong white bishop on c4.

12 ♘xe5 ♘xc4 13 ♕a4+ &d7

If 13...c6 then 14 ♘xc4 takes advantage of the hole on d6. 14...&c7 15 d5 ♘xd5 16 ♖ad1 ♘xc3 17 ♖xd8+ &xd8 18 ♕b4 ♘d5 19 ♖d1 ♖e8 20 ♘e3 and the black position collapses.

14 ♕xc4 &e6 (D)

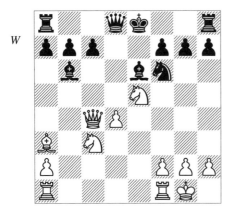

15 d5!

Open files for the rooks and the gain of one further tempo are worth more than a pawn.

15...&xd5

After 15...♘xd5 16 ♖ad1 c6 17 ♘xd5 &xd5 18 ♕e2 the discovered check will be decisive.

16 ♕a4+ c6 17 ♖ad1 ♘d7 18 ♘xd7

White could have won in many ways but chose the most aesthetically pleasing conclusion.

18...♕xd7 19 ♘xd5 cxd5 20 ♖xd5! 1-0

In view of 20...♕xa4 21 ♖e1+ with mate to follow.

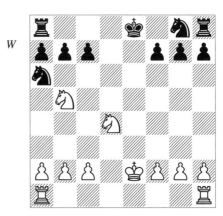

Siegbert Tarrasch – Jacques Mieses
Gothenburg 1920

The position is symmetrical and Black only needs to castle kingside in order to equalize completely. However, White is ahead in development and finds a way to transform his advantage.

13 ♖he1

To prevent Black from castling by giving a discovered check.

13...0-0-0

The only way to avoid the king being caught in the centre.

14 ♘xa7+ &b8

Black's idea is that now 15 ♘ab5? loses a piece to 15...c6, but White has seen even further.

15 ♘ac6+ bxc6 16 ♘xc6+ &c8 17 ♘xd8 &xd8 18 ♖ad1+ &c8 19 &f3

With a material advantage, two passed pawns on the queenside, great open files for the rooks and no outposts for the knights in the centre, White is clearly better.

8) The Initiative – The Conductor Who Dictates the Tempo of the Game

This advantage is hard to define. You usually say that the player who is making threats has the initiative and the player who is parrying does not have it. Therefore a player with one type of advantage also has the initiative, as in Epishin-Hall. In most games, though, the sides have their pros and cons and then it is common for a player to sacrifice a pawn to grab the initiative, as in Lehmann-Müller.

Here are two not so brutal examples.

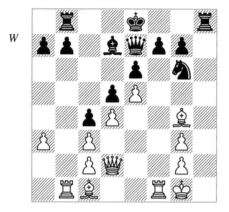

Leonid Stein – Tigran Petrosian
USSR Ch, Moscow 1961

Black has a long-term advantage in his better pawn-structure. White lacks the usual breakthrough with f4 and f5 and has to rely on his piece play. The rooks have good opportunities on the b- and f-files; the light-squared bishop has the possible post on h5, pointing towards the weak f7-square. The only piece left is the child of sorrows on c1.

19 a4!

A common idea in this position-type. At the cost of a pawn the white bishop can reach the attractive a3-f8 diagonal. Note that if it were Black's move in the diagram he would have played ...♗a4, a great move that would have given him the better chances.

19...♗xa4 20 ♖a1 b5 21 ♗a3 ♕d7 22 ♖f2 ♖b7 23 ♖af1 ♕d8 24 ♕d1!

With his last few moves, White has gradually increased the pressure and with the intervention of the queen the game is decided. The move makes possible ♗h5, ♕b1-b4 and ♗xe6.

24...♖h6 25 ♗c1 ♖h7 26 ♗xe6! 1-0

The end could have been 26...fxe6 27 ♕g4 ♖h8 28 ♕xg6+ ♔d7 29 ♖f7+ ♔c8 30 ♕xe6+ ♔b8 31 ♗a3 with threats like ♖f8, ♗d6+ and ♕xd5, winning.

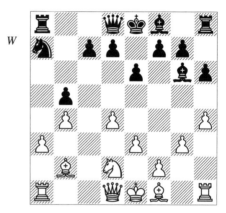

Garry Kasparov – Ulf Andersson
Tilburg 1981

"How do you learn to handle the initiative?" one of the pupils asked GM Tom Wedberg during a training session. "It is both simple and difficult. Just play like Kasparov," was his advice. And it is true. During his long period as World Champion, Kasparov has brought chess into the era of the initiative. Both with Black and White he strives to challenge his opponent by seeking the initiative. His style of play has also had a clear effect on the top players coming after him, such as Anand, Shirov, and Morozevich.

To demonstrate what he meant, Wedberg showed this position where the 18-year-old

Kasparov, with his modern approach to chess, outplayed the Swedish master of strategy Ulf Andersson. Black has opted for an interesting positional idea: to play ...d5 and then bring the knight to c4 via c8 and b6. Black will then have the better prospects as White's b2-bishop is penned in by its own pawns. Time for Kasparov to act.

14 d5!

Kasparov opens the position up for the b2-bishop and thereby makes it difficult for Black to get his king into safety. White now has a lead in development; he has natural moves like ♗g2, 0-0, ♖e1 and e4, going for an attack on the black king. All for the price of a mere pawn.

14...exd5 15 ♗g2 c6 16 0-0 f6

Black is forced to accept new weaknesses to get his dark-squared bishop out.

17 ♖e1 ♗e7 18 ♕g4

White will not let Black castle. Kasparov is a master of keeping up the pressure and by mini-operations he makes life difficult for his opponent.

18...♔f7 19 h5!

White's idea is to play e4, but when that is done he has to find a new plan to continue the attack. With the text-move, Kasparov prepares to take control of the light squares.

19...♗h7 20 e4 dxe4 21 ♗xe4 ♗xe4 22 ♘xe4 ♘c8

Black desperately tries to get the knight into the defence. The problem is that the most obvious move, 22...d5, leads to a lost position after 23 ♘c5 ♗xc5 24 ♕e6+ ♔f8 25 bxc5 – Black can hardly move. For example, 25...♕c8 26 ♕d6+ ♔g8 27 ♖e7 is crushing.

23 ♖ad1

Players who are good at handling the initiative know the importance of using all the pieces in their attack. Take a look at the activity of each piece on the board. All White's pieces are more active than Black's.

23...♖a7 *(D)*

23...d5 24 ♘c5 ♗xc5 25 ♕e6+ ♔f8 26 bxc5 ♖a6 (26...♘e7 27 ♗xf6 gxf6 28 ♕xf6+ ♔g8 29 ♖xe7 and White wins) 27 ♖d3 and Black can do nothing against ideas like ♖f3 followed by ♗xf6 or ♖de3 and ♕e8+.

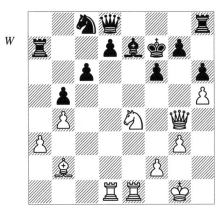

24 ♘xf6!

With all his pieces placed on their best squares, Kasparov is ready for the final breakthrough.

24...gxf6

Forced. If 24...♗xf6 25 ♕g6+ ♔f8 26 ♗xf6 gxf6 (26...♕xf6 27 ♖e8#), then 27 ♖e6 is the key move that wins immediately.

25 ♕g6+ ♔f8 26 ♗c1 d5

26...♕e8 27 ♗xh6+ ♖xh6 28 ♕xh6+ ♔f7 29 ♕h7+ ♔f8 30 h6 ♕f7 31 ♕f5 ♘d6 32 ♕g4 and Black can do nothing against the threat of ♕g7+, when the e7-bishop will be lost.

27 ♖d4

Again Kasparov prefers keeping up the pressure and the initiative to cashing in on material. The h6-pawn will not run away.

27...♘d6 28 ♖g4 ♘f7 29 ♗xh6+ ♔e8

Or: 29...♖xh6 30 ♕g8#; 29...♘xh6 30 ♕g7+ ♔e8 31 ♕xh8+ ♔d7 32 ♕xh6 and White wins.

30 ♗g7 1-0

The h-pawn will soon decide the game after 30...♖g8 31 h6.

An impressive game by Kasparov. Once he had seized the initiative he had the creativity to keep up the pressure and destroy all efforts to defend.

Temporary or Long-Term Advantage

When you know that you have an advantage and you have identified what type it is, it is important to appreciate whether it is a temporary or a long-term one. Material advantage, advantage in space and superior pawn-structure usually entail a long-term advantage as they seldom risk disappearing in a move or two. If your opponent has a weak king-position, you have a lead in development or you have the initiative, these are advantages that might easily disappear after some inexact moves. If you have one of these advantages it is important to watch out and keep up the pressure or to transform the advantage into a longer-term one.

The advantage of better pieces, or control of a key file or rank, can be either temporary or long-term depending on the position. Your opponent can, e.g., exchange a passive piece for an active one or maybe neutralize your control of a key square or a key file by the same method.

"See What is Left, Not What You Got"

During a game you normally pick out the various advantages quickly. There are two other questions that you have to struggle with to understand the position.

First of all you often have to pay a price to obtain an advantage. There your opponent sits with one type of advantage, and you have another. Which one is the best in the specific position? This area is handled in the next chapter.

The other question is connected to the fact that you can often choose between various types of advantage when you have reached a better position. How should you think then? The most important guideline to follow is here *to see what is left, not what you got.*

Jesper Hall – Niclas Hjelm
Swedish Junior Ch, Stockholm 1986

I remember that before the tournament I had thought about how advantages can be transformed and how I should not be afraid to go from one position-type to another. This is easy to understand in theory, but it was in this game that I first understood it in practice.

1 ♘f3

With the positional education that I started to get at the age of thirteen I came to the realization that I must change my opening repertoire. As I was a hacker with tactically based openings I worked mainly with advantages like the initiative, weak opponent's king-position and extra material. I wanted to understand other advantages as well and therefore supplemented my aggressive 1 e4 with other moves.

1...♘f6 2 g3 g6 3 ♗g2 ♗g7 4 0-0 0-0 5 c4 d6 6 ♘c3 ♘c6

Black invites transposition to the King's Indian, which gives sharp play where White gets the centre and a space advantage, and Black tries to undermine it. But I wanted to play positional chess, therefore...

7 d3 e5 8 ♖b1

White's plan is clear. I want to play b4 with pressure against Black's queenside.

8...a5

A good move as Black can open the a-file when White plays a3 and b4. Black also gets rid of the weakness that the a7-pawn can be.

9 a3 h6 10 b4 axb4 11 axb4 ♗e6 12 b5 ♘e7 13 ♘d2!?

A logical move to make use of the long diagonal. Another move that, among others, GM Lars Karlsson has played is 13 e4, which may seem illogical if you think about the diagonal, but Black's best plan in this position-type is to play ...d5 with or without ...c6. 13 e4 puts an end to that idea.

13...♖b8?!

With Black's best plan in mind you understand that this move is dubious. More logical is 13...c6 14 ♕b3 d5 15 ♗a3 with an unclear game.

14 ♗a3 (D)

Now ...d5 would lose a pawn to ♗xe7.

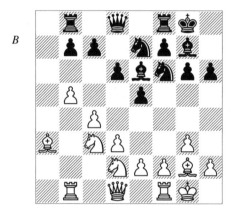

14...b6?

Maybe Black was afraid of White playing c5 or b6, but the move ...b6 gives White an even stronger diagonal and incurs weak light squares on c6 and d5. 14...♕d7 is a more natural and better move.

Here I thought for a while and came to the conclusion that I wanted to take control of the light squares in the centre and then try to get in on the a-file with the major pieces. But what is Black's idea? Well, he wants to create an attack on the kingside with such moves as ...♕d7, ...♗h3, ...♘h7, ...♘g5 and ...f5. How should I react to that?

15 ♕b3 ♕d7 16 ♘d5!

This move disturbs Black's planning as the e7-knight would now hang after ...♗h3. However, can't Black just exchange on d5 first?!

16...♘fxd5 17 cxd5 ♗h3 (D)

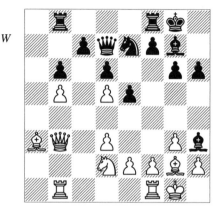

All of a sudden the position has changed. White's strong bishop is just a memory, but a new type of advantage for White has appeared – the backward black pawn on c7. I had seen that in this position White has a strong plan with the idea of trebling the major pieces on the c-file. This plan is difficult to counter.

18 ♖fc1 ♗xg2 19 ♔xg2 f5 20 ♖c4!

This strong move prepares the rook for a defence of the kingside on the fourth rank and of course for the attack on the c-pawn.

20...♖f7

After 20...♘xd5?! 21 e4 fxe4 22 dxe4 ♕f7 23 f3 ♘f6 24 ♖xc7 ♕xb3 25 ♖xb3 White has a superior position.

21 ♖bc1 ♖c8

Black cannot take on d5: 21...♘xd5? loses to 22 e4 fxe4 23 dxe4 ♘f6 24 ♖xc7.

22 e4 ♔h7?!

Black must be quicker with the counterattack. With a quick glance at the g7-bishop and the e7-knight you realize that it is the wrong moment to play a calm preparatory move. 22...f4 23 ♕c2 ♕xb5 24 ♗xd6 cxd6 25 ♖xc8+ ♘xc8 26 ♕xc8+ ♔h7 27 ♕c2 fxg3 28 hxg3 and the better minor piece implies that the position is advantageous for White.

23 ♖1c3 h5 24 ♕c2 ♘g8 25 ♖c6

An important finesse. Black cannot protect against ♖xd6 or ♖xb6.

25...♗f8 26 ♖xb6 cxb6 27 ♖xc8 ♕xb5 *(D)*

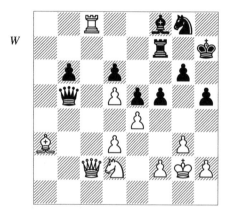

White obviously has a clear advantage with better minor pieces and control of the open file. But what is the best continuation?

28 ♖xf8! ♖xf8 29 ♗xd6

White gives away two types of advantage but gains others in return. The exchange sacrifice has given White a pawn on d6 and soon he will have another one on e5 since now 29...♖e8 would be very strongly answered 30 ♕c7+ followed by 31 ♗xe5. This gives White a mobile centre with two dangerous passed pawns, but even more important are the weak squares that Black has around his king. With a bishop on e5 and a knight on its way to g5, White will soon have a decisive attack against the black king.

29...♖f7 30 ♘f3 ♖d7 31 ♗xe5 ♘e7 32 ♘g5+ ♔h6

After 32...♔g8 33 d6 White will get a decisive attack along the a2-g8 diagonal. For example, 33...♕xe5 34 ♕c4+ ♔g7 35 ♕f7+ ♔h6 36 ♕h7+ ♔xg5 37 f4+ winning the queen.

33 ♘f7+ ♔h7 34 ♕d2 ♘g8

34...♔g8 35 ♘h6+ ♔f8 36 ♕g5 gives White a decisive attack.

35 ♘g5+ ♔h6 36 ♘e6+ 1-0

Black resigned because of 36...♔h7 37 ♘f8#.

My Training Tips

It is important to try to pick out and define the types of advantage that a player has during a game. Therefore try to explain with words the advantages that you discover as you analyse a game. Also, try to identify what players do to increase or oppose advantages. Collect instructive examples.

Suggestions for Further Reading

There are no books purely on this theme that I know of. Nevertheless, work on improving your ability to recognize an advantage must continue throughout your whole chess career. When the fundamentals are in place, the work is integrated in all other forms of chess activity. However, *How to Reassess Your Chess* by Jeremy Silman (Siles Press, 1993) is a good book for someone around 1700 in rating who wants to extend his understanding in the field. He speaks among other things about imbalances instead of advantages, something that appeals to me. The point is, for example, that the imbalance between a knight and a bishop in an endgame can be advantageous for the knight in one position-type and for the bishop in another. What matters, according to Silman, is to learn what the two sides strive towards in an unbalanced position. I prefer to speak about advantages, as that is an established concept. For more advanced players I can recommend the books by Mark Dvoretsky and Artur Yusupov. In this case maybe *Positional Play* (Batsford, 1996) suits best, even though it does not exactly follow the theme.

7   A Russian Doll Hides Many Secrets

On the struggle for advantage

It is both frustrating and central to the game itself that you can always look further and deeper.

I was seven years old and had just reached my peak in chess. I had won all my games in a district tournament, which gave me first place. It was the prize-giving ceremony and my arms were in the air with my fingers in V-signs. It was my trainer who had told me that this is what you do when you win a tournament in an overwhelming manner. I was full to the brim with victory and I thought as I received the plaquette that I knew everything about the game.

My experiences throughout the years have made me more humble and since my first triumph I have never relived that feeling of self-confidence. However, another occasion when I was carried away with optimism was after I read *Think Like a Grandmaster* by Kotov (Batsford, 1971). The annotations were even deeper than those of Larsen, and Kotov methodically mapped out the various aspects of chess. I gained much enlightenment by reading the book, and burned with eagerness to use the models in my games. The stumbling block was to make the ideas work in practice. It is precisely that point we have reached in this book. We have gone through tactics, strategy, and positional advantages, and have tried to look at all the elements separately. It is time to put all the ideas into the melting pot, and use them all at once.

A Way to Structure the Search

I have gained one type of advantage, my opponent another. We have both formulated plans and have our dream positions in mind, and consequently we know what we are heading for. Logically, we can't both succeed.

We have now come to the critical point where plans, tactics and advantages meet. It is here that real ability to think deeply is tested. It is both frustrating and central to the game itself that you can always look further and deeper. Nobody will ever be able to play chess without mistakes. This means that there are no standard recipes to follow when you are trying to work out the details. What you can do is to structure the search with the help of some concepts:

Main theme – the theme that dominates the position.

Partial goal – a position a little bit better than the one you have on the board, working within the overall plan.

Mini-operations – small manoeuvres on the way to partial goals.

Key positions – positions where everything is critical; this is where games are generally decided.

Tactics as a strategic tool – tactics that support the overall plan.

A Practical Example

Personally, I realize that I have had a glimpse of something a little bit deeper in the mystery of chess when my cheeks are flaming red after a loss. That is why I have emphasized the importance of analysing your own games, to gain new insights and learn from your mistakes.

In the following game I was reminded of the gap between my knowledge and that of a Russian grandmaster in the position-type that arose. Afterwards I was totally exhausted by all the calculating that I had done and the surprises that I had been confronted with. I thought, and I still think, that I played well, found logical plans and saw the right structures and ideas. The only problem was that my opponent was always one step ahead, and move after move I had to wrack my brain to keep up with him.

Mikhail Ulybin – Jesper Hall
Rilton Cup, Stockholm 1998/9

This game is very sharp and tactical as we have two types of advantage in conflict with each other. Black has the superior pawn-structure and thus the long-term advantage, but White has an advantage in development and therefore has the initiative on his side. These are temporary advantages. In the series of critical positions that arise, White always manages to find tactical mini-operations that keep the pot boiling. This game helped me to appreciate that ultimately strategies and plans require concrete analysis.

1 e4 c5 2 ♘f3 ♘c6 3 d4 cxd4 4 ♘xd4 ♘f6 5 ♘c3 d6 6 ♗e3

I had prepared the Classical Variation of the Sicilian for this tournament, and knew the main variations (the Richter-Rauzer and Sozin) pretty thoroughly. Here I was confronted with an unusual variation and really had to prove my strength against a Russian grandmaster.

6...♘g4 7 ♗g5!?

If White wants to play with the structure that arises in the game, it is more common to play 7 ♗c4 here. Now I could have chosen 7...h6 8 ♗h4 g5, which gives a Najdorf variation with ...♘c6 instead of ...a6, which must be in Black's favour. However, it was not the Najdorf variation I had prepared for the tournament, so I came up with an alternative move.

7...♕b6 8 ♗b5 ♗d7 9 0-0 h6!?

Here I calculated 9...♕xd4 10 ♗xc6 ♕xd1 11 ♗xd7+ ♔xd7 12 ♖axd1 h6 13 ♗c1 g5 14 h3 ♘e5 15 f4 gxf4 16 ♗xf4 and came to the conclusion that White is better as 16...♘g6 can be met by 17 e5, when my central pawn-structure is destroyed. However, if I start with ...h6, the variation is possible after ♗h4. White, though, has other plans.

10 ♗e3!

After 10 ♗h4 ♕xd4 11 ♗xc6 ♕xd1 12 ♗xd7+ ♔xd7 13 ♖axd1 g5 14 ♗g3 ♗g7, Black is at least equal.

10...♘xe3 11 fxe3 (D)

A very interesting and complicated position-type has appeared. White has a bad central pawn-structure but in return he has the open f-file and a lead in development. White therefore must act quickly and keep up the pressure, because if pieces are exchanged or if the play is simplified, Black will have a great advantage. Ulybin demonstrates in the remainder of the game how modern chess should be played.

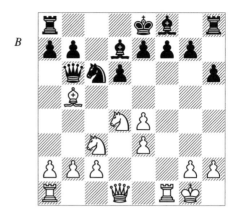

11...e6 12 ♕f3 ♘e5 13 ♗xd7+ ♔xd7 14 ♕h3 ♖e8 (D)

Up to this point everything was forced as 14...♗e7? would have been answered by the brutal 15 ♖xf7 ♘xf7 16 ♕xe6+ ♔e8 17 ♘d5 ♕d8 18 ♘f5 ♕d7 19 ♘xg7+ ♔d8 20 ♕xf7, when White is winning. My plan was therefore to move the king into safety with ...♔c8 and ...♔b8 before developing the bishop with ...♗e7 and ...♗f6. I could not see how White would be able to increase the pressure and therefore drew the conclusion that Black was better.

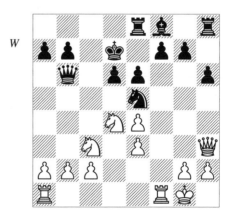

15 a4!

A wonderful move. White foresees Black's plan and makes an attacking move before the king has even arrived in the area – a prophylactic attacking move. The problem for Black is that he has no other way to develop.

15...♔c8

Note that a move like 15...♕xb2? is not a good idea while the black pieces are undeveloped and the king is still in the centre. In this particular case the queen is even trapped after 16 ♘d5 followed by ♖fb1. 15...a6 16 a5 gives White a square on b6 for the knight and the opportunity to break up the queenside by advancing his b-pawn (b4-b5).

16 a5 ♕d8 17 a6 b6 *(D)*

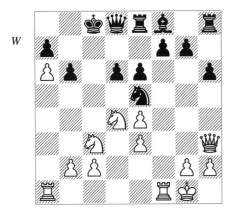

After 15 a4 it was this position I was heading for. Now I could not find any way for White to break me down, despite the weak light squares around my king. If Black could play ...♕d7, ...♗e7, ...♗f6, ...♔b8, and ...♖c8 it would not be easy for White to find compensation for the weakness of his pawn-structure.

18 b4!

Starting a beautiful plan to take advantage of the weak light squares before Black has consolidated.

18...♕d7 19 b5 ♗e7 20 ♘a2

With the target c6.

20...♗f6 21 ♘b4 ♔b8 22 ♘dc6+ ♔a8 23 ♖ad1

With 19 b5 I understood that White wanted to put a knight on c6. I had to find a new counter-plan. The idea I had found was to sacrifice the exchange on c6. In a position without open files my bishop could be as strong as a rook. And then there is the weak white pawn-structure...

23...♖c8 24 ♘xe5 ♗xe5 25 ♘c6 ♖xc6 26 bxc6 ♕e7 *(D)*

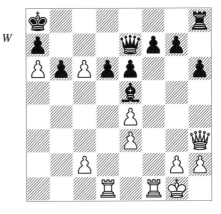

...and I play ...♖c8 and ...♖xc6 and Black is better, I thought. Again I had missed that in this key position White had a way to bring his pieces to life.

27 c4!

This move breaks up the position and gives the white rooks open files to operate on.

27...♖c8 28 c5

Just in time, before Black's rook reaches c6.

28...bxc5

Or:

a) 28...dxc5 29 ♖d7 followed by ♖fxf7 is disastrous for Black.

b) 28...♖xc6 29 cxd6 ♗xd6 30 e5 ♗xe5 31 ♕f3 ♕c7 32 ♖d8+ ♕xd8 33 ♕xc6+ ♔b8

34 ♕b7# shows how effective the rooks could be if Black does not manage to keep the position closed.

29 ♖b1 ♖xc6 30 ♖b7 ♖c7

After White's pawn sacrifice we are level on material, but the position has been opened, so the white rooks have the b-file to work on and therefore the black king is anything but secure.

31 ♖xc7!

Here I had only looked at 31 ♖fb1 ♕d8 with the point that after 32 ♕f3 c4 the passed c-pawn gives Black some hope of surviving.

31...♕xc7 *(D)*

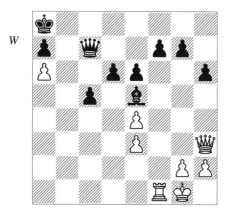

32 ♕h5!

The move I had missed. The point is that 32...♗f6 33 e5! dxe5 34 ♕f3+ ♔b8 35 ♖b1+ wins for White and 32...f6 loses to 33 ♕e8+. I now realized that I was lost and therefore set a final trap:

32...♕c8 33 ♕xf7 ♗f6 34 ♖b1 c4 35 ♖b7 c3 36 ♖xa7+ ♔b8 37 ♖b7+ ♔a8 38 ♖c7 ♕b8 39 ♖b7 ♕c8 40 ♕c7!

However, White did not of course fall into it. I had hoped for 40 ♖c7 ♕b8 41 ♕d7? ♕b1+ 42 ♔f2 ♗h4+! 43 g3 ♗xg3+, which leads to perpetual check after both 44 ♔xg3

♕g1+ 45 ♔f3 ♕f1+ and 44 hxg3 ♕c2+ 45 ♔f3 ♕d1+ 46 ♔g2 ♕e2+ 47 ♔h3 ♕h5+.

40...♕xc7 41 ♖xc7 ♔b8 42 ♖c6! ♗e5 43 ♔f2 ♔a7 44 h3 1-0

White wins easily as the white rook and a-pawn have walled in the black king. Black must therefore exchange the c-pawn for the a-pawn, which gives a lost endgame the exchange down with level pawns. After the game my opponent said modestly "During the whole game you stood well positionally, but you forgot that in the end chess is based on exact calculation." What he meant was that I had stared blindly at his weak pawn-structure, forgetting that chess is an exacting game where temporary and long-term advantages must be weighed precisely.

The Main Theme of the Position

Amongst the throng of advantages and weaknesses it was necessary for Ulybin to keep up the pressure imaginatively, not letting Black's pieces coordinate and thereby neutralize White's initiative. The main theme ran like a thread through the game and constantly gave rise to partial goals: "If I can get my king to b8 and then develop the bishop, I stand well" or "If I can sacrifice the exchange, taking on c6 with the rook without opening any files, I have a better position". Both my opponent and I had formulated the main theme and understood what to search for and what to avoid. These formulations developed into a struggle to attain various partial goals, then into sequences of concrete lines. Only very rarely is the same theme dominant throughout an entire game.

Mini-Operations

I wrote earlier that the thinking process in chess begins and ends with concrete analysis. When you know the main theme, have found a partial goal and want to achieve it, you reach the concept of mini-operations. It has been said that carrying out a plan correctly is as hard as finding the right plan in the first place. This is connected to the question "Can I take a step in the right direction?" in the method of eight questions. Artur Yusupov has stated that it is only this aspect that a grandmaster works out during a game. The reason is that a lot of what we have been speaking about is already internalized. The grandmaster is aware of the overall plans, searches intuitively for combinative themes that are of particular interest and knows the relevant standard positions. He can therefore devote his energy to the details.

Key Positions

Mini-operations are connected to the concept of key positions. In the struggle to attain partial goals White and Black use mini-operations. Naturally you reach a position where their plans are in direct confrontation. The mini-operations collide and a single move can decide which of the players will take control, or whether the plans will cancel each other with a draw as the result. These are the moments that constitute key positions and it is here that games are decided. The play now rises above the intuitive moves and the overall plans. It becomes exact and concrete and you must analyse the finesses without generalizing. What made my game against Ulybin so special was that there were successive key positions that I misjudged and where tactical mini-operations decided in his favour.

Tactics as a Positional Tool

In key positions and in mini-operations, tactics and strategy are woven together. In tactically complicated positions, the main theme is directly connected to the concrete calculation, so even the small strategic ideas are in the background. In quieter position-types you focus on manoeuvres according to plans that are based on structure and weaknesses. Even here the players must always be aware of hidden tactical finesses, not least when key positions are getting closer and the manoeuvring and mini-operations become concrete. In this situation I usually say that the tactics support the strategy, so tactics become a strategic tool.

Daniel King – Jesper Hall
Bundesliga 1998/9

1 e4 e6 2 d4 d5 3 ♘c3 ♗b4 4 e5 ♕d7
The idea of this move is to meet ♕g4 with ...f5, protecting the g7-pawn.

5 ♗d2
White can also choose to play with doubled pawns on the c-file after 5 a3. Play usually continues 5...♗xc3+ 6 bxc3 b6 7 ♕g4 f5 8 ♕g3 ♗a6 9 ♗xa6 ♘xa6 10 ♘h3 and White has an advantage in space and some pressure against the kingside. Black will bring his knight from a6 to c4 and start exchanging pieces to try to reach a better ending.

5...b6 6 ♗b5
White does not want to allow an exchange of light-squared bishops, but is trying to transfer the bishop to c2.

6...c6 7 ♗a4 ♗a6 8 ♘ce2
A standard manoeuvre. The dark-squared bishops are exchanged and c3 becomes a possibility.

8...♗xd2+ 9 ♕xd2 ♗b5 10 ♗b3 c5
Here I did not want to go down the line 10...♗c4 11 ♗xc4 dxc4 12 ♕g5 f6 13 exf6 ♘xf6 14 ♘f3, where Black's pawn-chain has been destroyed, leaving many weaknesses.

11 c3 ♘c6 12 ♘f3 ♘ge7 13 0-0 ♘a5
Black has to play actively because if White can play ♗c2, ♖fe1 and ♘f4, he has good prospects on the kingside.

14 &d1

Forced, as 14 &c2? ②c4 15 ♕c1 ②xb2 gives Black an extra pawn.

14...0-0 15 ♖e1 *(D)*

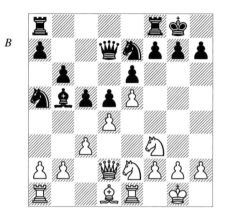

This is an important moment in the game, as the opening ends and the middlegame begins. It is time to form a plan. White has several natural moves at his disposal to start an attack on the kingside, but it is more difficult for Black. I thought like this: as White has not yet coordinated his pieces, I want to play ...f6 quickly to force White to exchange his central pawn. Beyond that, my thoughts became more concrete. After the natural continuation 15...②g6 he will certainly play 16 h4 to chase away the knight and add the h-pawn to the attack. Neither 16...f6 nor 16...h5 is then possible. 16...♕e7 remains. It took me a while to find my way through all the variations.

15...②g6 16 h4 ♕e7 17 h5

17 g3 f6 18 h5 fxe5 19 hxg6 ♖xf3 20 gxh7+ ♔h8 21 ②f4 ♖xf4 22 gxf4 ②c4 23 ♕e2 e4 24 b3 ②d6 *(D)*.

I sat and analysed this position for some time after 15 ♖e1 and came to the conclusion that Black has compensation for the exchange. Black can definitely take command

of the kingside with such moves as ...♕h4, ...♖f8 and ...②f5.

17...②h4 18 ②h2

A logical move, as the attacker usually wants to keep the pieces on the board. After the exchange of knights with 18 ②xh4 ♕xh4 I thought that White's attack was over before it had even started and Black should have an equal game.

18...f6 19 exf6?!

19 ②g4 f5 (after 19...②c4? 20 exf6! gxf6 21 ♕c1 e5 22 b3 ②d6 23 ②f4 Black's position falls apart; for example, 23...cxd4 24 cxd4 ♖ac8 25 ②xd5 ♕g7 26 ♕a3) 20 ②h2 &xe2 21 &xe2 f4 22 &g4 cxd4 23 cxd4 ♖ac8 with an approximately equal position.

19...♕xf6 20 ②g4? *(D)*

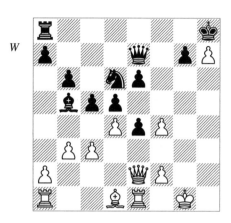

20 ②g3 was the only move that gave hope for an advantage. I had then planned 20...cxd4 21 ②g4 ♕f4 22 ♕xd4 ♕xd4 23 cxd4 ②c6 24 ♖xe6 ②xd4 25 ♖e5 &c6 26 ♖c1 ♖ae8 27 ♖xe8 ♖xe8 with an equal game. But why not bring the knight to e5 with tempo?

20...♕f3!!

It was this tactical finesse that took a while to find after 15 ♖e1. If Black had to go in for 20...♕f7? 21 ♕g5 ②f5 22 ②f4, White would have his attack and a clear advantage. Therefore I needed tactics to support my

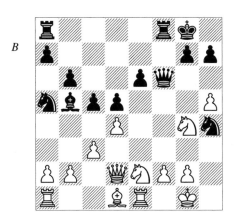

positional idea. The rest is a matter of technique.

21 gxf3 ♘xf3+ 22 ♔g2 ♘xd2 23 ♘g3 ♖ae8 24 ♘e5 ♘dc4 25 ♗g4 ♘xe5 26 ♖xe5 ♖f6 27 ♖ae1 ♔f7 28 dxc5 bxc5 *(D)*

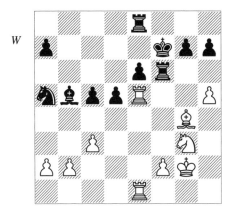

29 b3 ♘c6 30 ♖g5 ♗d3 31 ♗e2 ♗xe2 32 ♖xe2 ♖f4 33 ♘f1 h6 34 ♖g3 ♖f5 35 ♖f3 ♖xf3 36 ♔xf3 e5 37 ♘e3 ♔e6 38 ♔g3 ♖f8 39 f3 d4 40 ♘c4 ♖f5 0-1

To Learn is to Question

Fundamental to learning more about the difficult concepts that we have considered is the will to analyse and extend one's knowledge,

both in a game and in training. It is always worthwhile to try to find a little bit more. You can compare the work with that of a detective. A mistake has been made, but it is shown after analysis of the key position that it was much earlier. In this way you work backwards to find new key positions. In my game against Ulybin I played 18...♕d7. Perhaps 18...♕c7 is a way to strengthen Black's play? And like this you can proceed.

In addition to working on your own games and their key positions, you should study standard positions. The more you have in your memory, the better you will become, as there will be more positions you can judge by intuition.

An important piece of advice

An important part of the driving force and will to understand is that you must dare to question everything and everyone. You are the one that must understand! Therefore do not believe analysis or suggestions in magazines and newspapers without having first convinced yourself that they are correct. Moreover, do not trust computer analysis without having formulated and described it in your own words.

My Training Tips

As well as being critical and wanting to extend your knowledge, it is important to learn from the masters. Try to spot the small battles that are constantly going on when they play a game. Read their comments carefully and try to work from the general down to the specific when you follow their annotations. Then you will understand that the whole position might be linked to a single key move, because if that move is made, one side will obtain an important advantage.

Suggestions for Further Reading

The best way to study the various themes of this chapter is to analyse a large number of critical positions where small details decide the games. Specialized books that I use include *Analyse to Win* by Byron Jacobs (Batsford, 1997), *John Nunn's Chess Puzzle Book* by John Nunn (Gambit, 1999), *The Best Move* by Vlastimil Jansa and Vlastimil Hort (RHM, 1980) and *Test Your Positional Play* by Robert Bellin and Pietro Ponzetto (Batsford, 1985). The first two are mainly tactical and the last more positional, while the two Vlastimils have mixed both types of exercise.

For theoretical guidance I recommend the series of books by Dvoretsky and Yusupov, all of which offer advice on how you should think when chess gets really difficult. Yuri Averbakh's books are also excellent; for example, *Schachlehrbuch Für Fortgeschrittene* (Sportverlag Berlin, 1973).

8 Have I Not Seen You Before?

On how to study position-types

*If you understand a position-type thoroughly and well,
it can be a terrifying point-scoring machine.*

When the summer came we just went. Four friends in a rusty brown Volvo 240. We had planned to travel around Europe for several months hunting adventures and IM norms. It was a wonderful time that included some important lessons. One I got in the Galician town of La Coruña on the northern coast of Spain.

At the board beside me sat my Yugoslav rival for first place. He moved quickly, confidently and played amazingly well although his position was far from simple to handle. He won easily, but I was not surprised,

having followed him through the tournament. He played the same position-type in every game, both as White and Black. He knew the positions like the back of his hand – something I had found out for myself in the previous round.

In the beginning my friends and I coined the somewhat disparaging expression 'system player' for him, and thought that his play was one-sided and boring. This was until we realized that if you understand a position-type so thoroughly and well, it can be a terrifying point-scoring machine. After the tournament

I therefore started to systemize my study of typical positions to become as good as my rival. Today it is one of my main forms of training. Explained simply, you learn the patterns and standard moves that the position has. In a game it is then easier to identify the partial goals, find mini-operations and calculate the key positions, as you know exactly what to look for.

As I wrote earlier in Chapter 5, every opening has its own structure and strategy. This strategy often lasts throughout the whole game, from opening to endgame, encompassing plans and tactical possibilities. Some position-types can arise from several different openings: the isolani structure, the hedgehog, and hanging pawns. Just like Branko Damljanović and his beloved King's Indian set-up from above, there are many players who have specialized in one structure and try to reach it from various openings, often both as White and Black.

What I did then in Spain was to start to analyse the typical positions that arise when the opening transforms into the middlegame. I gained a clearer understanding of what to look for in the opening and what kind of endings to strive for. I realized that every part of a chess game was connected and that you must understand the correspondence.

My method was as follows:

1) Collect and go through several annotated games with the specific position-type.

2) Write down what is typical of the position, for White and for Black.

3) Write down the plans and normal outposts for the pieces for White and Black.

4) Pick out dream positions and advantageous standard positions for White and Black.

5) Write down typical tactical themes for White and Black.

6) Pick out key positions and important key moves.

7) Collect and go through several endings that might arise from the specific position, to see in what situations White or Black is better.

Isolation Can Be a Source of Strength or Weakness

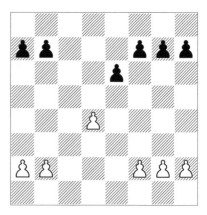

The isolani structure in the centre is defined by White or Black having an isolated pawn on the d-file. It can arise from many openings, such as the Queen's Gambit, the c3 Sicilian or the Caro-Kann. The structure is therefore common and consequently good to know about.

The two sides have entirely different goals and plans. Therefore I find it appropriate to use this structure to demonstrate how to study position-types. Below I give some games, endings, tactical themes and exercises that you can use as basic material to test my method.

In the following diagram, White has arrived at a typically advantageous position when playing against an isolani. Two pairs of minor pieces have been exchanged,

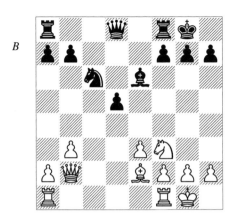

Mikhail Botvinnik – Evgeny Zagoriansky
Sverdlovsk 1943

including the dark-squared bishops. The remaining black bishop is restricted by its own pawn on d5. The c6-knight is far from the ideal e4-square and all in all Black has difficulties in finding the activity that might compensate for the isolated pawn in the centre. The other plan that Black usually has, namely to play ...d4, is not realistic here. White's plan is simple: he wants to put pressure on the d5-pawn, forcing the black pieces into passivity.

14...♕a5 15 ♖fd1 ♖ad8 16 ♖d2 ♖d7 17 ♖ad1 ♖fd8 18 h3 h6

White's first task is accomplished. Black had to put his rooks on the d-file to guard the pawn instead of placing them actively on the c- or e-file. But what next? What to do with the knight and the bishop? The ideal continuation would be to put the knight on f4 and the bishop on f3. However, 19 ♘e1 d4 20 exd4 ♘xd4 21 ♖xd4 ♖xd4 22 ♖xd4 ♖xd4 23 ♕xd4 ♕xe1+ only gives an equal position. As well as thinking about where to put the pieces, you can always ask yourself which pieces you want to exchange. Generally speaking, White does not mind exchanges

as the isolani structure will be weaker the closer you get to an ending. With regard to the minor pieces, White would prefer Black to be left with the bishop, so he wants to exchange knights: d4 would be the ideal square for this to take place, but after 19 ♘d4 it is not clear that Black has to exchange. Thus...

19 ♘e5! ♘xe5

After 19...♖d6 20 ♘c4 White wins the exchange.

20 ♕xe5 ♕c5 21 ♗f3 b6 *(D)*

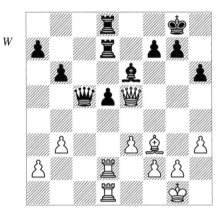

There is no doubt that White has a firm grip on the game. All Black's pieces are tied to the defence of the d-pawn. But what next? When your opponent has a clear weakness and you have control of it, as in this game, it is time to think about the *principle of two weaknesses*. This is one of the most important concepts in chess, especially in the endgame. The question is where should White try to create a second weakness. The answer: on the kingside!

22 ♕b2 ♖c8 23 ♕e5 ♖cd8 24 ♖d4!

The pawn is forever put behind bars and the rook is ready for action on the fourth rank.

24...a5 25 g4!

White plans to break up the position with g5 to attack the black king with the major pieces. This kind of move is possible because Black's pieces are so committed to defence that they cannot take advantage of White opening up the squares in front of his own king.

25...♕c6 26 g5 hxg5

26...♕c2!? is a possibility to try to get the queen into the defence: 27 gxh6 ♕g6+ 28 ♔h2 ♕xh6 with better chances of surviving.

27 ♕xg5 (D)

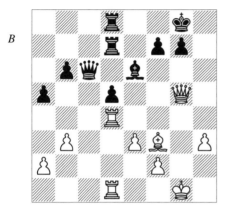

27...f6

Or:

a) 27...♗xh3?! is the kamikaze defence, but it is not so easy to crack even though it gives White extra tempi for his attack. However, after 28 ♖h4 ♖d6 29 ♔h2 ♗c8 30 ♖h1 f5 31 ♔g1 White has a winning attack.

b) 27...♕c2 is the grovelling defence. After 28 ♕h5 ♕h7 29 ♕xh7+ ♔xh7 30 ♔g2 White has a clear advantage in the endgame, with opportunities to infiltrate on the c-file or to play e4 at the right moment. Nasty, but better than getting mated.

28 ♕g6 ♗f7 29 ♕g3 f5?!

With this move Black incurs a third weakness and is doomed from a basic positional point of view (look at his bishop). This move does not even hinder White's attack. 29...♕c2

is a better way to get the queen into the defence.

30 ♕g5 ♕e6 31 ♔h1 ♕e5 32 ♖g1 ♖f8 33 ♕h6 ♖b8 34 ♖h4 ♔f8 35 ♕h8+ ♗g8 36 ♖f4!

The third weakness is the first to fall.

36...♖bb7 37 ♖g5 ♖f7 38 ♕h5 ♕a1+ 39 ♔g2 g6 40 ♕xg6 ♗h7 41 ♕d6+ ♖fe7 42 ♕d8+ 1-0

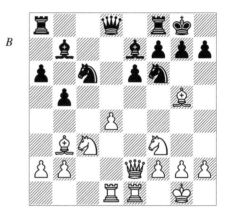

Isaak Boleslavsky – Alexander Kotov
Candidates tournament, Zurich 1953

I saw this position for the first time in a 25-minute game between Andersson and Karpov. Karpov played the normal-looking 13...♘b4? and faced the unpleasant 14 d5!. I thought that Black must be OK in the diagram and tried to understand the mysteries of the isolani structure. I soon noticed what a central role the move d5 has. Often it can work tactically even when at first sight it does not look clear. That is why Black has really serious problems in the position, as the threat of d5 is difficult to prevent given that the natural method with ...♘b4 does not work.

13...♘a5?!

Or:

a) 13...♘b4? 14 d5! ♘fxd5 (14...♘bxd5 15 ♘xd5 ♗xd5 16 ♗xd5 ♘xd5 17 ♗xe7 ♕xe7 18 ♖xd5 and White is a piece up) 15 ♘xd5 ♗xg5 16 ♘xb4 ♕e7 17 ♘d5 ♗xd5 18 ♗xd5 1-0 Andersson-Karpov, Rapidplay, Österskär 1995.

b) I rejected 13...♖e8! for some reason, but now I think it is Black's best choice. 14 d5 ♘xd5! leads to nothing clear, while the messy line 14 ♗xe6 ♗b4 15 d5 ♘a5 16 ♘e5 fxe6 17 dxe6 ♕e7 18 ♘g4 gives White an attack and a passed pawn for the piece, but I don't think it is any more than sufficient compensation.

c) 13...♘d5!? is the move that I concluded gave the best chances. Then 14 ♗xd5 ♗xg5 15 ♗e4! is the only way to create problems for Black. The best possibility seems to be 15...♗h6 since on f6 the bishop would probably be threatened by a knight on d5. 16 a4! (16 d5 exd5 17 ♘xd5 g6 18 ♘b4 ♕c7 19 ♘xc6 ♗xc6 gives Black good chances to equalize) 16...bxa4 (after 16...b4 17 d5 exd5 18 ♘xd5 Black has problems with the b4-pawn) 17 ♘xa4 ♘a5 18 ♘e5 (18 b4 ♗xe4 19 ♕xe4 ♘c4 20 d5 ♘d6 21 ♕d3 exd5 22 ♕xd5 ♘b5 and Black hangs on) 18...♗xe4 19 ♕xe4, and Black still has some problems with the coordination of his pieces.

14 d5 ♘xb3

After 14...♘xd5? 15 ♗xd5 ♗xd5 16 ♗xe7 ♕xe7 17 ♘xd5 White wins a piece.

15 dxe6 ♕b6

15...♗xf3 16 exf7+ ♔h8 17 ♖xd8 ♗xe2 18 ♖xa8 ♖xa8 19 ♖xe2 and White regains the piece on b3 or e7 and remains two pawns up.

16 axb3 fxe6 17 ♘d4 ♗d6 18 ♕xe6+ ♔h8 19 ♘f3 ♖ad8 (D)

20 ♗f4!

I like this move a lot, as it shows that a good player always has the ending in mind. There was no reason to play 20 ♘e5, which

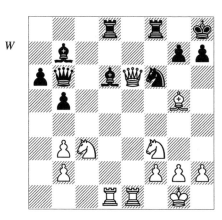

leads to a worse version of the ending after 20...♕c7 21 ♗f4 ♗c8 22 ♘g6+ hxg6 23 ♗xd6 ♗xe6 24 ♗xc7 ♖xd1 25 ♘xd1 ♗xb3.

20...♗xf3 21 ♖xd6 ♖xd6 22 ♕xd6 ♕xd6 23 ♗xd6 ♖e8 24 ♖xe8+ ♘xe8 (D)

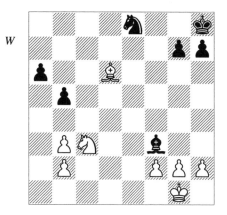

25 ♗e5!

Boleslavsky must have seen this move when he played 20 ♗f4. Now the bishop dominates the knight.

25...♗c6 26 b4!

With another strong move, White fixes Black's queenside pawns on the same colour squares as the black bishop. The idea is that if the knight moves, White will exchange it and obtain a winning ending with a good knight against a bad bishop.

26...h5 27 f3

Opening up a diagonal for a royal procession towards the queenside.

27...♔h7 28 ♘e2 g5 29 ♔f2 h4 30 g3 hxg3+ 31 hxg3 ♔g6 32 g4

Another weakness is fixed. Now the knight will go to e4 to tie the black king to the defence of the g-pawn, and the white king will travel his royal road towards the pawns.

32...♗b7 33 ♔e3 ♗c6 34 ♘c3 ♗b7 35 ♘e4 ♗d5 36 ♘c5

This is an important aspect of planning. If your opponent tries to resist your plan, he might have to accept other weaknesses. White wins a pawn.

36...♔f7 37 ♘xa6 ♔e6 38 ♗c3 ♗a8

The knight could not move due to ♘c7+.

39 ♘c5+ ♔f7 40 ♘e4 ♔g6 41 ♗e5

Back again. It is time for ♘d2, followed by ♔d4 and ♔c5.

41...♗d5 42 ♘d2 ♔f7 1-0

Two Endgames with Isolanis

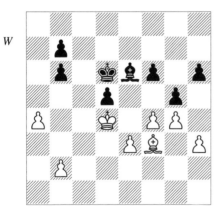

Alexander Wojtkiewicz – Alexander Khalifman
Rakvere 1993

An isolani endgame with same-coloured bishops has arisen. Black has a second weakness on the b-file. If the b7-pawn were instead on a7, I doubt that White could break through. In the actual position, White found a nice plan to profit from his advantage.

33 f5!

White chooses to put his pawn on the 'wrong' colour to give the black bishop less space to manoeuvre. Observe that this idea is viable only because the black bishop is well and truly locked in.

33...♗f7

After 33...♗d7 34 b3 ♗c6 35 ♗h1 Black is in zugzwang, and so White wins the d5-pawn.

34 b4 ♗e8 35 b5 ♗f7 36 ♗d1!

Starting the winning manoeuvre.

36...♗g8 37 ♗b3 ♗f7 *(D)*

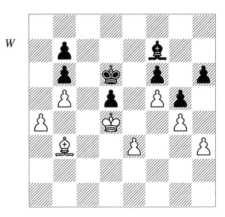

38 e4!

A method worth remembering when playing against the isolani: put your bishop on the same diagonal as your opponent's and then attack using the pawn.

38...♗g8 39 ♗a2

White calculates the forthcoming ending before he forces the play.

39...♗f7 40 ♗xd5 ♗xd5 41 exd5 ♔c7

White has a pawn more but has problems finding squares on which to penetrate. The only plan is to exchange pawns with a5 at the right moment. A triangulating manoeuvre is needed to make this work.

42 ♔c3! ♔d6 43 ♔c4! ♔e5 *(D)*

43...♔c7 44 ♔b4 ♔d6 45 a5 ♔xd5 (after 45...bxa5+ 46 ♔xa5 ♔xd5 47 ♔b6 ♔c4 48 ♔xb7 ♔xb5 49 ♔c7 ♔c5 50 ♔d7 ♔d5 51 ♔e7 ♔e5 52 ♔f7 White wins the f-pawn and the game) 46 a6 bxa6 47 bxa6 ♔c6 48 ♔a4 and White wins.

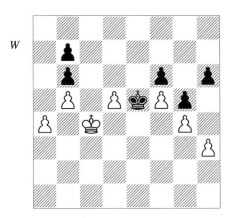

44 a5!

This breakthrough forces a won queen ending.

44...bxa5 45 ♔c5 a4 46 d6 b6+

Black has to sacrifice a pawn; otherwise he is mated on d4.

47 ♔c6 a3 48 d7 a2 49 d8♕ a1♕ 50 ♕d6+ ♔e4 51 ♔xb6

Black cannot prevent White from promoting his b-pawn.

51...♔f3 52 ♔b7 ♔g2 53 ♕d3 ♕c1 54 b6 ♕c5 55 ♔b3 ♔h2 56 ♕f3 ♕d4 57 ♕c6 ♔xh3 58 ♔c8 ♕b4 59 b7 ♕f8+ 60 ♔d7 ♔xg4 61 ♕c8 1-0

After 61...♕f7+ 62 ♔d6 there are no checks left.

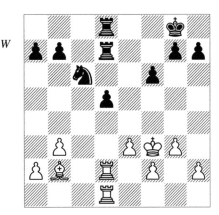

Zoltan Ribli – Jozsef Pinter
Zonal tournament, Baile Herculane 1982

Although White does not have the light-squared bishop left to put pressure on d5, his remaining bishop is strong. It controls the long diagonal and keeps the d5-pawn restrained. Moreover, Black cannot guard the isolani with ...♘e7, because ♗a3 will drive the knight away. White immediately tries to create a new weakness by a pawn advance on the kingside.

27 g4!

A strong move. It takes space on the kingside with the idea of ♔e2 and a pawn-push to f5, counteracting Black's natural plan to bring the king to e6 to protect the d5-pawn and release the rooks. Also, ideas like h4 and g5, to open the position up even more for the bishop, will be of interest.

27...♔f7 28 ♔e2 ♔e6 29 f4 f5?!

Preventing White from playing f5, but at the cost of opening the diagonal for the bishop and giving the white rooks a target on g7. 29...g6 is better.

30 gxf5+ ♔xf5 31 ♔f3 ♔e6 32 h4!

With the idea of nailing down the weakness on g7 with h5.

32...♖f8 33 ♔g4 g6?!

It is hard to defend when your opponent can manoeuvre between the two weaknesses, and Black misses the threat after ♔g4. After 33...♖fd8 White can either go back or try to strengthen his position with 34 h5.

34 e4 *(D)*

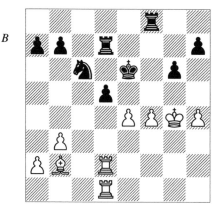

34...h5+?!

Black judges 34...♖fd8 35 exd5+ ♖xd5 36 ♖xd5 ♖xd5 37 ♖xd5 ♔xd5 38 f5 gxf5+ 39 ♔xf5 as lost. Probably that is correct but White must then be very careful. 39...♘e7+ 40 ♔f6 ♘g6 and now:

a) White cannot play 41 h5 immediately, because the king would be locked in if it took the h7-pawn with the black king on f7.

b) 41 ♔g5! ♔e4 42 h5 ♘f4 43 ♗c1 ♘d3 44 ♗d2 ♔f3 (to meet 45 ♔h6? by 45...♔g4) 45 ♔f6 and White is winning as the black h-pawn is lost and the black king does not reach f7 in time.

In the game Black stakes everything on one card, but with some brave and exact king moves White decides the game.

35 ♔g5 d4 36 ♗xd4 ♘d8 37 ♗g7!

This is the key move, which destroys Black's hope of a successful attack.

37...♘f7+ 38 ♔xg6 ♘h8+ 39 ♔h6 ♘f7+ 40 ♔xh5 1-0

Isolani Combinations

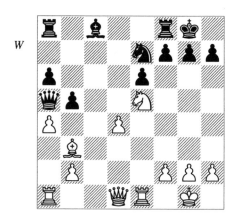

1 d5! ♘xd5

Forced as 1...exd5 loses to 2 ♘xf7! ♖xf7 3 ♗xd5 (3 ♖xe7 ♖xe7 4 ♕xd5+ ♗e6 5 ♕xa8+ ♔f7 6 ♕f3+ also wins) 3...♕xe1+ (3...♖a7 4 ♕f3 ♗f5 5 ♕xf5 ♘xf5 6 ♖e8#) 4 ♕xe1 ♘xd5 5 ♕e8+ ♖f8 6 ♕c6.

2 ♗xd5 exd5 3 ♘xf7! *(D)*

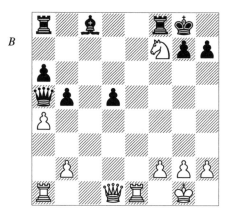

3...b4 4 ♘e5 ♗b7 5 ♕g4

White is better, as Black has weaknesses on d5 and b4 and White has a good knight on e5 compared with Black's b7-bishop.

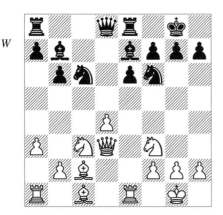

Kezli Ong – Miriam Olsen
Esbo 2000

1 d5! exd5 2 ♗g5 g6?

After 2...♘e4! (forced) 3 ♘xe4 dxe4 4 ♕xe4 g6 5 ♖ad1 ♕c7 6 ♕e3 White has great pressure with ideas like b4 and ♗b3.

3 ♖xe7 ♘xe7 4 ♗xf6 ♕d6 5 ♗e5 ♕e6 6 ♘b5 ♗a6 7 ♕d2 1-0

7...♗xb5 8 ♕h6 f6 9 ♘g5 wins the queen.

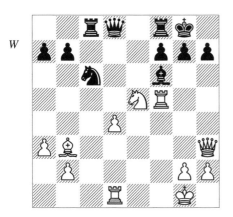

1 ♕xh7+ ♔xh7 2 ♖h5+ ♔g8 3 ♘g6 ♗xd4+ 4 ♔h1

Mate on h8 follows.

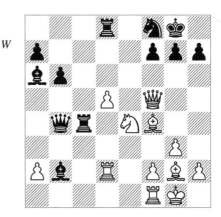

1 ♖xb2! ♕xb2 2 ♗e5 ♕e2

2...♕c1!? loses to 3 ♗xg7 ♘g6 4 ♗a1.

3 ♕g5!

With a double threat on d8 and g7.

3...f6 4 ♘xf6+ ♔f7 *(D)*

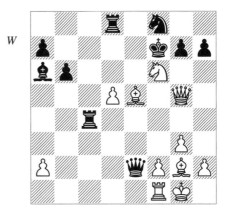

5 ♘xh7 ♘xh7 6 ♕xg7+ ♔e8 7 ♕g6+ ♔f8 8 ♕h6+ ♔e8 9 ♕e6+ ♔f8 10 ♗g7+ ♔xg7 11 ♕xe2 and White is winning.

Exercises

Here are two positions for you to investigate. Solutions are given on page 172.

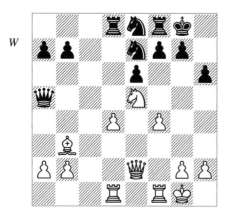

W

**Gideon Ståhlberg – José Raúl
Capablanca**
Moscow 1935

1) How should White continue?

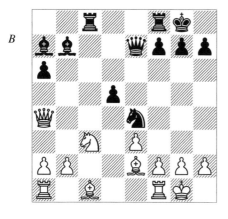

B

2) How should Black continue?

Isolani Themes

*The following comments apply to the side
with the isolani.*

1) This side has a space advantage.

2) There is one open and one half-open
file for the rooks.

3) There are two key squares for the
pieces obliquely in front of the pawn (e5 and
c5 if the pawn is on d4).

4) This side is often better if the pawn can
advance and free the pieces behind. An open
centre requires active pieces. As well as advancing the d-pawn, a common plan is to
start an attack on the king. All the pieces join
in, often even a rook on the third rank. Common breakthroughs are sacrifices on f7, e6,
g6 and advances with the f-pawn or the h-
pawn to undermine Black's position.

5) This side wants to keep as many pieces
on the board as possible, so that the attack
does not lose its strength.

*The following, on the other hand, apply to
the side playing against the isolani.*

1) There is a strong square in front of the
isolated pawn.

2) This side has a natural plan of exerting
pressure on the 'weak' isolated pawn and ty-
ing the opponent's pieces to its defence.

3) This side seldom has any tactical
themes to strive for, but must be alert to the
opponent's. Beware the advance of the pawn.

My Training Tips

Studying position-types is closely connected
to work on openings. If you do not understand the position-type that will arise from
your opening, you will soon be in trouble
when the moves that you have learned by

heart have all been played. I therefore always start with the typical position before I learn the specific moves. This also gives you a chance to find your own ideas and new moves, as you develop a better understanding for what to look for.

To me the computer seems an important tool for studying position-types. Using (e.g.) ChessBase, examples, endings and combinations can be easily collected into specific databases. In some of my openings I have chosen to merge the opening analysis and the material related to position-types together into one database. These are openings that are characterized by the fact that they almost always contain only one position-type – such as the Benoni. For something like the Trompowsky, I have separated the typical positions into various databases.

The best you can do is to try to find a system of your own, linking the opening and the position-types that can arise from it.

Suggestions for Further Reading

Usually opening books deal with the typical positions, but this is seldom done in a systematic way and often explanations of the position-type that the opening generates in the middlegame are left out. There is one specialized book on position-types, *Winning Pawn Structures* by Alexander Baburin (Batsford, 1998). This covers the isolani structure and also hanging pawns. In *The Power Chess Program 2* by Nigel Davies (Batsford, 1999) there are three good chapters on these areas together with one about the hedgehog system. These three structures can arise from most openings and are a good start for you if you want to study position-types.

In *Positional Play* by Mark Dvoretsky and Artur Yusupov (Batsford, 1996) there is a section on position-types. Here the concept is extended to factors other than the pawn-structure. I would like to recommend the chapter 'Opposite-Coloured Bishops in the Middlegame', which I personally think is one of the best pieces ever written about a specific type of middlegame.

9 Move One: The First Crossroad

On openings

A deep understanding is different from instant and superficial information.

The arrival of computers in the chess world was nothing less than a revolution in access to information. The greatest influence that this had on chess was probably to enable ambitious players to prepare for their opponents' openings. Hysteria soon surrounded the openings and spread down to lower levels. The consequence has been that the most common way to study chess today is to hammer a lot of variations into your head.

Personally, I believe that the computer has made it even more important to understand the openings properly, so that even if you are confronted with a new move you can find a good answer. This deeper understanding is something other than instant and superficial information. What matters is to know what to look for and to understand the position-type that will arise. Therefore, a player who is good at openings is also a player who can master the middlegame that follows. I therefore link the work with openings to the study of position-types, as this deeper knowledge is needed before the memorizing starts.

When I am going to learn a new opening I use a scheme rather like the one in the previous chapter. I start with a couple of well-annotated games played by strong players. I try to choose games with commentaries in words, not just a stack of variations – games where the ideas and the plans are presented in an instructive way.

My Opening Questions

I use the following questions to structure my thinking process systematically:

- What pawn-structures and position-types can arise?
- What positional plans and tactical ideas do White and Black have?
- What do White's and Black's dream positions and advantageous standard positions look like?
- Which are the key positions and key moves? (Here I add concrete variations that illustrate the critical positions.)
- What are the most common combinative themes?
- What types of ending can arise from the opening? When are they good for White and when for Black?
- What variations do I have to learn by heart? (Often it is sharp forced lines with aggressive themes.)
- What variations are critical for the opening? (These are the variations that theory judges the most difficult to face.)

Trompowsky – A Blank Area on the Map?

There is an explanation for my embarrassing opening play in the games of Chapter 2. The temptation is to play an opening where theory is still in its childhood and where I have several of my own ideas and novelties. But the answer to the question is nevertheless "No!". Since Anand played the variation against Karpov in the final of the FIDE World Championship in 1998 a lot has happened, as the popularity of a variation is connected to whether the world elite are playing it. Probably there is no uncharted area on the chess map, only areas that are rather less explored.

I have always liked the feeling of being an explorer in the opening and have tried to find exciting and playable openings that have not been analysed to death. Some are in my normal repertoire and some I use as a surprise weapon. To you and to my opponents in the games of Chapter 2, my love for the Trompowsky is no secret.

Time to prepare with a chessboard, pen and paper.

1 d4 ♞f6 2 ♗g5 *(D)*

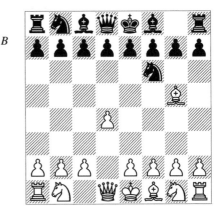

This is the initial position of the Trompowsky. Immediately you notice that Black has several moves to choose from, which give rise to various pawn-structures, plans and ideas. White's opening is often played to avoid the thoroughly analysed variations of the King's Indian and the Grünfeld. White therefore normally meets 2...g6 with 3 ♗xf6. This gives a position where Black has doubled pawns but the bishop-pair. Black wants to open up the centre to let his bishops come to life, and White wants a more solid structure in the centre to play against the bishops and the weakened pawn-structure. A totally different idea is to play 3 e3 followed by f4 and a type of Stonewall position, where the dark-squared bishop is outside the pawn-chain.

Probably you have already written down on your piece of paper that a characteristic of the Trompowsky is that it can give rise to several different types of game. To understand and to be ready to play various position-types is therefore a prerequisite for playing the Trompowsky. In addition to the 2...g6 variation, there are three common ways to meet it. I will now try to give you the basic ideas by showing three of my own games. To the comments I add the notes that I wrote down after the games. Don't believe my comments blindly, but try to draw your own conclusions.

Jesper Hall – Igor Khenkin
La Coruña 1992

The reasons why you play a certain opening can have an almost banal history; perhaps a friend once showed you a trap five minutes before an important game. However, the reason that some openings stay with you throughout your career is linked to a feeling of being at home in the positions that arise, and of course to successes.

1 d4 ♞f6 2 ♗g5

I was not even an IM when this game was played and the strong Russian grandmaster glanced up quickly before he delivered the well-known theoretical moves.

2...♞e4

This set-up became especially popular after the game Van der Wiel-Kasparov, Interzonal tournament, Moscow 1982, where White got crushed.

3 ♗f4

3 ♗h4 is not so popular any more. Black seems to have at least equal play in the sharp variations after 3...c5 4 f3 g5 5 fxe4 gxh4 6 e3 when he can continue with ...♗h6 or ...♗g7 and exert pressure on the centre with ...♞c6 and ...♛b6. 3 h4 was once a speciality

of Julian Hodgson, but my opinion is that the move is only effective if Black takes the bishop. After normal development, h4 might easily become a weakness.

3...c5 4 f3 ♛a5+

With the idea of destroying the coordination of the white pieces. 4...♞f6 5 dxc5 ♛a5+ 6 ♞c3 ♛xc5 7 ♛d2 gives a position from which I have won many games. White continues with e4, castles queenside, and has good attacking prospects whether Black fianchettoes the bishop with ...g6 or tries some other structure.

5 c3

After 5 ♞d2 ♞f6, Black threatens both the d4-pawn and to play ...♞d5.

5...♞f6 6 d5

6 ♞d2 cxd4 7 ♞b3 ♛b6 (7...♛f5 8 ♗xb8 ♖xb8 9 ♛xd4 gives White a dangerous initiative as e5 is about to follow) 8 ♛xd4 ♞c6 9 ♛xb6 axb6 10 ♞d4 e5 11 ♞xc6 exf4 12 ♞d4 gives a sharp ending where the question is whether Black's activity, open files for the rooks, bishop-pair and the strong e3-square compensate for his miserable pawn-structure.

6...♛b6 7 b3

This was my own move and a novelty when the game was played. Now, some years later, I believe that White should play 7 ♗c1.

7...e6 8 e4!?

Hitherto, only 8 dxe6 fxe6 had been suggested, giving Black a good game with ...d5, ...♗e7/d6, ...♞c6 and ...0-0.

8...exd5 9 exd5 ♗d6!

To gain a tempo and prevent d6. Black wants to exchange the dark-squared bishops as the squares f2, e3 and c3 will lose their defender.

10 ♗g5 (D)
10...0-0?

My opponent played this move quickly, but it is a mistake as he unnecessarily gives

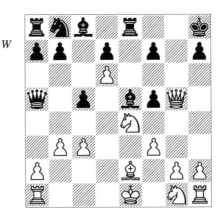

himself a bad pawn-structure. He thought that the attacking chances on the dark squares compensated for this. However, the pieces on the queenside are so crippled that the attack fades out before it has even started. Current theory says that Black is supposed to have the better chances after 10...♗e7 as White has problems with development. The pawns on d5 and c3 are weak, while Black has natural moves like ...0-0 and ...d6 at his disposal.

11 ♗xf6 ♖e8+ 12 ♗e2 gxf6 13 ♘d2!

After this move Black's position is already critical. White threatens ♘c4, and the even more dangerous ♘e4.

13...♕c7 14 ♘e4 ♗e5

After 14...♔g7 15 ♘h3 it is hard to see how Black will be able to get his queenside pieces out. If the d6-bishop moves, I will play d6, and on ...f5 White takes on d6 and plays ♕d2 with a more or less winning position.

15 d6 ♕a5 16 ♕d2

White threatens f4. Black therefore makes a last desperate effort to attack.

16...f5 17 ♕g5+ ♔h8? (D)

17...♔f8 is better, though White retains a strong attack.

18 ♕xf5!

This counterattack decides the game. ♘g5 is a move to take seriously.

18...♗xc3+ 19 ♔f1 ♖xe4

19...♗xa1 20 ♘g5 ♔g7 21 ♕xh7+ ♔f6 22 f4! ♖e7 23 ♘e4+ ♖xe4 24 ♕h6+ ♔f5 25 g4#.

20 ♕xe4 ♗xa1 21 ♗d3 ♔g7 22 ♕xh7+ ♔f8

This move both surprised and pleased me as I had been absorbed in analysing the consequences of 22...♔f6 23 ♕f5+ ♔g7 24 ♕g5+ ♔f8 25 ♕e7+ ♔g7 26 ♗c4; I came to the conclusion that White won after 26...♕d2 27 ♕xf7+ ♔h6 28 g4 ♗d4 29 ♘e2 with h4 and g5+ to follow.

23 ♗c4 1-0

The end could have been 23...♔g7 24 ♕h5 ♔g8 25 ♕xf7+ ♔h7 26 ♗d3+ ♔h8 27 ♕e8+ and mate next move.

My Notes

In this variation Black avoids the doubled pawns by playing ...♘e4 and wants to put the d4-pawn under pressure by means of ...c5 and ...♕b6. The check on a5 is played to disturb White's development and create weaknesses. White wants to coordinate his pieces and exploit Black's lost tempi with the queen. If White succeeds in this then he can start a strong attack against Black's king. White has an important choice at move six: 6 d5 or 6 ♘d2 are possible, leading to different types of game. Currently, you should examine 6...♕b6 7 ♗c1 after the former and 6...cxd4 7 ♘b3 ♕b6 8 ♕xd4 ♘c6 9 ♕xb6 after the latter.

Jesper Hall – Alexander Khalifman
Vienna 1996

1 d4 ♘f6 2 ♗g5 e6

Black avoids the doubled pawns and gains the bishop-pair, but White gets a lead in development and a space advantage in the centre. Black's style of play is reminiscent of the ideas of Basman: he plays ...a6, ...b5 on one side and ...h6, ...g5 on the other, followed by fianchettoing the bishops to put pressure on the centre. The system chosen by Black in the game became popular, with new ideas from Karpov at the beginning of the 1990s.

3 e4 h6 4 ♗xf6 ♕xf6 5 ♘c3 d6

5...♗b4!? is interesting, and in my opinion gives Black good chances of equality. After 6 ♕d2 c5 7 a3 ♗xc3 8 bxc3 d6 9 f4 e5 10 ♗b5+ ♗d7 11 ♖b1, de Firmian played the dubious 11...exf4 against me at Malmö 1999; White got a good game with 12 ♘f3. In the post-mortem we found the better line 11...exd4 12 ♗xd7+ ♘xd7 13 cxd4 ♕xd4 14 ♕xd4 cxd4 15 ♖xb7 ♘c5 16 ♖b4 0-0 17 ♖xd4 ♖fe8, with equality.

6 ♕d2

White delays ♘f3, as it would be strongly met by ...g5 and ...♗g7. This was Karpov's main idea.

6...a6

If Black now plays 6...g5, White has a better set-up with ♗c4, ♘ge2, 0-0 and f4 with good chances.

7 0-0-0 ♕e7?!

This stereotyped move does not really belong here. With the knight on f3 and the pawn

on f2, Black often has time for this type of passive manoeuvring, but in this game White can start an attack with the f-pawn.

8 f4! g6 9 ♘f3 ♗g7 10 ♗d3

Black has chosen a wait-and-see strategy, planning to counterattack at the right moment. However, with the f4-pawn ready to roll, this is a risky policy. White now wants to play e5 and meet ...d5 with g4 and f5. Black's position would not survive another inexact move – but Khalifman does not make another in the rest of the game.

10...♘d7 11 e5 d5 12 g4 c5 13 dxc5 g5!

Khalifman has woken up. On 13...♘xc5? there follows 14 f5 and White's attack breaks through. Therefore, Black must try to undermine White's centre.

14 fxg5 hxg5 15 ♖de1 ♘xc5 16 ♔b1

Preparing ♕xg5.

16...b5 17 ♖hf1

After 17 ♘xg5 ♗h6 18 h4 ♗b7 19 ♖hf1 0-0-0 I thought that Black had survived better than he should but with, e.g., 20 ♕f4 White still has a great advantage.

17...♗h6 (D)

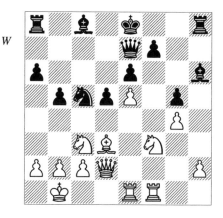

18 ♘d4?

So far White has played in accordance with the demands of the opening. Black has not managed to undermine the centre so that the bishops can start working, and they have so far been acting as supernumeraries. However, White's advantage is connected to his lead in development, which is temporary. Therefore it is important to act quickly. 18 h4! was the move. After the game Khalifman did not want to analyse the variations but stated "White is winning". That the attack is dangerous is shown by the following variations: 18...♘xd3 19 ♕xd3 gxh4 (the alternative 19...♗b7 loses to 20 hxg5 ♗xg5 21 ♘xg5 ♕xg5 22 ♘xb5) 20 g5 ♗g7 (after 20...♗xg5 21 ♘xg5 ♕xg5 22 ♘xd5 exd5 23 ♕xd5 ♖a7 24 ♕c5 White is winning) 21 g6 ♖f8 (21...fxg6 22 ♕xg6+ ♕f7 23 ♕g4 h3 24 ♘d4 ♕g8 25 ♕g6+ ♔d8 26 ♘xd5 exd5 27 ♘c6+ ♔c7 28 ♕d6+ ♔b7 29 ♘a5+ ♔a7 30 ♕c7+ ♗b7 31 ♕xb7#) 22 gxf7+ ♖xf7?! 23 ♕g6 ♔d8 24 ♘d4 and White wins.

The reason why I did not find 18 h4 was that I almost immediately found an appealing sacrificial idea instead. I didn't calculate sufficiently, nor did I see the candidate moves in the position. At this point Khalifman only had five minutes left to the time-control. I was excited by the possibility of winning and the thought crept into my head that he could never calculate all the complicated variations with so many moves still to make.

18...♗b7 19 ♗xb5+ axb5 20 ♘cxb5 0-0 21 ♖f6 ♗g7 22 ♕xg5 ♘e4 23 ♖xe4 dxe4 24 ♘d6 *(D)*

When I played the sacrifice, it was this position that I was heading for and I could not see any defence for Black against a new sacrifice with ♘f5. This was a key position that I completely misjudged.

24...♖fd8!

Not a particularly difficult move to find, preparing a back-rank mate. With some good defensive moves, Black neutralizes White's attack and wins easily.

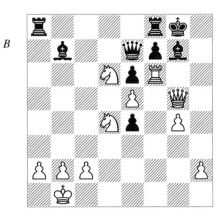

B

25 ♘xf7 ♖xd4 26 c3 e3 27 ♘h6+ ♔h8 28 ♘f7+ ♔g8 29 ♘h6+ ♔h7 30 ♕g6+ ♔h8 31 cxd4

31 ♘f7+ ♕xf7 32 ♕xf7 ♗e4+ 33 ♔c1 e2 34 ♕h5+ ♗h7 and the game is over.

31...e2 0-1

My Notes

White has the centre and a lead in development and Black the bishop-pair. Black's strategy is guerrilla warfare with the bayonet stabs ...b5 and ...g5 and the guns on b7 and g7. White wants either to make use of his lead in development and break through, or to obtain a closed structure in the centre where the bishop-pair cannot be effective. Delaying ♘f3 meant an extra pawn in the attack on the kingside, and Black should probably have played ...g5 anyway. The other interesting possibility is to play 5...♗b4 with the idea of continuing ...d6 and ...e5.

Jesper Hall – Samir Lejlić
Swedish Ch, Ronneby 1998

1 d4 ♘f6 2 ♗g5 d5 3 ♗xf6 gxf6

3...exf6 is also possible, and leads to a positional game. White then plays c4 to make use of his extra pawn in the centre.

4 e3 c5 5 ♘c3 cxd4 6 exd4 ♘c6

This variation was the reason why I took a long break from the Trompowsky. After 7 ♘ge2 ♗f5 Black has a natural plan of development with ...e6, ...♕b6, ...♗d6 or ...♗h6 and White has problems with the coordination of his pieces. However, then a friend tipped me off about 7 ♕h5. The idea is to shut Black's light-squared bishop inside his pawn-chain. After that, White castles queenside and attacks on the kingside and in the centre with knights and queen supported by the f- and g-pawns.

7 ♕h5 e6

This is forced, since 7...♘xd4 8 0-0-0 gives White a quick attack. For example, 8...e5 9 ♘f3 ♗c5 (9...♘xf3 loses to 10 ♗b5+ ♗d7 11 ♖xd5) 10 ♘xe5 fxe5 11 ♕xe5+ and White is winning.

8 0-0-0 ♕a5 *(D)*

This was a key position for me during the game. In my preparation, I had only looked at 8...♕b6 with the idea of ...♗d7 and ...♖c8 or ...0-0-0.

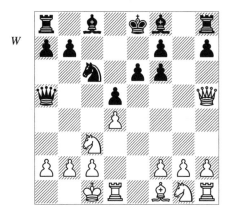

9 ♘ge2

My first thought was to play 9 ♔b1 in order to guard a2, but suddenly I saw the reply 9...♕b6 10 ♘ge2 ♗a3. After 11 b3 Black

has managed to weaken my queenside and has good prospects for his attack. The natural move that I chose leads to a very sharp game and I had to think deeply about the consequences. Remember what I said about how difficult it is to build up a combination and foresee what is happening before the combination is delivered.

9...b5?!

With hindsight, Black should have played 9...♗d7 followed by ...♖c8 and ...♘b4. White would play the same ideas as in the game.

10 ♘f4 b4 11 ♘cxd5!

This was the sacrifice I had to calculate on my ninth move.

11...b3!?

After 11...exd5 12 ♘xd5 ♗e6 13 ♘xf6+ ♔e7 14 d5 ♗xf6 (14...b3 15 cxb3) 15 ♕h4+ ♔g6 16 ♗d3+ f5 17 dxe6, with threats like g4, White should be winning.

12 axb3

12 ♘xf6+!? ♔e7 13 axb3 (13 cxb3!?) 13...♕a1+ 14 ♔d2 ♕xb2 15 ♕c5+ ♔xf6 16 ♘h5+ ♔g6 17 ♗d3+ f5 18 ♕xc6 ♕xd4 is one of many possible lines in this game that would be difficult to judge correctly over the board.

12...exd5 13 ♘xd5 ♕a1+ 14 ♔d2 ♕a5+ 15 c3 ♗e6 16 ♗b5

16 ♘xf6+ ♔e7 17 d5 ♖d8 18 ♔c1 ♗g7 19 ♗b5!? (after 19 dxe6 ♕a1+ 20 ♔c2 ♕xd1+ 21 ♕xd1 ♖xd1 22 ♔xd1 ♗xf6 23 exf7 it is not completely clear that White has an advantage) 19...♗xf6 20 ♗xc6 ♗xc3 21 ♔c2 ♖hg8 22 bxc3 ♕a2+ 23 ♔d3 might be strong for White, but in a game situation it is almost impossible to assess.

16...0-0-0 17 ♗xc6 ♖xd5?!

We both thought that after 17...♗xd5!?, 18 ♖a1 won back the piece, but Black has the fantastic 18...♕c5 and even though I think White is better after 19 dxc5 ♗f3+ 20 ♔c2 ♗xh5 21 b4 ♔b8 22 ♖he1 since Black's pieces are difficult to develop, I doubt I would have found the correct path after such a surprising move.

18 ♗xd5 ♕xd5 19 ♕xd5 ♗xd5 20 ♖hg1 ♗xb3 21 ♖a1 ♔b7 22 ♖a5 ♗c4 (D)

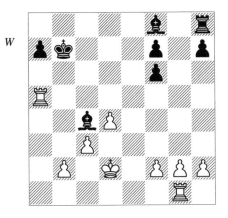

23 ♖ga1?

In moderate time-trouble, I completely underestimated Black's threats. The priorities for White are to coordinate his rooks, secure his king and to get the queenside pawns moving with b3 and c4. The pawn sacrifice 23 b3! is therefore correct: 23...♔b6 24 ♖ga1 ♗xb3 25 ♖a6+ ♔c7 (25...♔b5 26 ♖1a5+ ♔c4 27 ♖c6+ with mate to follow; it was this mate that I had missed and therefore I did not dare to play the pawn sacrifice) 26 ♖xa7+ ♔c6 27 ♔d3 ♗h6 28 c4 ♖b8 29 ♖xf7 and White is winning.

23...♗h6+ 24 ♔d1?!

24 ♔c2 is better: 24...♖e8 25 ♖xa7+ ♔b6 26 b3 ♖e2+ 27 ♔d1 ♖d2+ 28 ♔e1 ♖e2+ 29 ♔f1 ♖a2+ 30 bxc4 ♖xa7 31 c5+ ♔b7 32 ♖xa7+ ♔xa7 33 ♔e2 with a very interesting ending in which White has the better prospects.

24...♖e8

Black's pieces have come to life so much that 25...♗b3# is threatened.

25 ♖xa7+ ♔b6 26 ♖7a3 ♖e2 27 b3 ♖d2+ 28 ♔e1 ♖e2+ 29 ♔f1 ♗d3 30 ♔g1 ♗d2 31 c4 ♗c3 32 ♖a6+ ♔b7 33 ♖a7+ ♔b8 34 ♖a8+ ♔b7 35 ♖1a7+ ♔c6!

Not 35...♔b6? 36 c5+ ♔c6 37 ♖c8+ ♔d5 38 ♖d8+ ♔e4 (38...♔c6 39 ♖d6+ ♔b5 40 ♖b6#) 39 ♖e7+, after which White swaps rooks and wins.

36 ♖a6+

White has to go for the perpetual because 36 d5+ ♔c5 37 h3 ♖e1+ 38 ♔h2 ♗e5+ 39 g3 ♗e4 is only dangerous for White.

36...♔b7 37 ♖6a7+ ♔c6 38 ♖a6+ ♔b7
½-½

My Notes

The game left theory at an early stage and became sharp. It should be possible to find important novelties here. White forced Black to restrict his light-squared bishop by playing the slightly unusual move 7 ♕h5. After that, White wanted to castle queenside and attack with the f- and g-pawns, or open files for the rooks against Black's king by means of a piece sacrifice in the centre. After the sacrifice on d5, the game left positional play behind: what mattered was to analyse further and better. Almost every position was critical and even far into the ending the players were forced to calculate tactics.

A Summary of the Trompowsky

When I read my notes made after the games it seems hard to understand the opening. The play seems a bit rough and unpolished. The clear strategic ideas that you usually find are reduced to a medley of possibilities. That is why I continue to play the opening even after the surprise factor has disappeared. If you choose to study it even further and explore the latest theory, you will notice that despite the fact that the amount of theory has increased, it is still possible to find new moves at an early stage. Therefore this opening suits someone who wants to start to think for himself early on and who is prepared to play various position-types. However, in your excitement do not forget to prepare something against 1...d5.

Building Up a Repertoire

I try to create a basic repertoire, openings that I have played for a long time and where I try to keep up with theory. I also always try to find new moves and improvements in order to keep ahead. Then I have a box of surprises: openings that I have looked at a bit. These openings reflect my craving for adventure and inspiration when I venture out on the slippery ice. The thought is, of course, that the ice will be even more slippery for my opponent...

What to Think About When You Learn a New Opening

The pawn-structure. Are there many types of pawn-structure, like in the Trompowsky, to keep me interested? If that doesn't appeal, then it is better to seek an opening with fewer possibilities.

The tempo. If the opening quickly leads to a complicated battle that demands thorough preparation and you do not like learning lots of theory, then you should find more unusual or slower openings.

Exchanges. If the opening quickly leads to an ending, you have to ask yourself if this is something that suits you.

My Training Tips

If you systematically write down and categorize your openings, then you can add material as you find new interesting games or gain practical experience in the opening. The computer is a great tool for this, but be selective and critical. It is better to have one well-annotated game that explains structures and ideas than ten without comments.

Build a bridge between your openings. If you are working with openings having one position-type, you can often find comprehensive structures and ideas in related opening variations. Then you have already done the basic work and it will be easy to learn. In my repertoire I have tried to have one solid positional choice and one more tactical line in every opening. With two parallel choices, you can shift according to mood and opponent.

Suggestions for Further Reading

Every year many books on openings come on the market. My recommendations therefore cannot be absolutely up-to-date, but more an explanation of what to look for. I have one book for each opening. All the books have annotated games that explain the basics. These I update using the *Informator* series. Very seldom do I buy a new book on the same opening, but of course sometimes there is a book coming out that you just have to have.

Personally I like Matthew Sadler's book *The Slav* (Chess Press/Cadogan, 1996); it is instructive, clear and useful. I also like *Mastering the Spanish* by Daniel King and Pietro Ponzetto (Batsford, 1993) as the discussion centres around pawn-structures. I have to mention *Beating the Sicilian 3* by John Nunn and Joe Gallagher (Batsford, 1995), which gives White a repertoire against the Sicilian. It has come out in several revised editions and every time Nunn (and for the third edition Gallagher) has found great novelties which have given Black headaches. This is probably the openings book I have read most myself.

If you want to get more of an overall perspective on openings and build a complete repertoire, I recommend the first chapters in *The Soviet Chess Conveyor* by Mikhail Shereshevsky (Semko, 1994). His fundamental premise is that young players should start to work with their openings and create a repertoire, as this is something they will use in their whole careers. However, the study of openings should not overshadow the other parts of the game, and you should not just hammer variations into your head.

The Road to Chess Improvement by Alex Yermolinsky (Gambit, 1999) is another book that has inspired me with its personal tone and good advice, not least in the area of openings.

10 Fewer Pieces, More Problems

On the endgame and overall themes

The first task is to learn how to think in the endgame.

Many lower-rated players are afraid of the endgame. The reason is probably that openings and middlegames occur in every game, but endgames only sometimes and then often with such a material imbalance that deeper knowledge is not needed. Therefore the endgame is something unusual and frightening. The fear affects your playing strength in the earlier parts of the game too, because you lose an important dimension in your calculations if you don't consider the subsequent endings.

There is a way to deal with the problem, even though as usual it is not possible to avoid hard work. The first thing to do is to learn how to think in this part of the game. I believe that the most common erroneous notion concerning the endgame is that you have to learn everything by heart. This makes you give up before you have even had the energy to finish the first task in a weighty endgame book. However, our brains cannot keep track of too much exact information, so instead I suggest that you work with overall themes, basic positions and guidelines to help structure your thinking process:

Overall themes. General ideas for all types of endgames.

Basic positions. The positions that you have to learn by heart.

Guidelines. The most important ideas for a specific type of ending.

Overall Themes

The King is a Very Powerful Piece in the Endgame

More or less from the moment that we leave the beginner's level we know that the king is a very powerful piece in the endgame. Often the king is also the most active. It should be placed as far up the board as possible to attack the pawns or to participate in an attack on the other king. The first thing to do in an endgame is therefore to bring the king to an active post, often in the centre. All my examples of endgames are based on this theme, so let me show you how a strong player can be preparing for an endgame even when still in the middlegame.

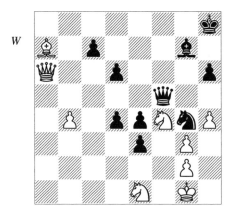

Evgeny Agrest – Jesper Hall
Swedish Ch, Ronneby 1998

A decisive moment in the 1998 Swedish Championship. Following an error by White just out of the opening, Black had good play with a massive pawn-centre in return for a piece. I had aimed for this position and believed my advantage decisive. Black threatens 32...d3 33 ᐤexd3 exd3 34 ♕xd3 ♕xd3 35 ᐤxd3 e2, when White's king is cut off.

32 ♔f1!

This strong move was difficult to foresee since White breaks the sharp tactical rhythm of the game with a quiet positional move. Moreover, he voluntarily moves the king in front of the black pawns and pins his own knight. I had mainly been looking at 32 ♕a5? and came to the conclusion that Black was winning after 32...♕xa5 33 bxa5 e2 34 a6 (34 ᐤxe2 loses after 34...d3! 35 ♔f1 d2!) 34...♔h7 35 ♗c5 d3 36 ᐤexd3 exd3 37 ᐤxd3 dxc5 38 a7 ♗d4+ 39 ♔h1 ᐤf2+.

32...ᐤh2+

32...♗e5 is a better way to retain winning chances.

33 ♔g1 ᐤg4 34 ♔f1 ♔h7?

This was a stupid way to try to avoid the draw, and could have ended badly.

35 ♕c4 d3 36 ᐤexd3 exd3 37 ♕xd3 ♕xd3+ 38 ᐤxd3 ᐤe5?!

38...♔g6 is better.

39 ♔e2??

Relieved to have escaped, Agrest misses a chance to play for a win: 39 ᐤxe5 ♗xe5 40 b5 ♗c3 (a sad necessity; 40...♗xg3? loses to 41 ♗b8 d5 42 b6) 41 g4 ♗d2 42 ♔e2 ♔g6 43 ♗b8 ♗a5 44 ♔e3 ♔f6 45 ♔e4 ♔e6 and White has good winning prospects.

39...ᐤxd3 40 ♔xd3 e2 41 ♔xe2 c6 ½-½

Take It Easy

There is a classic aphorism that all too often comes true: the first move after the time-control is a mistake. What happens is that it is difficult to slow down after a hectic time-scramble. The brain is in a high gear and the player lashes out another move in the same spirit. The aphorism could also be valid for the transformation from middlegame to ending.

The endgame has its own rhythm and demands a different way of thinking. The multitude of tactical and strategic possibilities of the middlegame are transformed, not into anything easier (in fact many would say just the opposite) but the assumptions become different and hence also the thinking process. The first thing you must do when the game moves towards an endgame is to feel this rhythm and be aware of the changes.

One change is that the king, who has been skulking out of danger of attack, should now be activated. It becomes even more important to find the optimum post for each piece and to coordinate those that remain as efficiently as possible. New elements such as zugzwang, stalemate, and the opposition are added, and other elements become more important, such as structural and thematic thinking. The question "Where do I want my pieces?" and the several-moves-in-a-row principle therefore increase in importance. The following is a classic example of how to think in an ending:

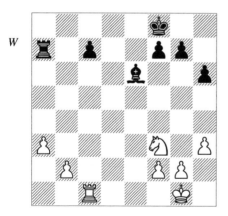

**José Raúl Capablanca –
Viacheslav Ragozin**
Moscow 1936

What has made this ending so famous is the way Capablanca annotated it. He wrote: "White's plan is to prevent the c-pawn from advancing and to control the board up to the fifth rank. To do this it is necessary to move the king to e3, put the rook on c3, the knight on d4 and the pawns on b4 and f4. When this position has been achieved, it will be time to move the queenside pawns." Capablanca asks himself: "Where should my pieces stand?" and uses the several-moves-in-a-row rule. He gave no specific variations, nor did he seem bothered about how long it would take to achieve this. With his comments, Capablanca demonstrated a new way of thinking in the endgame.

33 ♘d4 ♖b7 34 b4 ♗d7 35 f4 ♚e7 36 ♚f2 ♖a7 37 ♖c3 ♚d6 38 ♖d3 ♚e7 39 ♚e3 ♖a4 40 ♖c3

After 40 ♚e4?! Black can free himself with 40...c5. The take-it-easy concept involves always trying to keep your opponent's counterplay to a minimum. After 41 bxc5 ♗c6+ 42 ♚e5 f6+ 43 ♚f5 ♗xg2 44 ♖g3 ♗d5 Black has chances to hold the position.

40...♚d6 41 ♖d3 ♚e7 42 ♖c3 ♚d6

Repetition is a good tool when you are following the take-it-easy rule. It puts you in the right mood, and gives you some extra time to think about how to proceed. It also has a psychological function. When I play against an opponent who repeats the position, I feel a glimmer of hope: "Maybe I will get a draw after all." It is then depressing when the position is not repeated for a third time. Instead, I realize that my opponent has just been teasing me to show his superiority. At this stage you often do something desperate.

43 ♘e2 g6 44 ♖d3+ ♚e6 45 ♚d4 ♖a6 46 ♖e3+ ♚d6 47 ♘c3 f5 *(D)*

The dream position has been reached. Time to advance the pawns.

48 b5 ♖a8

48...♖xa3 49 ♘e4+ fxe4 50 ♖xa3 ♗xb5 51 ♖g3 and White wins.

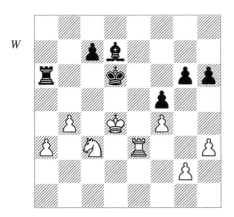

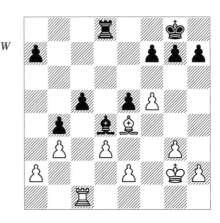

49 ♔c4 ♗e6+ 50 ♔b4 c5+ 51 bxc6 ♗g8 52 ♘b5+ ♔xc6 53 ♖d3

Black's problem is not only the a-pawn, but the kingside pawns as well.

53...g5 54 ♖d6+ ♔b7 55 fxg5

55 ♖xh6 gxf4 with the idea of ...♗d5 is not clear.

55...hxg5 56 ♖g6 ♖f8 57 ♖xg5 f4 58 ♘d4

Again Capablanca takes time to prevent any counterplay involving ...f3 before he takes the next step. The take-it-easy principle is used over and over again in this ending.

58...♖c8 59 ♖g7+ ♔b6 60 ♖g6+ ♔b7 61 ♘b5 ♖f8 62 ♘d6+ ♔b8 63 h4 1-0

The following diagram is from one of my favourite endings. It instructively demonstrates the importance of finding the best squares for your pieces combined with methodical progress towards a breakthrough. What makes the ending a masterpiece are the great twists at the end. In the diagram you get the feeling that a draw is close as there are opposite-coloured bishops in a closed position that lacks squares for any breakthrough. However, White has some advantage as his king can proceed along the diagonal from f3 to d5, and the bishop has good

Richard Réti – Peter Romanovsky
Moscow 1925

prospects. But what about the rook? And where should he break through? White finds a beautiful mini-operation that activates his pieces.

28 ♖c4!

Otherwise Black plays ...♗c3, locking the rook out.

28...♔f8 29 ♔f3 ♖c8

Black is forced to displace his rook as White threatens to win the c5-pawn by playing e3.

30 e3 ♗c3

With some exact moves White has placed his pieces actively and rendered Black's passive. Now it is time for phase two in the planning. What White wants to do is to get around Black's pawn-chain with the rook. It is not easy to break through on the queenside or in the centre, so only the kingside option remains. White wants to proceed with ♗d5, ♖h4, ♔e4 and ♖h5 forcing ...h6, and then h4, g4 and g5 to get the rook in. Before he does that, he eliminates his only weakness – the a2-pawn. Perhaps Black should have played 30...♗b2.

31 a4!

A great prophylactic move. If White had put his plan into operation immediately, Black would have obtained counterplay by playing his rook to a6.

31...♔e7 32 ♗d5 ♖c7 33 ♖h4 h6 34 ♔e4 ♔f6 35 ♖h5 ♖d7! 36 g4

If White had guessed the counterplay that Black had planned he would probably have made some further take-it-easy moves, such as ♗c4 and h3, before playing g4. Going through the game today, we can be happy that Réti forgot the prophylactic question "What is my opponent planning?" this time.

36...g6

Black has found a nasty trap.

37 ♖xh6 ♔g5 38 ♖h7 ♔xg4 *(D)*

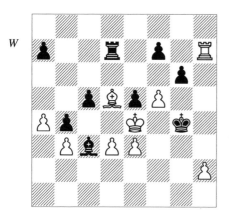

Now what? 39 fxg6?? f5# and 39 ♗xf7?? gxf5# are two highly unattractive finishes from White's viewpoint. Réti keeps his cool and finds a beautiful continuation.

39 ♗e6! fxe6 40 fxg6

Not 40 ♖xd7?? gxf5#.

40...♖d8 41 ♖xa7

White's winning idea is simply to push his passed pawns. The black bishop and king are too far away to help the defending black rook.

41...♔g5 42 g7 ♔h6 43 a5 ♔h7 44 a6 ♖d6 45 h4 ♗e1 46 h5 ♗h4 47 h6

The only way to stop 48 ♖a8 is 47...♖d8 but then 48 ♖b7 followed by a7 and ♖b8 wins. Therefore...

1-0

The Principle of Two Weaknesses

One of the most important concepts in the endgame is that of the two weaknesses. If you have an advantage and exert pressure against a weakness in your opponent's position, he can usually find a defence. However, if you can create another weakness and combine your threats against the weaknesses, the defence will almost always fail. That is why the concept should always be in the back of your mind: small in-between moves can be used to force your opponent to make new concessions. In many of my favourite examples this idea, just like the take-it-easy rule, is used in addition to the main theme.

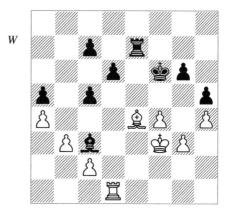

Vadim Faibisovich – Heikki Westerinen
Vilnius 1969

Black has two weaknesses, a5 and g6. The first partial goal is to put them under as heavy pressure as possible to tie Black up. The next step is to combine the threats and try to win one of the pawns. You should already have noticed the possibility of a breakthrough by f5 with the rook on g5. With the king on b5, the idea of ♖d3 followed by c3 to cut off the black bishop's protection of the a5-pawn might be practical.

44 ♖d5 ♖g7 45 ♖g5 ♗d2

To prevent f5. After 45...♔f7? 46 f5 gxf5 47 ♖xf5+ White wins a pawn.

46 ♔e2 ♗c3 47 ♔d3

Now f5 does not achieve anything, as the g3-pawn is not protected.

47...♗e1 48 ♔c4 ♔f7 49 ♔b5 ♗c3?!

Black overlooks White's possibility of combining threats against the two weaknesses. The win would have been more difficult after 49...♔f6, after which White must go for the third weakness on c7: 50 ♔c6 ♗d2 51 ♗g2 ♖e7 52 ♗h3. The idea is to play the bishop to d7 and win the c7-pawn. There follows 52...♗e1 53 f5 ♖g7 (53...gxf5 54 ♖xh5 ♖e5 55 ♔xc7 ♗xg3 56 ♔xd6 affords White winning chances as the black rook cannot give an effective check) 54 fxg6 ♖xg6 55 ♖xh5 ♖xg3 56 ♗f5 with good chances for White.

50 ♖d5!

With the king on f7, the counterplay with ...♖e7 comes too late. In the game White therefore manages to execute the manoeuvre ♖d3 and c3.

50...♗e1 51 ♖d3 ♔f6 52 c3 ♖e7 53 ♗b7 ♖e2 54 ♔xa5 ♖c2 55 ♔b5 ♗xc3 *(D)*

Black has won back the pawn, but the white a-pawn is not far from promotion.

56 a5?

Recklessly played. 56 ♗d5 is correct, leading to the same type of play as we see in the game.

56...♗e1?

Black had a chance to make the ending distinctly unclear with 56...c4!:

a) 57 bxc4? ♖b2+ 58 ♔a6 ♗xa5 and Black is even better as the white king is badly placed on the a-file.

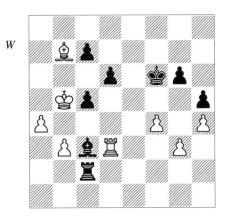

b) 57 ♖d1 cxb3 58 a6 b2 (58...♖a2? 59 ♔c4 b2 60 ♔xc3 ♖a1 61 ♔xb2 ♖xd1 62 a7 and the a-pawn decides the game) 59 a7 ♖c1 60 ♗e4 ♖xd1 61 a8♕ b1♕+ 62 ♗xb1 ♖xb1+ 63 ♔c6! leads to a difficult ending where Black has some practical chances to draw by snatching the g3-pawn and then building a fortress on the kingside. For example, 63...♔g7 64 ♕d8 ♔h7 65 ♕xc7+?! (65 f5 gxf5 66 ♕d7+ is better, as Black's kingside pawns fall) 65...♔g7 66 ♕xd6 ♖b3 67 f5 gxf5 68 ♕f4 ♖c3+ 69 ♔d5 ♔g8 70 ♕xf5 ♖xg3 71 ♕xh5 and Black should get a draw by putting his rook on f6.

57 a6 c4

One move too late.

58 bxc4 ♗f2 59 ♖a3 c6+

59...♗a7 loses to 60 ♗d5 followed by ♔c6.

60 ♔xc6 ♖xc4+ 61 ♔xd6 ♗a7 62 ♗c6 ♖b4 63 ♔d7 ♖b1 64 ♖a5 ♖b3 65 ♖g5

The idea of combining threats against various weaknesses continues even when White is two pawns up. It is time to harass the g6-pawn once more.

65...♖e3 66 ♔c7 ♖e7+ 67 ♗d7 ♗f2

Allowing the thematic f5, but it was too late to find a defence. For example, 67...♖e3 68 ♔b7 ♗d4 69 ♗b5 ♖e7+ 70 ♔c6 ♖e6+ 71

♔d5 ♗f2 72 ♖xg6+ ♔xg6 73 ♔xe6 and White is winning.

68 f5 ♖e3 69 ♖xg6+ ♔f7 70 ♗e6+ ♔e7 71 ♖g7+ ♔f8 72 ♖f7+ ♔e8 73 a7 1-0

This game is an excellent example of how to play against two weaknesses, but also reminds us that tactics are always present. It might only take a minor tactical finesse to remove one or other of the weaknesses. The possibility of 56...c4!, although based on relatively straightforward tactics, was missed by both players, and by Shereshevsky when he annotated the ending. This suggests that when players are in a frame of mind to consider positional manoeuvring, their tactical awareness can drop dramatically. Therefore it is important to make a special effort in the endgame, whether attacking or defending, to be especially alert.

My Training Tips

The three overall themes that I have discussed are the basic ones, but besides them there are the fight for the initiative in the ending, attack against the king, schematic thinking, and so on. When you go through instructive endings try to think about which themes the players are using. Catalogue the ones that were especially good.

A good way to study this type of endgame is to take an interesting position from a book and play it against someone of equal strength in a 45-minute game. Analyse it thoroughly afterwards and compare your game and your analysis with the book.

Suggestions for Further Reading

Most endgame books illustrate the basic positions that I write about in the next chapter, but lack the overall themes. The reason is probably that these themes use a similar way of thinking as in the middlegame and are therefore difficult to explain. One of my favourite books is in this field: *Endgame Strategy* by Mikhail Shereshevsky (Pergamon, 1985). The book goes through various general themes and has good examples with explanations and guidelines. The last three examples in this chapter are from this book, as they were simply the most instructive ones I could find. This is a book I really recommend.

Before I found this book, I used *Exploring the Endgame* by Peter Griffiths (A. & C. Black, 1984). Decent, but in another division. *Winning Endgame Technique* by Alexander Beliavsky and Adrian Mikhalchishin (Batsford, 1995) can be used as an alternative or a complement to *Endgame Strategy*. There is also *Mastering the Endgame* by Mikhail Shereshevsky and Leonid Slutsky (published in two volumes by Cadogan).

11 Basic Positions and Guidelines

On a method to study specific endgames

The basic positions, requiring exact knowledge, are complemented with guidelines.

Basic positions are positions that you need to know by heart. There should only be so many that you can handle them and be sure that if they arise you can play them correctly. It is the basic position that is the skeleton for the analysis; players try to reach or avoid them, as appropriate, when they calculate an ending.

The basic positions which require exact knowledge are complemented with guidelines. The use of guidelines is a technique that helps you remember and manipulate knowledge. When you calculate far into a certain ending, you extract the relevant material from your memory. It is useful to have some short key phrases to help you with this. You should try to remember these phrases; this is not usually a problem. I remember that when I was studying German at school we made up some short songs and rhymes out of the prepositions "an, auf, hinter, in, neben, über, unter, vor, zwischen" in order to remember them. Those songs and rhymes are even today securely anchored in the back of my mind, even though I have forgotten what role these German prepositions played. Maybe you will do the same and put a tune to the phrases that you find in your analysis.

Pawn Endings

Many people think that studying pawn endings is the best way to learn how to calculate. The play is concrete as the variations are few and an assessment of unclear is very rare. It is usually possible to calculate to the very end. Therefore the guidelines often lead directly to exact basic positions. Knowledge of these is of great importance, so that you know what to look for. That creativity is also needed is demonstrated by the following study.

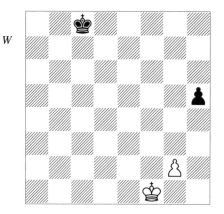

Josef Moravec
Československský Šach, 1952

1 ♔f2!

White has two ideas: to go towards the h-pawn via either f2 or g1. To go via g1 gives Black the chance to get there in time after 1 ♔g1? ♔d7 2 ♔h2 ♔e6 3 ♔h3 ♔f5 4 ♔h4 ♔g6 with an easy draw.

1...h4!

With the idea of sacrificing the pawn with ...h3 and then running to h8 with the king.

2 ♔g1!

White combines the two ideas that he had in the initial position. After 2 ♔f3 h3 3 g4

♔d7 4 ♔g3 ♔e6 5 ♔xh3 ♔f6 6 ♔h4 ♔g6 it is a draw.

2...♔d7

2...h3 3 g3 ♔d7 4 ♔h2 ♔e6 5 ♔xh3 ♔f6 6 ♔h4 and White has the diagonal opposition and thereby a win.

3 ♔h2 ♔e6 4 ♔h3 ♔f6 5 ♔xh4

White is winning.

The Opposition

This concept is fundamental for pawn endings. Opposition is the situation when the kings stand in front of each other, fighting for important squares. The one that has the opposition is the one that forces the opponent to give away. There are also other versions of the opposition, such as diagonal opposition and virtual opposition, while anti-opposition (e.g. kings a knight's move apart) can be important in positions where there are spare tempi. Distant opposition is a form that is often used in studies, but the most simple form of opposition is the most important in a real-game situation. But watch out; sometimes someone will challenge you with a position that he says is a draw with White to move but that Black to play loses. Then it is probably a question of distant or virtual opposition, where the whole board has corresponding squares, which means that if one of the kings is on one square there is only one other square that the other king can stand on to hold the draw.

Can White win in the following diagram?

1 ♔d5 ♔c8 2 c7

Yes! By sacrificing the c-pawn and then grabbing the b-pawn it is possible. Even though Black will get the opposition, he is lost if the attacking king is on its sixth rank. Note the stalemate after 2 ♔d6 ♔d8 3 c7+ ♔c8 4 ♔c6??.

2...♔xc7 3 ♔e6 ♔c8 4 ♔d6 ♔b8 5 ♔c6 ♔a7 6 ♔c7 ♔a8 7 ♔xb6 ♔b8 8 ♔a6

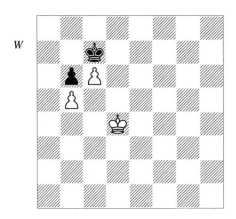

Giambatista Lolli
1763

It is important to observe that 8 ♔c6?! ♚a7 9 ♔c7 ♚a8 10 b6?? is stalemate (to win, White must retrace his steps with 10 ♔b6).

8...♚a8 9 b6 ♚b8 10 b7

White is winning.

Here is a practical example where distant opposition played a role:

Svetozar Gligorić – Bobby Fischer
Candidates Tournament,
Bled/Zagreb/Belgrade 1959

Black's king is cut off, but nevertheless he has a way to save himself.

53...♖b8+ 54 ♔a4 ♖a8+

These checks force White's king to retreat.

55 ♔b3 ♖c8! 56 ♖xc8 ♚xc8 57 ♔c4

White has the distant opposition. However, thanks to the b-pawn's position on b4, White is unable to maintain it after Black's next move.

57...♚b8! ½-½

The Royal Diagonal

I have always been fascinated by the fact that it takes the same number of moves for a king on e2 to reach e6 via c4 as to go straight down the e-file. This can be used to advantage, by threatening something on the way or hindering the opponent's king from getting closer.

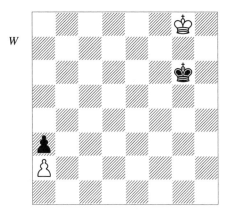

Franz Sackmann
Deutsche Schachblätter, 1924

When Black takes on a2, White must be able to play ♔c2 or ♔c1 to hold the draw. Therefore:

1 ♔h8!

Not 1 ♔f8?? ♚f6!, when via his royal diagonal Black's king marches towards b2 and stops White's king reaching c2 in time. Black wins by 2 ♔e8 ♔e5 3 ♔e7 ♔d4 4 ♔d6 ♔c3 5 ♔c5 ♔b2 6 ♔c4 ♔xa2 7 ♔c3 ♔b1.

1...♔f6 2 ♔h7

White's king has found his royal diagonal.

2...♔e5 3 ♔g6 ♔d4 4 ♔f5 ♔c3 5 ♔e4 ♔b2 6 ♔d3 ♔xa2 7 ♔c2

White secures a draw.

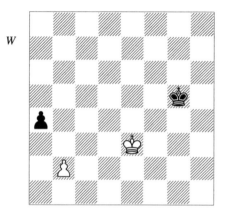

W

Josef Moravec
Československý Šach, 1952

1 ♔d4 ♔f5 2 ♔c5!

White uses the idea of the royal diagonal and gives the king two tasks: to grab the a-pawn and keep the opponent's king away. 2 ♔c4 a3 3 bxa3 ♔e6 4 ♔b5 ♔d7 5 ♔b6 ♔c8 and Black has used his royal diagonal to reach the drawing square c8.

2...a3 3 bxa3 ♔e6 4 ♔c6

Black's royal diagonal is cut off.

4...♔e7 5 ♔b7

It is impossible to stop the a-pawn.

The Distant Passed Pawn

In an ending with pawns on both sides this is the most important rule: the side which has its passed pawn further from the other pawns usually wins. When the kings have taken the passed pawns, one will be that much closer to the remaining pawns.

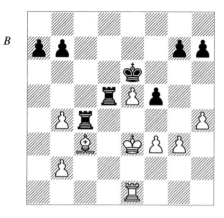

B

William Lombardy – Bobby Fischer
USA Ch, New York 1960/1

Black is an exchange up, but what is the easiest way to win?

30...♖xc3+!

The answer is to sacrifice back the material advantage to obtain an ending with the more distant passed pawn.

31 bxc3 ♖xe5+ 32 ♔d2 ♖xe1 33 ♔xe1 ♔d5 34 ♔d2 ♔c4 35 h5 *(D)*

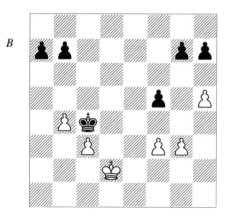

B

35...b6

Black's plan is simple. He fixes the king-side pawns, and then advances the a-pawn. In the end White will have to take Black's a-pawn, which gives Black the c-pawn. This exchange will give Black an advantage in the race to reach the kingside pawns. It is this that makes the idea of the distant passed pawn so important.

36 ♔c2 g5 37 h6 f4 38 g4 a5 39 bxa5 bxa5 40 ♔b2 a4 41 ♔a3 ♔xc3 42 ♔xa4 ♔d4 43 ♔b4 ♔e3 0-1

Practical Examples

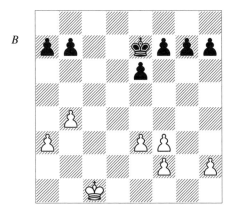

Erich Cohn – Akiba Rubinstein
St Petersburg 1909

When you look for the weaknesses it easy to spot the white h-pawn, but the slightly advanced pawns on the queenside are also worth noting. However, the most important reason that this ending is won for Black is that his king can advance far up the board. How do you then make progress? The method that Rubinstein uses is worth remembering. If you get such an advantage it is often good to exchange pawns on the same side as you

have the opposition. This opens up a route for the king sideways, so you can attack the other pawns. Here the weakness on the queenside might be of importance. A king on h3 can try to reach the a3-pawn by moving across the board, which would not have been possible without the move b4.

25...♔f6! 26 ♔d2 ♔g5 27 ♔e2

27 ♔d3 was the only variation that Black had to check apart from the game continuation. 27...♔h4 28 ♔d4 ♔h3 29 ♔c5 ♔xh2 30 b5 ♔g2 31 ♔d6 h5 32 ♔c7 b6 (even 32...h4 wins after 33 ♔xb7 h3 34 ♔xa7 h2 35 b6 h1♕ 36 b7 ♕a1 37 b8♕ ♕xa3+ 38 ♔b7 ♕b3+ 39 ♔a7 ♕xb8+; the black king picks up the pawns on f2 and f3 and the g-pawn will advance) 33 ♔b7 h4 34 ♔xa7 h3 35 ♔xb6 h2 and Black is winning.

27...♔h4 28 ♔f1 ♔h3 29 ♔g1 e5 *(D)*

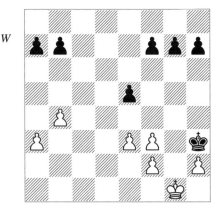

Part one is accomplished; the king has penetrated as far as possible. Now it is time for the pawns to advance. Both ...e5 and ...g5 are natural as they restrict White's f3-pawn.

30 ♔h1

30 e4 g5 31 ♔h1 h5 32 ♔g1 and now:

a) 32...g4 33 fxg4 ♔xg4 34 ♔g2 ♔f4 35 f3 ♔e3 is sufficient to win, but is unnecessarily complicated.

b) 32...h4! is a simpler and clearer win, as Black can hold the white king back with ...h3, viz. 33 ♔h1 g4 34 fxg4 ♔xg4 35 ♔g2 h3+ 36 ♔f1 ♔f3, and Black wins.

30...b5 31 ♔g1 f5 32 ♔h1 g5 33 ♔g1 h5 34 ♔h1 g4 35 e4

Or 35 fxg4:

a) 35...hxg4?! 36 ♔g1 f4 37 exf4 exf4 38 ♔h1 g3? (Black can still win by 38...f3!, with the idea of manoeuvring the king around, but it is much closer than it needed to be) 39 hxg3 fxg3 40 fxg3 ♔xg3 41 ♔g1 ♔f3 42 ♔f1 ♔e3 43 ♔e1 ♔d3 44 ♔d1 ♔c3 45 a4! bxa4 46 ♔c1 and Black cannot win as White has reached the key c1-square.

b) 35...fxg4! (preventing the e-pawns from being exchanged) 36 ♔g1 h4 37 ♔h1 e4 38 ♔g1 g3 39 hxg3 hxg3 40 ♔f1 ♔h2 (40...g2+ 41 ♔g1 a6 also wins) 41 fxg3 ♔xg3 42 ♔e2 ♔g2 and Black wins.

35...fxe4 36 fxe4 h4 37 ♔g1 g3 38 hxg3 hxg3 0-1

White resigned because of 39 f4 exf4 40 e5 f3 41 e6 g2 42 e7 ♔g3 43 e8♛ f2#. On any other try, Black's g-pawn and White's f-pawn will be exchanged and Black will grab the e-pawn, winning.

The following diagram features a decisive moment in the 1992 Oakham tournament.

53...♗xf3?

Akopian had missed the decisive finesse in the pawn ending that now follows. The point is that White can get a passed pawn by the sacrifice c5 at the right moment – a possibility worth remembering. Instead:

a) 53...♔e6? loses to 54 ♔g3 ♔e5 55 c5 bxc5 56 a5! ♔d5 57 b6 since 57...axb6?! 58 a6 ♔c6 59 ♘d6 forces the a-pawn through.

b) 53...♔f4! 54 ♘d2 ♗h1 55 ♔g1 ♗g2 (55...♗xf3? 56 ♘xf3 ♔xf3 57 c5 bxc5 58 a5 c4 59 b6 axb6 60 a6 and White queens with check) 56 c5 ♔g3! (56...bxc5? 57 a5 ♔g3 58

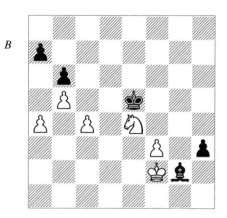

B

Alexei Shirov – Vladimir Akopian
Oakham 1992

♘e4+ ♔xf3 59 b6 and a pawn queens) 57 ♘e4+ ♔f4 appears to draw; e.g., 58 c6 ♗xf3 59 ♘d6 ♗g4 60 ♔h2 ♔e5 61 ♘c4+ ♔d4 62 ♘xb6 ♔c5 63 ♘d7+ ♔b4 64 ♘e5 ♗c8 65 ♘f7 ♔xa4 66 ♘d6 ♗e6 67 c7 ♔a5 68 c8♛ ♗xc8 69 ♘xc8 ♔xb5.

54 ♔xf3 h2 55 ♔g2 ♔xe4 56 c5 ♔d5

56...bxc5 57 a5 ♔d5 (D) (57...c4 58 b6 axb6 59 a6 and the pawn will promote with check) and now:

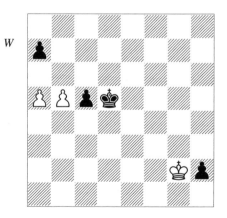

W

a) After 58 b6? Black has 58...♔c6.

b) 58 a6! was the finesse that Akopian had missed: now the black king cannot take a step in the right direction on the royal diagonal. 58...c4 59 b6 c3 (59...axb6 loses to 60 a7) 60 bxa7 h1♕+ 61 ♔xh1 c2 62 a8♕+ and White wins.

57 c6 ♔d6 58 ♔xh2 ♔c7 59 ♔g3 ♔d6 60 ♔f4 ♔e6 61 ♔e4 ♔d6 1-0

Black did not want to face ♔f5.

Guidelines

- It is good to have the opposition as far up the board as possible.
- A distant passed pawn is good.
- Always keep an eye on how the king can make use of the diagonal. It is often possible to threaten two things at the same time and gain a tempo.
- Zugzwang is common in pawn endings. Tempo moves are therefore valuable. If a pawn can take one step or two, think a little longer before you move it.

Rook Endings

Rooks are generally the last pieces to be developed, and unlike the other pieces, there generally need to be open files for rooks to be exchanged. Therefore rooks tend to stay on the board longer than most other pieces, with the consequence that rook endings occur extremely frequently. As they are also often hard to handle, it is important to study them thoroughly. Grandmasters and even world champions have made striking mistakes in rook endings. The difficulties are caused by the fact that you need to know a lot of basic positions precisely, and that there are a lot of positions which are very close to being basic positions, where both guidelines and exact calculation are required to handle correctly.

If even the world champions make mistakes, how shall we mortals be able to understand rook endings?

The first thing you must do is to study the basic positions with rook and pawn against rook, where the third rank is an important defensive rank and you must also know how to build a bridge (or create a shield). Then gradually you have to learn new basic positions and additional guidelines. As this is not an endgame book we have to make do with the most important examples, but I recommend that you proceed with the work that begins here.

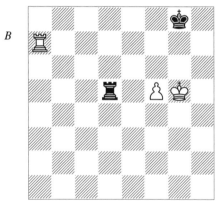

The third-rank defence (Philidor)

This is the most important drawing idea in an ending with rook against rook + pawn.

1...♖d6!

A game continuation I have seen from this position is 1...♖d8? 2 ♔g6 ♖c8 3 f6 ♖d8 4 ♖g7+! ♔f8 5 ♖h7 1-0, since 5...♔g8 6 f7+ decides the game.

2 f6

If Black continues to cover his third rank, this is the only way for White to try to make progress.

2...♖d1

Black is planning to check the white king from behind and as the f-pawn has moved forward it cannot provide shelter from the checks. White cannot make any progress and Black therefore draws. This is the simplest way to draw rook vs rook and pawn, and if there is time to set up this defence, it is certainly the method to choose.

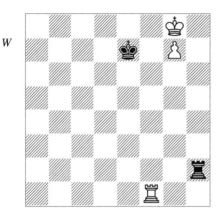

Build a bridge / Create a shield ('Lucena')

This is the most important way of promoting a pawn. In the diagram Black tries to prevent White's king from coming out. Step one therefore is to give the king space.

1 ♖e1+ ♔d7

1...♔d6 2 ♖e4 ♔d5 is an attempt to hinder White's idea, but with 3 ♖g4 White can win as the black king cannot prevent the white king from coming out. 3...♔e6 4 ♔f8 ♖f2+ 5 ♔e8 and White wins.

2 ♖e4!

The key move. If 2 ♔f7 Black starts giving checks with 2...♖f2+ and the white king cannot escape (he must return to g8 and then revert to the correct winning method). The idea of the text-move is to create a shield

against the checks, or (the more common expression) to build a bridge, before the king comes out.

2...♔d6 3 ♔f7 ♖f2+ 4 ♔g6 ♖g2+ 5 ♔f6 ♖f2+ 6 ♔g5 ♖g2+ 7 ♖g4

The pawn will queen.

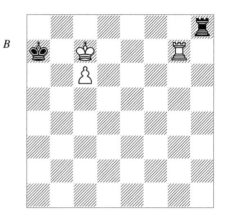

The first-rank defence

This is a basic position where White cannot make progress. The black rook is perfectly placed on h8. General advice in this position-type is that the rook should be as far away as possible from the king when it gives check.

1...♔a6 2 ♖e7 ♔a7 3 ♖e1

The white rook leaves the seventh rank, and Black can use it to check the king.

3...♖h7+ 4 ♔d6 ♖h6+ 5 ♔d7 ♖h7+ 6 ♖e7 ♖h8 7 ♔c7

Or:

a) 7 c7 ♔b7 8 ♖e1 ♖h7+ and Black wins the c-pawn.

b) 7 ♔d6+ ♔a6 8 ♖b7 ♖h6+ and White will not escape from the checks.

7...♔a6 8 ♖e1 ♖h7+ 9 ♔d6 ♖h6+ 10 ♔d7 ♖h7+ 11 ♖e7 ♖h8

White has not made any progress.

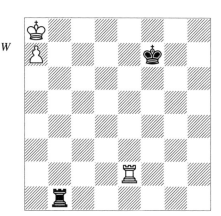

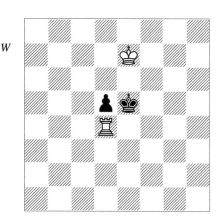

It is harder to promote a rook's pawn as the opposing rook alone can cut the king off in the corner. The most important method of winning is the method of four files. If there are four files or more between the opposing king and the pawn, the rook can be redeployed without allowing the opposing king to hinder the white king's escape.

1 ♖c2 ♔e7 2 ♖c8 ♔d6!

The best defence. After 2...♔d7 3 ♖b8 ♖h1 4 ♔b7 ♖b1+ 5 ♔a6 ♖a1+ 6 ♔b6 ♖b1+ 7 ♔c5 White's king sneaks out and the pawn will promote.

3 ♖b8 ♖h1 4 ♔b7

If the black king had been one file closer in the initial position, it would now have reached c7, preventing the white king from coming out.

4...♖b1+ 5 ♔c8 ♖c1+ 6 ♔d8 ♖h1 7 ♖b6+ ♔c5 8 ♖c6+!

The final key point.

8...♔b5

Or:

a) 8...♔d5 9 ♖a6 ♖h8+ 10 ♔c7 ♖h7+ 11 ♔b6 ♖h6+ 12 ♔a5 and the pawn promotes.

b) 8...♔xc6 9 a8♕+ ♔d6 10 ♕xh1 wins for White.

9 ♖c8 ♖h8+ 10 ♔c7 ♖h7+ 11 ♔b8

White achieves his goal.

Richard Réti
Münchener Neueste Nachrichten, 1928

1 ♖d2!

1 ♖d3! also works.

1...d4 2 ♖d1!!

The point is that Black has to choose a side for the king and then White can go to the other side with his. The rook will be on d1 when the pawn moves forward so that Black cannot gain a tempo on it.

2...♔d5 3 ♔d7 ♔c4 4 ♔e6 ♔c3

With the rook on d2 in this position Black would have gained the extra tempo by threatening it, and achieved a draw.

5 ♔e5 d3 6 ♔e4 d2 7 ♔e3

White wins the pawn.

Practical Examples

The following game shows that even the most prominent players can miss a basic position (*see next diagram*). Piket knew what to search for, but Kasparov underestimated the danger.

Rook + four pawns against rook + three pawns is a rather easy draw when the defender is able to put his pawns on f7, g6, and h5. However, there is one basic position that you have to know.

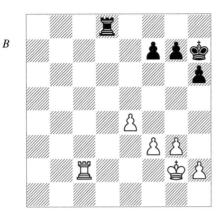

Jeroen Piket – Garry Kasparov
Internet 2000

39...h5 40 f4 g6 41 e5 ♖d3 42 ♔h3 ♖e3?

The right defence is 42...♖d7 with the idea of moving the rook along its second rank. After 43 ♔h4 ♔h6! the only thing that Black must watch out for is that the white king does not reach g5. For example, 44 ♖c6 ♖e7 45 ♖d6 ♖a7 46 f5 ♖a4+ 47 ♔h3 ♖e4 and Black has nothing to fear.

43 ♔h4 ♔g7?!

It seems like Black could also have drawn here, with 43...♔h6. For example:

a) 44 ♖c6 ♖e2 45 h3 ♖d2 46 ♖f6 ♖d4 47 g4 hxg4 48 hxg4 (48 ♖xf7 gxh3 49 ♔xh3 ♖e4 and Black seems to draw by keeping the rook on the e-file) 48...♖xf4 49 ♖xf4 g5+ 50 ♔g3 gxf4+ 51 ♔xf4 ♔g6 52 g5 ♔h7 53 ♔f5 ♔g7 with a draw.

b) 44 ♖c7 ♖e2 and then:

b1) 45 h3 and now 45....♖xe5 is the real point of Black's defence. 46 ♖xf7 (46 fxe5?? g5#) 46...♖e4 47 g4 ♖xf4 48 ♖xf4 g5+ 49 ♔g3 gxf4+ 50 ♔xf4 hxg4 51 hxg4 ♔g6 with a draw.

b2) 45 g4 ♖xh2+ 46 ♔g3 ♖h1 47 ♖xf7 (47 g5+ ♔g7 48 e6 ♖e1 49 ♖xf7+ ♔g8 50 ♖f6 ♔g7 51 ♔f2 ♖e4 52 ♔f3 ♖e1 and White

cannot make progress) 47...hxg4 48 ♔xg4 (48 e6 ♖e1 49 e7 ♖e4 50 ♔xg4 ♖e3 51 f5 ♖e4+ 52 ♔f3 gxf5 with a draw) 48...♖e1 49 ♖e7 (49 ♔f3 g5 50 ♖f6+ ♔g7 with a draw) 49...♖e3 50 e6 ♖e4 51 ♖e8 ♖e3 with a draw. However, there is certainly no margin for error.

44 ♔g5 *(D)*

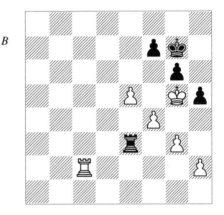

Now Black is lost as a known winning basic position has arisen. White's plan is to put the rook on e7 and then to play e6. The point is that the complicated pawn ending which is forced is winning for White. Even if Black had his rook on its second rank the position could be won with the same idea.

44...♖e1 45 ♖c7 ♖e2 46 ♖e7 ♖a2

Desperation, but Kasparov did not want to go in for 46...♖e3 47 e6! (this starts a long forced variation that Kasparov must have calculated incorrectly several moves earlier) 47...♖xe6 48 ♖xe6 fxe6 49 h3 ♔f7 50 ♔h6 ♔f6 51 g4 h4 (51...hxg4 52 hxg4 ♔f7 53 g5 and White wins the g-pawn) 52 g5+ ♔f5 53 ♔g7 ♔xf4 54 ♔xg6 e5 55 ♔h5 e4 56 g6 e3 57 g7 e2 58 g8♕ e1♕ 59 ♕g5+ ♔f3 60 ♕g4+ ♔e3 61 ♕e6+ ♔d2 62 ♕xe1+ ♔xe1 63 ♔xh4 ♔f2 64 ♔g4 and the pawn will become a queen.

47 f5!

To take away Black's check on a5. 47 e6? Ra5+ 48 ♔h4 ♔f6 does not give White any winning chances.

47...gxf5 48 e6 h4 49 Rxf7+ ♔g8 50 ♔f6 1-0

Black cannot stop Rb7 followed by Rb8+ and e7.

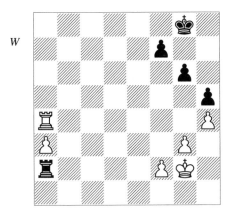

Vladimir Akopian – Kiril Georgiev
FIDE KO World Ch, Las Vegas 1999

This is a classic type of ending that often occurs in practice. It is supposed to be a clear draw as the black rook is active and can carry out many duties, in contrast to White's rook, which can only help the a-pawn to move forward. However, you have to know the ideas and know which basic positions are drawn, even if you are a super-grandmaster. I have therefore chosen to illustrate with variations where the other important basic positions are hidden, and where the defender should look for them. White's only way to make progress in the diagram position is to support the a-pawn with his king. Black's plan is therefore to snatch as many pawns as possible on the kingside when the white king leaves for the

queenside. Then Black's rook will be sacrificed for the a-pawn and Black will draw by forcing White to sacrifice his rook back for a passed black pawn on the kingside. Black is supposed to have a margin of two moves in this position, but Georgiev loses them quickly.

33 ♔f3 ♔g7 34 ♔e3 Ra1

Already here I think you can see that Georgiev does not feel at home in the ending. Black's rook belongs on a2.

35 Ra6 Ra2 36 Ra4 Ra1 37 Ra6 Ra2 38 a4 Ra3+?

There the first tempo is lost. Black should keep the rook on its seventh rank in order to take on f2 immediately when the white king advances. Black has two better possibilities: 38...f6 or 38...♔h7. The idea with 38...f6 is to get counterplay by playing ...g5. The idea of 38...♔h7 is to keep the f6-square free for the king so that Black can play ...♔f6 when the white rook leaves the sixth rank. Let's consider these moves in more detail:

a) 38...♔h7 39 a5 ♔g7 40 Ra8 ♔f6 41 a6 ♔f5 42 ♔d4 Rxf2 43 Rf8 Ra2 44 Rxf7+ ♔g4 45 Rf6 ♔xg3 46 Rxg6+ ♔xh4 with a draw.

b) 38...f6 39 Ra7+ ♔h6 40 a5 g5 41 hxg5+ fxg5 42 a6 h4 43 gxh4 gxh4 44 ♔f3 h3 45 ♔g3 h2 46 ♔xh2 Rxf2+ 47 ♔g3 Rf6 *(D)*.

We have reached an important basic position (a Vančura position) that is drawn. Black will put his king on h6 or h7 if White plays Ra8. The black rook will stay on its third rank. If White leaves the pawn on a6 and tries to bring his king closer, Black will start to give checks from the side and the white king will find no place to hide. If White plays Ra8 and a7, Black will play ...♔h7, ...Ra6 and ...Ra1. When White's king gets closer, Black will check from behind and again there is nowhere to hide. For example:

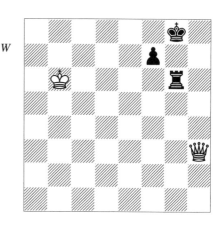

48 ♔g4 ♖g6+ 49 ♔f5 ♖g5+ 50 ♔f4 ♖g6 51 ♖a8 ♔h7 52 ♔f5 ♖b6 53 ♔e5 ♖g6.

39 ♔d4 f6?

Now this move is a mistake. Black must try to win the f2-pawn as quickly as possible. Therefore 39...♖a2! was the best move: 40 a5 (40 f4 ♖a3 41 a5 ♖xg3 42 ♖b6 ♔f3 43 ♔e4 ♖a3 44 a6 ♖a5 is a draw; 40 f3 ♖a3 is no improvement for White) 40...♖xf2 41 ♖c6 ♖g2 42 a6 ♖xg3 43 ♔c5 ♖a3 44 ♔b6 g5 45 hxg5 h4 46 a7 (46 ♖h6 h3 47 a7 ♖b3+ 48 ♔c7 ♖c3+ 49 ♔b7 ♖b3+ 50 ♖b6 h2 51 ♖xb3 h1♕+ 52 ♔b8 ♕h2+ and Black manages to save the game) 46...h3 47 ♖c3 ♖xc3 48 a8♕ ♖g3 49 ♕c6 ♖xg5 50 ♕c3+ ♔g8 51 ♕xh3 ♖g6+ *(D)*.

A new basic position has arisen that is drawn. Black can move his rook between e6 and g6 and White cannot make progress. Observe that if the pawn were on f6 and the rook on g5, it would be a winning position for White as the queen then has more space and can attack the pawn from behind.

40 ♖a7+ ♔h6 41 a5 g5 42 ♔c5 gxh4?

Black has stepped beyond the margin for error. As far as I can see, 42...♔g6! just draws. The main variation is 43 a6 ♔f5 44 hxg5 fxg5 45 ♖a8 ♔g4 46 a7 ♖a2 47 f4 gxf4 48 gxf4 ♔xf4 49 ♖f8+ ♔g3 50 a8♕ ♖xa8 51

♖xa8 h4 52 ♔d4 h3 53 ♔e3 ♔g2 54 ♖a2+ ♔g3 55 ♖a8 ♔g2 56 ♖g8+ ♔f1 and Black's threat to play ...h2 saves the game.

43 gxh4 ♖a4

43...♔g6 is a better try, even though White seems to be winning after 44 a6 ♔f5 45 ♖a8 ♔g4 46 ♔b6 ♖b3+ 47 ♔a7 ♔xh4 48 ♖b8 as he wins the h-pawn after both 48...♖a3 49 ♖b6 ♔h3 50 ♔b7 ♔g2 51 ♖xf6 ♖b3+ 52 ♖b6 ♖f3 53 a7 ♖f7+ 54 ♔a6 ♖xa7+ 55 ♔xa7 ♔xf2 56 ♖h6 and 48...♖f3 49 ♖b2 ♔h3 50 ♔b7 ♖a3 51 a7 h4 52 ♖b6 ♖xa7+ 53 ♔xa7 f5 54 ♖b4.

44 a6 ♖a2

Black realizes that 44...♖xh4 loses to 45 ♖a8 ♖a4 46 a7 ♔h7 47 ♔b6 h4 48 ♖d8 ♔g6 49 a8♕ ♖xa8 50 ♖xa8 ♔g5 51 ♔c5 ♔g4 52 ♖h8 as the pawn cannot be stopped.

45 ♖a8 ♔g6 46 ♔b6 ♖b2+ 47 ♔a7 ♖xf2 48 ♖b8 ♖f4 49 ♖b5 ♖xh4 50 ♔b6 ♖e4 51 a7 ♖e8 52 ♖a5 h4 53 a8♕ ♖xa8 54 ♖xa8 ♔g5 55 ♔c5 h3 56 ♖h8 ♔g4 57 ♔d4 ♔g3 58 ♔e3 ♔g2 59 ♔e2 h2 60 ♖g8+ ♔h3

60...♔h1 loses since the f-pawn lifts the stalemate: 61 ♔f2 f5 62 ♖d8 f4 63 ♖d1#.

61 ♔f2 h1♘+ *(D)*

Once more we have a basic position. A knight draws against a rook as long as it is not trapped in the corner. The problem here

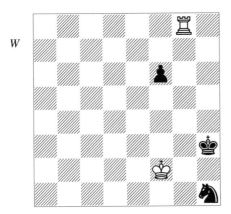

is that it is stuck without a chance to come out, because the rook dominates the position. The f-pawn is of no consequence.

62 ♔f3 ♔h2 63 ♖g2+ ♔h3 64 ♖g6 ♔h2 65 ♖xf6 ♔g1 66 ♖g6+ 1-0

If we put the white rook on e3 instead of a4 in the initial position we understand that this is better for White. The rook not only guards the a-pawn but also cuts the black king off from the queenside and can guard the kingside pawns. White's plan is therefore to play f4 to create a fortress impossible to destroy. Then the king moves to the queenside. With the rook on e3, the position is probably won but it is even better if White has his rook behind the pawn. Then Black is forced to keep his rook passively placed in front of the pawn. As soon as the black rook moves, the pawn will take a step forward. White can either play the king to the queenside to help his rook or try to win Black's kingside pawns if Black tries to cover the queenside with his king. This ending is supposed to be winning. If we instead put the a-pawn on the b-file we understand that this is better for White too. The white king will then be one step closer on his way to the queenside and one step closer on the way back in the race that occurs when Black

sacrifices his rook and pushes a kingside pawn, as in our game. This ending is still under discussion by theoreticians.

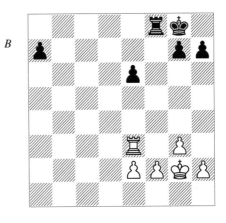

Anatoly Karpov – Vlastimil Hort
Waddinxveen 1979

White has fewer pawn-islands than Black (1 vs 3), which usually represents an advantage. However, the most important thing in rook endings is activity. If Black could play ...a5 and then put the rook on a6, White would have a tough time saving the game. Instead it is White who can become active with his rook on a6 or a5, then the king moves to the centre and the kingside pawns start to advance.

27...♖e8

After 27...♔f7 28 ♖a3 ♖a8 29 ♖a6 Black is pushed back.

28 ♖a3 ♖e7 29 ♖a5

White chooses to put the rook on a5 to ease the advance of the kingside pawns.

29...♔f7 30 h4

Black has no easy way to decide how he should react on the kingside. Should he just leave the pawns where they are, play ...g6, which allows White to break through with h5, or play ...h6 (as in the game)? If he just waits, White will put the king on e5 and the pawns on h5, g5, f4 and e4. After that there are several methods to break through; for example, infiltrating with the king by ♔d6, or playing h6 to put pressure on h7. I am not sure that this is won but the defender's task is very difficult.

30...h6

30...♖b7 31 ♔f3 ♔f6 32 g4 ♖c7 33 ♔f4 ♖b7 34 h5 ♖c7 35 g5+ ♔f7 36 ♔e5 ♖b7 37 f4 ♖c7 38 e4 ♔e7 39 ♖b5 ♔d7 (39...h6 40 ♖a5 ♖b7 41 gxh6 gxh6 42 f5 exf5 43 ♔xf5 ♔f7 44 ♖a6 ♔g7 45 e5 ♖c7 46 ♖g6+ ♔h7 47 e6 and White wins) 40 ♖b2, and White has the idea of playing h6 to open up a path for the king to walk in through f6. The rook will be ready to come in via the b- or the g-file. 40...♖c5+ 41 ♔d4 ♖c7 42 ♖h2 a5 43 h6 g6 44 ♖a2 ♖a7 45 ♔c5 and White wins the a-pawn and the game.

31 g4 ♔f6 32 f4

On 32 ♔f3 Black probably had planned 32...g5 in order to secure the f6-square for his king.

32...♖b7

32...e5 33 f5 followed by ♖a6+ is not in Black's interest.

33 ♔f3 ♖c7

Black has hindered White's plan to reach e5 but the price is some weaknesses on the kingside.

34 ♖a6

Now Black is forced to accept new weaknesses.

34...g6 *(D)*

After 34...♖b7 35 h5 ♖c7 36 ♖a5 ♖b7 37 g5+ hxg5 38 fxg5+ ♔f7 39 ♔f4 ♖c7 40 e4 ♖b7 41 g6+ ♔f6 42 e5+ ♔e7 43 ♔g5 White will get a decisive passed pawn with h6.

35 ♖a5!

Now White wants to play h5 to split the black pawns even more.

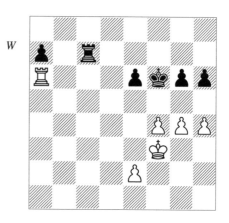

35...♖d7 36 e3 ♖b7 37 h5 g5 38 ♖a6 gxf4 39 exf4 ♖b3+ 40 ♔g2

White has the h4-square if Black continues to check.

40...♖b7 41 ♔g3 ♔f7 42 ♖a4 ♔g7 43 g5 ♖c7

43...e5 to split the white pawns does not work as the white king can support the e-pawn: 44 fxe5 hxg5 45 ♔g4 ♖e7 46 ♖a5! ♔h6 47 ♖a6+ ♔h7 48 ♔f5 g4 49 ♖g6 a5 50 e6 ♖e8 51 ♖xg4 and the white king will help the pawn advance.

44 ♖a5 ♔g8 45 ♖b5 ♔f7 46 ♔g4 a6 *(D)*

If Black continues to play passively, White's winning plan is to play g6+ and then bring the rook to e8. Black cannot guard all his weaknesses; for example, 46...♖d7 47 g6+ ♔g7 48 ♖b8 ♖c7 (48...♖e7 49 ♔f3 e5 50 f5 e4+ 51 ♔e3 ♔f6 52 ♖f8+ ♔g7 53 ♖c8 ♔f6 54 ♔f4 ♔g7 55 ♖c6 and 56 f6 will decide the game) 49 ♖e8 ♔f6 50 ♖h8 a5 (otherwise White simply takes on h6) 51 ♖a8! ♖c5 52 ♖a7 e5 53 ♖f7+ ♔e6 54 f5+ ♔d6 55 g7 ♖c4+ 56 ♔f3 ♖c3+ 57 ♔e2 ♖g3 58 ♖f6+ ♔e7 59 ♖g6 and White wins.

47 ♖b8

47 g6+ is also possible: 47...♔f6 (47...♔e7 48 ♖b8 ♖c1 49 ♖b7+ ♔f8 50 ♖h7 and White picks up Black's h6-pawn) 48 ♖b6 a5 49 ♖a6

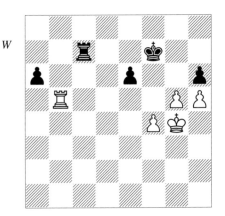

W

♖c5 50 ♖a7 e5 51 ♖f7+ ♔e6 52 f5+ ♔d5 53 ♖d7+ ♔e4 54 f6 and White wins.

47...♖c1

47...hxg5 also loses: 48 fxg5 ♖c4+ 49 ♔f3 ♖c3+ 50 ♔e4 ♖c4+ 51 ♔d3 ♖g4 (51...♖h4 52 ♖b7+ ♔g8 53 h6 ♖g4 54 ♖g7+ ♔h8 and White wins as in the main variation) 52 h6 ♖h4 (52...♔g6 53 ♖g8+ ♔h7 54 ♖g7+ and White wins) 53 ♖b7+ ♔g8 54 ♖a7 ♖g4 55 ♖g7+ ♔h8 56 ♔e3! and White wins by guarding the g-pawn with the king on f4 and picking up the a-pawn or pushing the g-pawn: 56...a5 57 ♔f3 ♖g1 58 ♔f4 a4 59 ♖a7 ♖f1+ 60 ♔g4 ♖g1+ 61 ♔h5 and White wins as the king can hide on g6.

48 g6+ ♔g7 49 ♖b7+ ♔f8 50 ♖b6 ♖g1+ 51 ♔f3 ♖f1+ 52 ♔e4 ♖e1+ 53 ♔d4 ♔e7 54 ♖xa6 ♔f6 55 ♖a7 e5+ 56 fxe5+ ♖xe5 57 ♖a6+ 1-0

If 57...♖e6 then 58 g7 is winning, and 57...♔f5 58 g7 ♖e4+ 59 ♔d3 ♖g4 60 ♖g6 is winning for White. In this game the difference between an active and a passive rook was clearly shown. All the time, White's rook had double duties: on the a-file it put pressure on the a-pawn and controlled the fifth or sixth rank. With the rook active, White was able to activate his king as well, and in the end Black was overwhelmed.

Guidelines

- Activity, activity, activity – the three most important guidelines.
- If you are under pressure it is often correct to sacrifice a pawn for activity.
- An old expression says "Rook endings are always drawn". In my version this becomes "In rook endings there is always a chance to draw."
- The rook prefers to be behind the passed pawn; second best is to cover it from the side and the least favourable position is in front of the pawn.

Minor-Piece Endings

In endings with minor pieces the guidelines are often more important than the basic positions, at least compared with pawn endings and rook endings. There are simply not so many basic positions. Therefore, this type of ending usually continues in a smooth transformation from the middlegame, as the general aspects continue to be of importance. Because of this, I will not be as detailed in my presentation of the various configurations of minor pieces as I was with the pawn and the rook endings.

Bishop vs Knight

The most important theme in an ending of bishop vs knight is dominance. Which piece dominates depends on the pawn-structure and whether there is play on both flanks. The following two examples illustrate when bishop or knight is to be preferred.

In the diagram overleaf, Black has an advantage. The most important reason is that the bishop is better than the knight in open positions with pawns on both sides. White really has problems because in addition the black king can reach the centre faster.

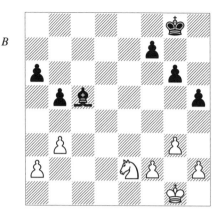

B

Alexandre Lesiège – Ulf Andersson
Olympiad, Elista 1998

33...♔f8

After 33...♔g7?! 34 ♘c3 White's knight stops the black king reaching the centre as 34...♔f6?? loses a piece to 35 ♘e4+.

34 ♔f1 ♔e7 35 f3

White must give up a tempo to put the f-pawn on a different colour to the bishop.

35...♔d6 36 ♔e1 ♗e3

The bishop move opens up a long royal diagonal that goes as far as a3. The move also hinders the white king's march to the centre.

37 ♔d1 ♔c5 38 ♔c2 ♗f2!

The idea with this move is to use the method of two weaknesses. Andersson wants to create a square through which the king can come in by playing ...h4. Then he will be able to oscillate between the two threats and win the a2-pawn or the kingside pawns. It is also important to appreciate that the side with the bishop does not want a fight for the opposition in this position-type. What he seeks is a position where the kings work on one side each. This is because a bishop can cover both sides at the same time whereas the knight is a cripple, limping slowly over an open board.

39 ♔c3 h4?!

I think Black should play 39...♗e1+.

The text-move gives White a chance to play 40 b4+, which takes space on the queenside. However, while White achieves one advantage he also flouts another rule: to put your own pawns on the opposite colour to the opposing bishop. It was therefore a hard choice to make in the time scramble and Lesiège did not dare to advance.

40 g4?!

It was more important to close the royal diagonal than to follow the other rule.

40...♗e1+ 41 ♔d3 ♗a5

The bishop has done its job and has created a new weakness. Time to make it as active as possible: yes, e5 will do.

42 h3 ♗c7 43 ♘d4 ♔d5!

Precisely played, as Black has problems proceeding after 43...♗e5 44 ♘c2.

44 ♘e2

44 ♘c2 ♔e5 45 ♔e3 ♗b6+ 46 ♔e2 ♔f4 and Black's king wins the g3-pawn.

44...♗e5 45 ♔e3 (D)

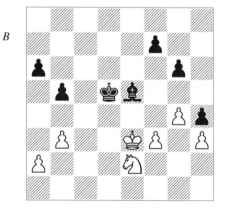

B

45...a5!

Andersson told me afterwards that he did not know whether the position was winning when the ending began. He just played in the correct manner and waited to see what would happen. However, in this position everything became clear and he saw the winning idea.

46 ⌷d3 ⌷c5 47 ⌷e4 ⌷g7 48 ⌷d3 ⌷b4 49 ⌷c2 ⌷a3 50 ⌷b1 a4!

The idea with this advance is to create a square for the king on c4. After that the king will gain entry by zugzwang. White is lost.

51 bxa4 bxa4 52 ⌷f4 ⌷b4 53 ⌷c2 ⌷c4 54 ⌷e2

Where should the bishop stand to set up zugzwang?

54...⌷e5 55 ⌷d2 ⌷c7 56 ⌷c2 (D)

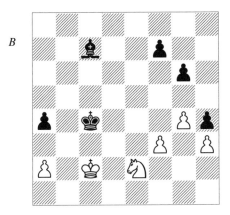

56...⌷a5

The answer to the question.

57 f4

If White moves the knight, the black king can come in via d4 and e3.

57...⌷b4 58 ⌷g1

White realizes that Black will go back and forth between a5 and b4 until White has run out of pawn moves. Therefore he goes for a last attack with the knight before everything comes to an end.

58...⌷d4 59 ⌷f3+ ⌷e4 60 ⌷g5+ ⌷xf4 61 ⌷xf7 ⌷g3 0-1

If 62 ⌷e5 then 62...g5 followed by ...⌷e7, winning. In this endgame Andersson used a lot of guidelines to find his way: there is the assumption that Black stands better with bishop against knight as there is play on both sides and as the centre is open; the idea that the king should be centralized; the principle of the two weaknesses; the use of zugzwang; the idea that the side with the bishop should manoeuvre so as to force an entry with the king.

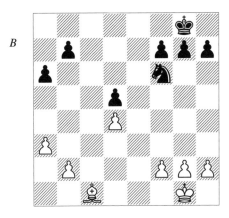

Anthony Saidy – Bobby Fischer
USA Ch, New York 1963/4

The reason why this game made such an impression on me is that I thought it must be an easy draw. Certainly, it is a draw if White defends correctly, but Fischer plays methodically and logically in accordance with his advantages, forcing Saidy into a more difficult defence than he had counted on. That is certainly the reason for Fischer's success. Saidy probably thought, just like me before I saw this game, that it was an easy draw, and he chose just to wait. Black has some advantage as the pawns in the centre restrict the movement of the bishop. Fischer asks himself where White has his weaknesses, which side of the board he should play on, and where he should put his pieces. He sees a weak point in the d4-pawn and understands that it is on the kingside where he has best chances to create another one. Therefore the knight should go to e6, where it threatens d4 and is ready to go to f4. The black king should go to the kingside.

23...♘d7! 24 ♔f1 ♘f8 25 ♔e2?!

Here I think that White should have taken the opportunity to gain space and important squares on the kingside with 25 g4. In the game continuation, Black completely dominates, and even though it should be a draw in any case, White's decision to do nothing is at the root of the forthcoming small mistakes.

25...♘e6 26 ♔d3 h5 27 ♗e3 ♔h7 28 f3 ♔g6 29 a4 ♔f5

Black's initial goals have been achieved. Black realizes that the weakness on d4 is not enough to win the game on its own, and starts to advance the kingside pawns. What Fischer tries to do is to arrive at an advantageous kingside structure, creating weaknesses and thereby obtaining entry squares for his king.

30 ♔e2 g5 31 ♔f2 ♘d8 32 ♗d2 ♔g6 33 ♔e3 ♘e6 34 ♔d3 ♔f5 35 ♗e3 f6 36 ♔e2 ♔g6 37 ♔d3 (D)

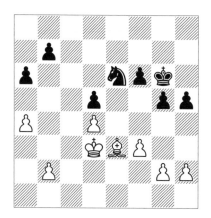

37...f5

Black needs to get help from one more pawn. Note that it is often good to take it really slowly before you force the play, so that you can calculate the consequences and also gain a psychological advantage over your opponent indirectly by saying 'I'm in charge; you can only wait'.

38 ♔e2

38 g3! is the right move. It is then hard to see how Black can break through. For example, 38...f4 39 gxf4 g4 40 fxg4 hxg4 41 ♗f2 ♘xf4+ 42 ♔e3 ♔f5 43 ♗g3 ♘e6 44 ♗e5 and White has built a fortress impossible to conquer.

38...f4 39 ♗f2 ♘g7?!

This gives White the chance to put up a good defence. 39...♔f5 is better.

40 h3?!

After 40 g4! fxg3 41 ♗xg3 ♘e6 42 ♗e5 it is hard to find any way to make progress for Black as the white bishop is well-placed on e5. However, the active 40 g4 is a difficult move to find if you have played a passive defence for so long.

40...♘f5 41 ♔d3 g4!

The breakthrough which Black has prepared for so long.

42 hxg4 hxg4 43 fxg4 ♘h6 (D)

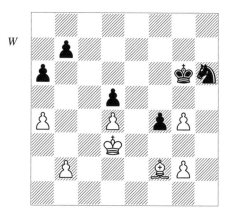

44 ♗e1?!

44 ♔e2 was the last chance to draw. After 44...♘xg4 45 ♗g1 ♔f5 46 ♔f3 ♘f6 47 ♗h2 ♘h5 48 a5! ♔g5 49 g4 fxg3 50 ♗xg3 Black can push White back, but cannot deliver the knockout blow. If you think about the fundamental principles, this is logical as the second weakness that Black tried to create on the kingside has disappeared. The following variation gives an illustration: 50...♘g7 51 ♗e5 ♘e6 52 ♔e3 ♔g4 53 ♗f6 ♘f4 54 ♗e7 ♘h5 55 b3 ♘g7 56 ♗f6 ♘f5+ 57 ♔d3 ♔f3 58 ♗e5 ♘h4 59 ♗f6 ♘g2 60 ♗e5 ♘e3 61 ♗f6 ♘g4 62 ♗h4 ♘f2+ 63 ♔c3 and Black cannot make progress as 63...♔e3? 64 ♗xf2+ ♔xf2 65 ♔b4 ♔e3 66 ♔c5 ♔e4 67 b4 even wins for White.

44...♘xg4 45 ♗d2 ♔f5 46 ♗e1 ♘f6

The next step is to win White's g-pawn by putting the king on g4 and the knight on h4.

47 ♗h4

After 47 g3 f3 48 ♔e3 ♔g4 Black will win the g3-pawn with 49...♘e4.

47...♘h5 48 ♗e1 ♔g4 49 ♔e2 ♘g3+ 50 ♔d3

50 ♔f2 ♘f5 51 ♗c3 ♘e3 52 a5 (after 52 ♗g1 f3 53 gxf3+ ♔xf3 Black wins the d4-pawn) 52...♘d1+ 53 ♔e2 ♘xc3+ 54 bxc3 ♔g3 55 ♔f1 f3 56 gxf3 ♔xf3 57 c4 ♔e4 and Black wins.

50...♘f5 51 ♗f2 ♘h4 52 a5 ♘xg2 53 ♔c3 ♔f3 54 ♗g1 ♔e2 55 ♗h2 f3 56 ♗g3 ♘e3!

White is not even given the chance to sacrifice his bishop for the f-pawn. Before Black moves the pawn, he will drive the bishop away by ...♘f5.

0-1

Guidelines

- The bishop prefers play with pawns on both sides. It wants an open centre and its

own pawns should usually be placed on the opposite colour to the bishop.
- The knight prefers play on one side or with a closed centre. It needs a secured outpost in the centre to be able to operate on both sides.

Bishop vs Bishop

Here there are two types of endings, endings with same-coloured bishops and endings with opposite-coloured bishops. The two types are fundamentally different and require a different way of thinking.

An important basic position

First we should consider the notorious issue of bishop and wrong rook's pawn.

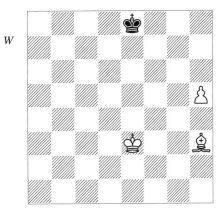

Aleksei Troitsky
Shakhmatny Ziurnal, 1896

If Black's king can reach h8, an important basic position arises that White cannot win. In this study you therefore have to keep the king away from the corner.

1 ♗e6! ♔e7

Or 1...♔f8 2 h6 and the white pawn promotes.

2 h6 ♔f6 3 ♗f5 ♔f7 4 ♗h7 ♔f6 5 ♔f4

White wins as his king can drive away the black king before the pawn advances.

Practical examples

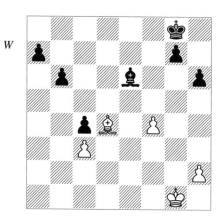

**Zurab Azmaiparashvili –
Ljubomir Ljubojević**
Leon 1994

Despite the fact that White is two pawns down there is still hope. White's d4-bishop dominates the position and can force Black's queenside pawns to move to light squares. There they can be blockaded. The most important method for the defender in endings with opposite-coloured bishops is to create a fortress with his opponent's pawns on the opposite colour to his own bishop.

36 ♔f2 ♔f7 37 ♔e3 g6 38 ♗e5 a5 39 ♔d2

39 ♗c7 a4 40 ♗xb6?? (40 ♗d6! resembles the game continuation) 40...a3 and the pawn cannot be stopped.

39...b5 40 ♔c1

White's plan is to stop the passed pawns with his king and guard the kingside with his bishop.

40...♗d7 41 ♗c7 a4 42 ♗d6 ♔e6 43 ♗f8

White wants to get access to the g5-square for the bishop, from where both White's king-side pawns can be protected after he plays h4.

43...h5 44 h4 ♔f5 45 ♗h6 ♔e4 (D)

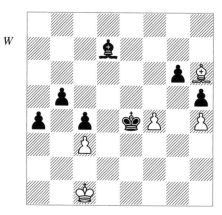

The two most important concepts for the player with an advantage in an opposite-coloured bishop ending are to create passed pawns and to play on both sides. If you manage that, you can usually storm the fortress. In our game Ljubojević first puts his pieces on optimum squares before he thinks about the breakthrough ...b4.

46 ♔c2 ♗f5 47 ♔b2 (D)

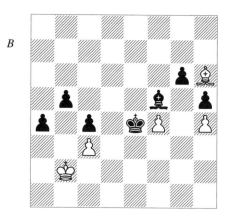

With the pieces on ideal squares, ...b4 now comes.

47...b4! 48 ♗f8!

A good defence. It is more important to keep the fortress intact than to win pawns. After 48 cxb4? ♔d3 49 ♗g7 c3+ 50 ♗xc3 a3+ 51 ♔b3 ♗e6+ Black wins a piece.

48...bxc3+?

Black stumbles just at the decisive moment:

a) Note that 48...b3? is bad as White has his fortress after 49 ♗h6 ♔d3 50 ♗f8, with a draw.

b) 48...a3+! 49 ♔a2 (after 49 ♔c1 a2 50 ♔b2 bxc3+ 51 ♔xa2 ♔xf4 Black wins with the same method as after 49 ♔a2; for example, 52 ♗g7 g5 53 ♗h6 ♔f3 54 ♗xg5 ♔e2 55 ♔a3 ♔d1 56 ♗h6 c2 57 ♔b2 c3+ 58 ♔xc3 c1♕+ 59 ♗xc1 ♔xc1 and Black's bishop has the right colour with respect to h1) 49...bxc3 50 ♗xa3 ♔xf4 and Black wins since White cannot handle both the threats, namely that Black can play ...g5 or advance his king to d1 or d2 and push the c3-pawn. For example, 51 ♗e7 ♔e3 52 ♗g5+ ♔e2 53 ♗f6 c2 54 ♔b2 ♔d1 55 ♗g5 c3+ and Black wins.

49 ♔xc3 ♗e6

Forced as 49...♔xf4 50 ♔xc4 g5 (otherwise White plays the bishop to g5 with a blockade) 51 ♗h6 is drawn.

50 ♗d6 ♗f7 51 ♗e7

White cannot prevent Black from winning one of the kingside pawns with ...♔g4 and chooses to let it go immediately.

51...♔xf4 52 ♔b4 ♔e4 53 ♔xa4 c3 54 ♔b4!

White's idea is to force the c-pawn to c2. Then he will put the king on b2 and the bishop on g5 with a blockade.

54...♔d3 55 ♗f6 c2 56 ♗g5 ♗e6 57 ♗h6 ♗f7 58 ♗g5 ♗e6 59 ♗h6 ♗d5 60 ♗g5 ♗g8 61 ♗h6 ½-½

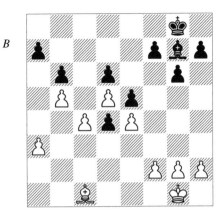

B

Boris Spassky – Robert Byrne
Candidates match (game 6), San Juan 1974

White has an advantage as his bishop is on the opposite colour to his own pawns and the same colour as the black pawns.

22...f6 23 ♔f1 ♗f8 24 a4 ♗e7 25 ♔e2 ♔f7 26 ♗d2 f5?!

If you have a worse position you should be careful not to create new weaknesses. Therefore, Black should have been focusing on the queenside. The reason why Byrne played 26...f5 was probably that he thought that Spassky would play 27 ♔d3 or 27 f3, when he can gain space with 27...f4.

27 exf5! gxf5 28 ♔d3 ♗f6 29 f3 h5

To prevent g4, which would have given White control of the light squares.

30 a5 ♔e8

Forced. After 30...bxa5? 31 ♗xa5 White wins with the manoeuvre ♗c7-b8.

31 a6!

This strong move prepares a future ♗a5. The bishop could not be taken because then White would win with b6, queening a pawn.

31...♔d7 *(D)*

32 g3

In accordance with the principle of two weaknesses, White must try to break through

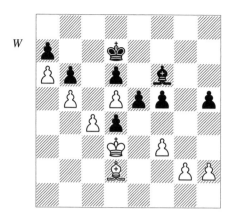

W

on the kingside, since Black already has one weakness on the queenside. White has two ideas at his disposal: either he can play h3 and g4 to open up a route for the king via e4 and f5, or he can play f4 to loosen up Black's centre. 32 h3? is wrong since it allows Black to kill off both ideas by 32...h4.

32...♔c7 33 h3 ♔d7 34 ♗a5

To entice away the black king before the bishop is placed on its best square.

34...♔c8

After 34...bxa5 35 b6 White will get a queen.

35 ♗e1 ♔d7 36 ♗f2 ♔e8 37 ♗e1 ♔f7?!

If Black had continued to wait passively with 37...♔d7, White would have had to try the breakthrough 38 g4. Exact calculation would then be needed for White to win. After 38...fxg4 39 fxg4 hxg4 40 hxg4 ♔e8 41 ♔e4 ♔f7 42 ♔f5 ♗d8 43 ♗d2 ♔e7 44 ♗b4 Black is in zugzwang because ...♗f8 is answered by ♗a5. He therefore has to allow the white king to come to e6: 44...♔g7 45 ♔e6 ♗f8 46 ♗a5 bxa5 47 b6 d3 48 bxa7 d2 49 a8♛ d1♛ (White is a piece down, but the advanced a-pawn is decisive) 50 ♛b7+ ♔h6 51 ♔d7 ♛xg4+ 52 ♔e8 and White is winning.

38 ♗b4 ♗e7 39 f4 exf4

This is forced since 39...♔e8 loses to 40 fxe5 dxe5 41 ♗xe7 ♔xe7 42 c5 bxc5 43 b6, with a decisive breakthrough.

40 gxf4 ♔e8 41 ♔xd4

White has won a pawn, but as the white king lacks any square via which to penetrate the position, he is faced with more difficulties.

41...♔d7 42 ♔d3 ♔c7

Here the game was adjourned, and Spassky could analyse a winning method in peace and quiet.

43 ♔e3 ♗f6 44 ♔f3 h4

Taking away the last square on the kingside for the white king. However, the pawn is now on the wrong coloured square. An important question now from the method of eight questions is whether White should exchange bishops. The answer is 'no': even though White has an extra pawn, Black has a fortress which is impossible to break down. The only possibility left is the move c5. Again it is the a6-pawn that is the main character.

45 ♔e3 ♗g7 46 ♔d3 ♗f6 47 ♗d2

As always when you play for a breakthrough you have to put the pieces in the right places before you force matters. The king's best place is d3, and the bishop's is f2, where it exerts pressure on both b6 and h4.

47...♔d7 48 ♗e3 ♔c7 49 ♗f2 ♔c8 (D)

This move allows White to break through, but if Black tries to mitigate the effects with 49...♗e7, White can manoeuvre his bishop to g5, winning the h4-pawn: 50 ♗d4 ♗d8 51 ♗g7 ♗e7 52 ♗h6 ♗d8 53 ♗g5 ♔d7 54 ♗d4 ♔c7 55 c5 dxc5+ (after 55...bxc5+ 56 ♔c4 White wins the pawn ending) 56 ♔e5 ♗xg5 57 fxg5 c4 58 ♔d4 and White wins.

50 c5!

The idea of the sacrifice is to create squares for the white king to come in on.

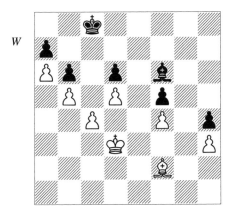

W

50...dxc5

50...bxc5 51 ♗e1 ♔c7 52 ♗a5+ ♔c8 53 ♔c4 ♗e7 54 b6 axb6 55 ♗xb6 and White wins by walking the king in via b5, c6, d7, and e6, winning the f5-pawn.

51 d6 ♔d7 52 ♗xc5 ♗d8 53 ♗b4 ♔e6

Black's last hope is to prevent the white king from reaching d5, but Spassky finds a new mini-operation that enables him to make further progress.

54 ♔c4 ♗f6 *(D)*

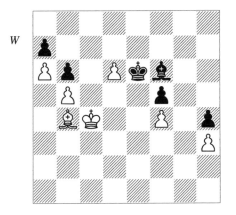

W

55 ♗c5!

The theme of offering the bishop in return for a breakthrough on the queenside repeats over and over again. Now Black's bishop must become passive.

55...♗d8 56 ♗d4

It is much more important to get the king to d5 than to keep the d6-pawn. Black is now in zugzwang.

56...♔xd6 57 ♗e5+ ♔e6 58 ♗b8 ♔d7 59 ♔d5

White's king has reached the key square and Black cannot prevent it from advancing even further.

1-0

Guidelines

In endings with opposite-coloured bishops the defender puts his pawns on the same colour as his own bishop and builds a fortress that the opponent cannot break down. The chances of a draw are considerable even if you are some pawns down.

In endings with same-coloured bishops, both players want to put the pawns on the opposite colour to the bishops. Here the prospects are greater for a win for the player with a better position.

Knight vs Knight

Knight endings are usually compared with pawn endings, because the knight can reach all the squares on the board and the knight is 'slow' just like the king. Therefore, as in pawn endings, calculation is of great importance, together with criteria such as an active knight, active king, and favourable pawn-structure.

There are no real basic positions, but it is useful to know that three pawns against two on the same side is a draw if the defending side has no real weaknesses. Four against three is a borderline case where the theoreticians still do not agree on a final judgement.

A knight ending has arisen where White has an extra pawn on the queenside. The first

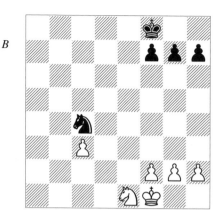

Paul Keres – Samuel Reshevsky
Leningrad/Moscow 1939

moves are obvious as both White and Black move their kings to the centre.

34...♔e7 35 ♔e2 ♔d6 36 ♘c2 ♔e5 37 ♘e3 ♘b2 38 ♘d1 ♘a4 39 ♔d3 ♔d5 40 ♘e3+ ♔c5 41 ♘f5!

In pawn endings with a distant passed pawn, the plan for the side with the extra pawn is to sacrifice it and then win the others left on the opposite side. In this type of knight ending the plan is the same, so the knight tries to create squares to get in on.

41...g6 42 ♘h6 f5 43 ♘f7 ♔d5 44 ♘g5 ♘c5+ 45 ♔e3 h6 46 ♘f3 g5?!

I prefer 46...♘e4 and cannot then find any clear win for White. For example, 47 c4+ (47 g3 ♘xc3 48 ♘h4 f4+ 49 gxf4 g5 50 ♘f5 ♔e6 51 ♘xh6 ♘d5+ 52 ♔f3 ♘xf4 53 h4 ♔f6 54 ♔g4 ♘e6 55 h5 ♘f4 56 f3 ♘d3 with a draw) 47...♔xc4 48 ♘e5+ ♔d5 49 ♘xg6 ♔e6 50 f3 ♘d6 51 ♘f4+ and Black has good drawing chances despite the split pawns. If the f-pawn had been on the g-file it would have been a theoretical draw. Now White can try to exploit the weak pawns, but I guess that it is possible to hold the position anyway.

47 g3 ♘e4 48 ♘d4 ♘xc3 49 ♘xf5

If Black could use his king to guard the pawns it would be a draw. Now they are forced to advance.

49...h5 *(D)*

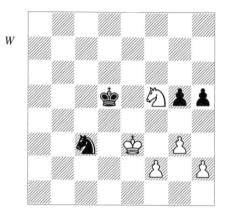

50 ♘g7?

White stumbles at the last hurdle. After 50 f4! g4 (50...gxf4+ 51 ♔xf4 ♘e4 52 h4 ♘c3 53 ♘g7 ♘e2+ 54 ♔f3 ♘d4+ 55 ♔e3 and White wins the h5-pawn and the game) 51 ♘g7 ♔d6 52 ♘xh5 ♔e6 53 ♘g7+ ♔f6 54 ♘e8+ ♔e6 55 ♘c7+ ♔d6 56 ♘a6 the knight comes out and White will win.

50...h4 51 gxh4 gxh4 52 f4 h3!

The problem for White is that the split pawns make it impossible for him to win Black's h-pawn without losing one of his own.

53 ♘f5 ♔e6 54 ♘g3 ♔d5 55 ♔f3 ♔d4 56 ♘h1 ♘d1 57 ♘f2 ♘e3 58 ♔g3 ♔d5 59 ♔xh3 ♔e6 60 ♔g3 ♔f5 61 ♔f3

61 h3 ♘d5 62 ♘d3 ♔e4 63 h4 ♔xd3 leads to a draw.

61...♘f1

Even though White has won a pawn, Black can hold the position as White cannot prevent the black knight from getting one pawn back.

62 h3 ♘d2+ 63 ♔e2

63 ♔g3 ♘f1+ 64 ♔g2 ♘d2 65 ♘d3 ♔e4 66 ♔g3 ♔xd3 67 f5 ♔d4 68 ♔f4 ♘e4 69 h4 ♘f6 70 ♔g5 ♔e5 and White cannot make further progress.

63...♘c4 64 ♔d3 ♘b6

The f4-pawn is lost. Black will then sacrifice the knight for the remaining pawn with a draw. Therefore...

½-½

Guidelines

- Active knight and king are the key concepts.
- Assess the ending, broadly speaking, as if it were a pawn ending, if there is play on both sides.

Queen Endings

In queen endings there are usually loads of long variations to calculate and it is easy to go wrong among all the possibilities. A tip is to look for a position that you want to reach, for example where the checks end. It is then easier to know what to aim for in your calculations.

Basic Positions

There are three important basic positions that you need to know in the ending queen against pawn on the seventh rank (*see following diagram*):

If the pawn stands on the g-, e-, d-, or b-file (i.e. is not a rook's or bishop's pawn), the queen wins with the following method:

1 ♔h7

Black's idea is to force the white king to g8 and then to take a step forward with his own king. The procedure is repeated over and over again until the king has reached the pawn.

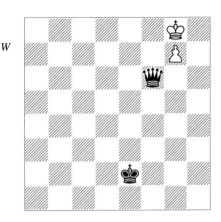

W

1...♕f7 2 ♔h8

After 2 ♔h6 ♕g8 Black wins by bringing his king closer.

2...♕h5+ 3 ♔g8 ♔e3 4 ♔f8 ♕f5+ 5 ♔e7 ♕g6 6 ♔f8 ♕f6+ 7 ♔g8 ♔e4 8 ♔h7 ♕f7 9 ♔h8 ♕h5+ 10 ♔g8 ♔e5 11 ♔f8 ♕h6 12 ♔f7 ♕e6+ 13 ♔f8 ♕f6+ 14 ♔g8 ♔e6 15 ♔h7 ♕f7 16 ♔h8 ♕h5+ 17 ♔g8 ♔f6 18 ♔f8 ♕f7#

B

1...♕g6+ 2 ♔h8

Black cannot make any progress, since if he brings his king closer, White will be stalemated. Thus the winning method used in the previous example does not work. Note that there are some positions where the queen wins against a rook's pawn on the seventh rank, but the king needs to be much closer.

1...♕g6+ 2 ♔h8!

Again, Black cannot make any progress because if he takes the pawn it is stalemate. As in the rook's pawn case, there are winning positions if the black king is closer.

Practical Examples

We will now throw light on one of the most difficult types of ending, queen and pawn vs queen. The games often last for many moves as the defender can check the opposing king all over the board. The player with the pawn must find a way to get out of the checks by covering squares with his own queen. An important method is to interpose the queen, giving a check in return. The basic principle for the defender is to try to get his own king in front of the pawn. It is then normally not difficult to achieve a draw. If this is not possible, the king should be as far away from the pawn as possible, to remove the possibility of an interposing check. As in all queen

Mikhail Botvinnik – Nikolai Minev
Olympiad, Amsterdam 1954

endings, a centralized queen is of great importance. The ending ♕ + ♙ vs ♕ is one of those that have been solved using computer tablebases. A tablebase is a list of all legal positions together with the result, which is derived by working backwards from terminal positions. The ending is a win with a c-, d-, e- or f-pawn unless the defending king can get in front of the pawn. Against an a-, b-, g- or h-pawn, it is also possible to draw if the king can reach the corner furthest from the pawn's queening square.

In practice, these endings are frequently mishandled, with both sides often failing to seize their chances. In the game below, we see what can happen if the defender does not know the right plan. As the black king cannot get in front of the pawn, he should try to move as far away as possible, which means a1. The game was played long before computers had solved this ending, which also explains the many mistakes that Botvinnik makes, especially when he gives a check at the wrong moment. These checks gave Minev the chance to reach the safe corner. Naturally, I would hardly dare to put so many question marks on the players' moves if I had not had silicon help.

57...♛h8+

The right plan is 57...♛h1+ 58 ♔g6 ♔b4, with the idea of going into the corner. Instead Minev chooses to keep contact with the a4-square. This makes it possible for White to use the threat of exchanging queens to push the pawn. This is carried out step by step. All the time White is seeking a position where he can interpose his queen with a counter-check.

58 ♔g6 ♛c3 59 g4 ♛d2 60 g5 ♛d4? *(D)*

It was not too late for 60...♔a4, in order to reach a1.

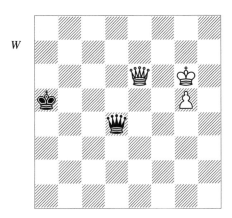

W

61 ♕f5+?

Forcing the black king to go in the right direction. Better was 61 ♔h7 with the idea 61...♛h4+ 62 ♕h6 and the pawn can take another step forward next move. In the rest of the game, Botvinnik's strategy is to centralize the queen and then move the pawn. A logical plan, very typical of Botvinnik the scientist, but he did not know the correct defence. On the other hand, Minev did not know it either.

61...♔a4 62 ♔h5 ♛h8+?

62...♔a3.

63 ♔g4 ♛h1?

63...♔a3.

64 ♕f4+!

Forcing the black king away from a1, because after 64...♔a3, 65 ♕f3+ exchanges queens.

64...♔a5 65 ♕e5+ ♔a4 66 g6 ♛d1+ 67 ♔g5 ♛d8+ 68 ♔f5 ♛c8+ 69 ♔f4 ♛c1+ 70 ♕e3 ♛c7+ 71 ♕e5 ♛c1+ 72 ♔f5 ♛c8+ 73 ♔g5 ♛d8+ 74 ♕f6 ♛d5+ 75 ♕f5 ♛d8+ 76 ♔h5 *(D)*

B

76...♛e8

76...♛h8+ 77 ♔g4 ♛g7 (77...♛d4+ is not possible because 78 ♕f4 forces an exchange of queens) 78 ♕f7 ♛c3 79 g7 ♛c8+ 80 ♔h4 ♛d8+ 81 ♔g3 ♛d3+ 82 ♕f3 ♛d8 and again we have a position where it is not possible for Black to give check as White can interpose with check. 83 ♕g4+ ♔a5 84 g8♕ and White wins.

77 ♕f4+?

Again a bad check from Botvinnik, but at this point he must have realized that Black did not plan to go to a1 with the king.

77...♔a5?

Commentary is superfluous.

78 ♕d2+ ♔a4 79 ♕d4+ ♔a5 80 ♔g5 ♛e7+ 81 ♔f5 ♛f8+ 82 ♔e4 ♛h6 83 ♕e5+

♔a4 84 g7 ♕h1+ 85 ♔d4 ♕d1+ 86 ♔c5 ♕c1+

After 86...♕c2+ 87 ♔d6 ♕d3+ 88 ♔e7 ♕c4 89 ♕a1+ ♔b5 90 ♕b1+ ♔a4 91 ♕d1+ ♔b5 92 ♕d7+ ♔b4 93 ♕b7+ ♔c3 94 ♕f3+ ♔b4 95 ♕f8 Black cannot prevent White from getting a queen as a check is answered by a counter-check.

87 ♔d6 ♕d2+ 88 ♔e6 ♕a2+ 89 ♕d5 ♕e2+ 90 ♔d6 ♕h2+ 91 ♔c5 1-0

Again White will be able to use the queen to interpose a black check. Black therefore cannot prevent White from getting a new queen.

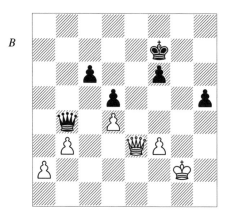

Robert Hübner – Henrique Mecking
Wijk aan Zee 1971

The game had been completely equal for a long time, but Hübner had kept on playing, and taken some risks.

60...c5!

In queen endings passed pawns are of great importance. It is more important to have a far-advanced passed pawn than to have three in their initial positions, as the queen can give very effective support to a passed pawn.

61 dxc5 d4 62 ♕e4

After 62 ♕c1 ♕c3 Black wins back the pawn.

62...♕xc5 63 a4

Black has a clear advantage as his d- and h-pawns are more dangerous than White's passed pawns on the queenside. The reason is that Black's pawns have advanced further, and the black queen can give the d-pawn good support. This gives Black the initiative. White must therefore look for perpetual check, but after the direct attempt 63 ♕h7+ ♔e6 64 ♕g8+ ♔f5 65 ♕h7+ ♔f4 66 ♕e4+ ♔g5 67 f4+ ♔h6 68 ♔f3 ♕c3+ 69 ♔g2 h4, the involvement of the h-pawn proves decisive.

63...♕g5+ 64 ♔f1 ♕c1+ 65 ♔g2?!

65 ♔e2 ♕b2+ 66 ♔e1 ♕xb3 67 ♕xd4 ♕xf3 68 a5 is better, starting the white pawn rolling. Probably the h- and a-pawns would have been swapped and a difficult theoretical ending would have arisen.

65...♕d2+ 66 ♔h3 d3 *(D)*

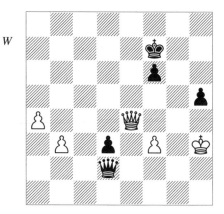

67 ♕d5+

The following checks that White now gives are a bit desperate. But what should White do? Black's plan is simply to play ...♕e2 and ...d2 when the checks stop. Therefore there are no alternatives. After 67 ♕h7+ ♔f8 68 ♕xh5 ♕e2 69 ♕c5+ ♔g7 70 ♕c7+ ♔g6 71 ♕g3+ ♔f5 72 ♕g4+ ♔e5 73 ♕g3+ ♔d5 the black king will hide behind White's queen-side pawns.

67...♔g6 68 ♕e4+

68 ♕g8+ ♔f5 69 ♕h7+ ♔e5 70 ♕xh5+ ♔d4 71 ♕h4+ ♔c3 72 ♕xf6+ ♔c2 and again the black king has found shelter behind White's own pawns.

68...♔g5 69 ♕h4+ ♔g6 70 ♕e4+ ♔h6 71 ♕d4 ♔g7 72 ♕d7+ ♔g6 73 ♕e8+ *(D)*

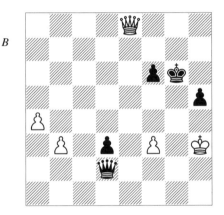

73...♔g5

Black's king fights to avoid the checks and therefore moves forward. As we have discovered from some of the variations given above, the king is just as well-placed behind White's pawns as in front of them. In addition, it might be used in an attack on the white king.

74 ♕b5+ ♔f4 75 ♕c6

75 ♕xh5 ♔e2 76 ♕g4+ ♔e3 77 ♕e6+ ♔f2 78 ♕b6+ ♔e3 and Black wins.

75...♕e1! 76 ♕xf6+ ♔e3 77 ♕e5+ ♔f2 78 ♕h2+ ♔xf3 79 ♕g2+ ♔f4 80 ♕h2+ ♔f5 81 ♕d6

This loses immediately, but after 81 ♕a2 (in order to check on c2 after ...d2), there

follows 81...♕h1+ 82 ♔g3 h4+ 83 ♔f2 ♕h2+ and Black wins the white queen.

81...♕f1+ 82 ♔g3 h4+ 0-1

83 ♔xh4 ♕f4+ wins for Black.

Guidelines

- An advanced passed pawn is worth its weight in gold.
- The queen is most often best placed in the centre where it has many opportunities.
- Perpetual check is a common theme.
- To have a secure king is of great importance.

Endings with Material Imbalance

The most common form of material imbalance is when one player has a pawn more. After this type of imbalance, the most common is rook against minor piece. I have chosen to take a closer look at rook against bishop.

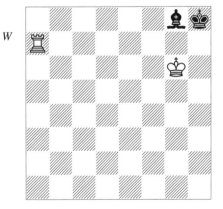

The easiest way to draw when you have an ending with bishop against rook is to retreat your king to a corner with the opposite colour to that of the bishop. The point is that there is then a stalemate with the rook pinning the bishop. White therefore cannot make any progress.

1 ♖c7 ♝b3 2 ♖h7+ ♔g8 3 ♖b7

After 3 ♖c7 ♔h8 White has not made any progress.

3...♝c2+

In addition to the stalemate idea, this check is important. The king is driven away and the mating threat is gone.

4 ♔h6 ♝e4 5 ♖b8+ ♔f7 6 ♔g5 ♔g7

The king is on its way to the corner again.

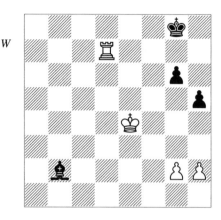

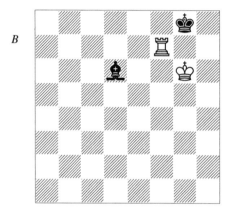

If the king is driven to a corner of the same colour as the bishop, the position is lost. The difference is that there is no stalemate. Therefore, White can chase the bishop and then give a decisive check on the back rank.

1...♝b4 2 ♖b7 ♝d6 3 ♖d7 ♝f8 4 ♖d8

Mate follows.

The following diagram is one of the rare positions where it is a draw with bishop and two pawns vs rook and two pawns. Note that it is necessary to have played ...h5 to make a proper fortress. With the black h-pawn on h7 and the white pawns on h4 and g4, the

position is won for White. The point in our position is that the white king cannot reach the g5- and f6-squares if Black plays correctly.

1 h4 ♝c3 2 ♔d5

After 2 ♔f4 ♝f6! White's king cannot penetrate.

2...♝b2 3 ♔e6 ♝c3 4 ♖f7 ♝b2 5 g4 hxg4 6 ♖f2 ♝c3 7 ♖g2 ♔h7 8 ♖xg4 ♔h6 9 ♔f7 ♔h5

Black will win the h4-pawn, with a draw.

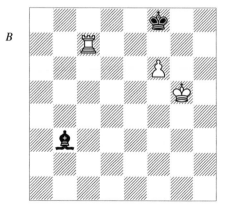

For this position to be a draw, the pawn must be a c- or f-pawn and it must have reached the sixth rank. The bishop must also cover the square beside the pawn. If the pawn were on the fifth rank, the king could move in front of the pawn, winning. If the pawn were on the b-, d-, e-, or g-file, then White would win by chasing the bishop away so that he could advance his king without being forced back. In the diagram position, the bishop has enough space to manoeuvre.

1...♗a2 2 ♖b7 ♗c4 3 f7

The only real try.

3...♔g7!

3...♗xf7? loses to 4 ♔f6.

4 f8♕++ ♔xf8 5 ♔f6 ♔g8

The king is in the right corner, so it is a draw.

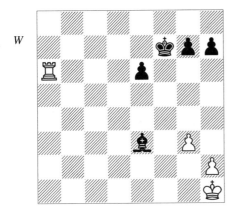

Patrick Wolff – Walter Browne
USA Ch, Durango 1992

We will now take a look at a game where the players were not aware of which basic positions they should try to reach or avoid. We can see immediately that Black is not far away from reaching the drawing position with two against two on the same side. At the same time you should notice that the bishop has the wrong colour to draw if all the pawns

were removed and the black king stuck on h8.

50 ♔g2?

50 g4, to hinder Black from achieving the basic drawing position, would have made the defence more difficult.

50...♗d4?

After 50...h5, with the idea of ...g6, it is a draw immediately.

51 ♔f3? g6? 52 ♔e4 ♗f6 53 ♖a7+ ♔g8 54 g4! *(D)*

Finally, White finds the best move in the position.

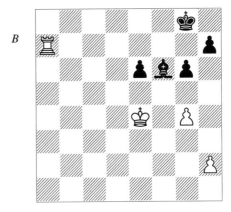

Now Black must try to find a new blockade that White cannot crack.

54...♗c3?

54...h6! is the correct move. The idea is that the bishop should cover the g5- and f6-squares from h4. This is another basic position that is drawn even if Black loses the e6-pawn. The point is that Black can prevent White from playing h4.

55 ♖e7?

Allowing Black to set up the basic position given above. 55 h4! was the right move; White would soon achieve a winning basic position because the h-pawn is not stuck on h2.

55...♗f6 56 ♖xe6 ♔f7 57 ♖a6 ♗c3?

Black again misses his chance to achieve the drawn basic position. He should play 57...♗h4 or 57...h6.

58 ♖a7+ ♔g8 59 ♖d7?

I hope you realize by now that 59 h4 would be a good move.

59...♗f6 60 ♔f4 ♗b2?

60...h6 61 ♔g3 ♗e5+ 62 ♔g2 ♗f6 63 ♖d5 (to be able to play 64 ♔g3 followed by h4) 63...♗h4 with a draw.

61 ♖c7? ♗f6 62 g5! ♗d4 63 h4 ♗b2 64 ♔g4 ♗e5

If Black tries to find a defence with the bishop on the a3-f8 diagonal, White wins by reaching another basic position. 64...♗a3 65 ♖b7 ♗f8 66 h5 and now:

a) 66...♗g7 allows White to create a decisive mating threat by putting the pawn on h6 and the king on e6: 67 h6 ♗c3 68 ♔f3 ♗d4 (68...♗d2 69 ♖b8+ ♔f7 70 ♖h8 ♗xg5 71 ♖xh7+ and the white h-pawn will decide the game: 71...♔f6 72 ♔g4 ♗e3 73 ♖h8 ♔f7 74 h7 ♔g7 75 ♖e8 and White wins) 69 ♔e4 ♗c3 70 ♔d5 ♗d2 71 ♔e6 and mate is unavoidable.

b) Black is therefore forced to take the h5-pawn before it can be advanced to h6: 66...gxh5+ 67 ♔xh5 (D).

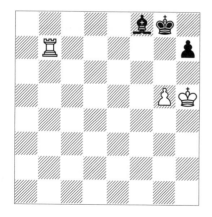

We have now reached a basic winning position. As you can probably guess, White should play g6 at the right moment to obtain a won ending with rook against bishop. The game might continue 67...♗a3 68 ♖b3 (before g6 is played, the black bishop is banished to a bad square and the white king redeployed on the more active f5-square) 68...♗d6 (68...♗f8 69 ♖b8 ♔f7 70 ♖b7+ ♔g8 71 g6 gives us the basic position where Black is lost if he takes the pawn) 69 ♔g4 ♗c5 70 ♖b5. Black's problem is that White can alternately threaten to play g6 or to put the king on f6; the bishop cannot prevent both:

b1) 70...♗d6 71 ♔f5 ♗c7 72 ♖d5 ♗b6 73 ♔f6 ♗c7 74 ♖d7 ♗a5 75 ♖g7+ ♔h8 76 ♔f7 h5 77 g6 with mate to follow.

b2) 70...♗f8 71 ♔f5 ♗g7 (if Black moves the bishop to another square then 72 ♔f6 wins) 72 g6 (Black's bishop and king are so badly placed that White is ready for an ending without pawns) 72...h6 (72...hxg6+ 73 ♔xg6 and the threat of ♖b8+ is winning) 73 ♖b8+ ♗f8 74 ♔f6 h5 75 g7 and White wins.

65 ♖c6 ♗b2 66 ♖a6 ♗c3 67 ♖a4 ♗e5 68 h5! ♗c3

68...gxh5+ 69 ♔xh5 ♗d6 (in order to take the h6-square away from the white king; after 69...♗c3 70 ♖a8+ ♔g7 71 ♖a7+ ♔g8 72 ♔h6 White wins the h-pawn) 70 ♖a8+ ♔g7 71 ♖a7+ ♔g8 72 g6 hxg6+ 73 ♔xg6 ♔f8 74 ♔f6 ♔e8 75 ♔e6 and White wins.

69 h6

We are now more or less into the variation that we discussed earlier. Black has to give up the h7-pawn, since otherwise White's king will march to e6.

69...♔f7 70 ♖c4 ♗e5 71 ♔f3 ♗d6 72 ♖c8 ♔e6 73 ♖h8 ♔f5 74 ♖xh7 ♔xg5 75 ♖d7 1-0

Black resigned since after 75...♗e5, 76 ♖d5 decides the game immediately.

Guidelines

The player with a rook wants to create a passed pawn, as the rook can provide good support. The player with the minor piece wants a blocked position with no passed pawns.

My Training Tips

My most important tips are to collect basic positions and guidelines that you think are important. I have compiled a book of endings for myself, based on the themes given above. When you have analysed an ending you should not just abandon it to its fate. It is important to refresh your memory every once in a while. That is easy with my method. Compiling a book of endings is a perfect job to do together with a friend. You can split up the endings between you, study them in depth, then present the results to each other.

Basic positions are perfect to use as the starting point for small competitions: either you solve them as exercises, or you play them out against a friend.

Suggestions for Further Reading

I think that most players only need *Essential Chess Endings* by James Howell (Batsford, 1997) for basic positions. The book is instructive and explains, with words, how you should think in the various types of endgame. Almost as good is *Chess Endings for the Practical Player* by Ludek Pachman (Routledge and Kegan Paul, 1983), which is a little bit more advanced and suitable for the more ambitious. Mark Dvoretsky and Artur Yusupov have often covered endgame themes, especially with *Technique for the Tournament Player* (Batsford, 1995).

12   I Can Give Check: I Am Not Afraid

On mental training

Chess is a mental sport where the focus is on the ability to concentrate.

The psychology of sport has developed considerably since the 1970s but in the chess world this is more or less an unknown concept, despite the fact that chess is a mental sport where the focus is on the ability to concentrate. I am not an educated psychologist, but I have read some texts that are relevant in this context. I have also used my own experiences in writing this chapter. As a consequence, it concentrates on practical advice such as how to create goals and be prepared mentally to play.

Personal Experiences

I walk slowly down the quiet main street in the little Galician town of Orense. I am aware of every step I take. I see every paving stone.

I am on the way to the playing hall for the final round in an open tournament where I share the lead. Some deep breaths, walk in, fill in the scoresheet, shake hands; the clock starts ticking. The board in front of me is the only thing that exists. I am totally focused.

Between my moves I sometimes leave the board, but even then I feel an almost physical participation in the game. When I go to the window to get some fresh air I look at my hand; it is firmly clenched. During the game my brain is clear; calculation is fast and effective. I feel that I have total control. I am concentrated and simply in top form. I win a convincing victory against a higher-rated opponent and share first place.

Setting Targets

The positive force that I experienced during that game in Spain can be constructed. In addition to chess training, it is important to train your mental strength. The first thing you have to do is to set targets. In the psychology of sport they talk about safety goals, working goals and barrier-breaking goals. If I use myself as an example it works like this: I am an IM with an Elo rating around 2500. My safety goal is to keep my rating, my working goal is to become a grandmaster and my barrier-breaking goal is to establish myself at 2600. This means that I have a lowest level of performance in each tournament where I maintain my rating. I have a carrot that is not out of reach and a vision far away that I can dream of. The barrier-breaking goal is needed because you should not be satisfied when the working goal is achieved. It is also important not to put the safety goal and the working goal so high that the pressure becomes too great. It is preferable to fulfil these goals and then set new, higher, ones.

Building Up One's Inner Strength

Many athletes visualize an inner picture in which they win important races and competitions. It should be a natural feeling to win. The same method works for chess-players. Myself, I used to run or swim. During the physical exercise I empty the brain of irrelevant thoughts and repeat to myself the following phrases:

- I am calm, relaxed, safe.
- My body feels strong and comfortable.
- I look forward to the game.
- I look forward to competing.
- I will concentrate one hundred percent, and not let my thoughts drift.
- I will put in all that I have.

When I feel focused, I evoke inner film clips: how I play a decisive combination, win a long endgame, find a strategy that gains a pawn, or how I accept first prize in a tournament. This is my way of training my ability to concentrate, but each of you has to find your own. Certainly yoga and tai chi can be just as good.

During a Game

The goal for mental training is partly to gain self-confidence, but mainly to become *as one* with the situation in a game. All irrelevant thoughts must be put aside, so that only the pieces and the board are left. If you look at the best players in the world during a game, it is often the total concentration that strikes you first. They have the feeling that I had in Spain in all their games.

When Things Just Go Wrong

I have had many tough losses and bad periods in my chess career. I have some tips for how to try to change the trend. The first thing I do is take a week off from chess, to get the hunger back. Then I use my book with grains of gold, which I told you about in Chapter 1. You could say that I try to get the inspiration back.

The next step is just to have fun with chess. I only do things that I enjoy and only so much that I do not lose the inspiration. After two or three weeks, I try to build up the motivation that I am going to come out strong from this. Just as when I analyse my own games, I think to myself "Good, now I have made these mistakes, I will not make them again." Most often a hard period of training will come after that where I analyse my games and all the mistakes. Perhaps I investigate a new opening or conduct in-depth analysis of a specific endgame. Remember that it is in these tough times that we are really tested. It is not the ones with greatest talent who climb highest, but those with the strength of will to use all the talent that they have.

The Psychological Side of Chess Training

Fundamental to making training effective is to make it fun. Fun must be woven into the serious study. However, chess is also a sport where winning matters, so you should try to recreate the element of competition in the training. If the exercise reminds you of a real game where it is important to do the best you can, the training will be of high quality. Solving combinations and problems under time-pressure is one way to do this, or you can challenge yourself to see as much as possible from a diagram in a book and then compare your analysis with the comments. It is important to concentrate as much in training sessions as in a game. If you are enervated when you train, then the feeling usually remains with you during a game.

Before a Tournament

Chess is a sport and therefore you have to be as prepared as other athletes. These are the four points that I try to follow before an important tournament.

1) Reserve time to prepare for the tournament.

2) Work on the mental side so that I feel strong and hungry for the challenge.

3) Prepare my openings well and review those of my opponents.

4) Practise combinations so that I can analyse quickly. This gives me a belief in my own ability.

During a Tournament

Personally I find it very difficult to keep up my concentration when I compete. If it is nice weather outside or if the tournament is being held in an interesting town that I would like to visit as a tourist, then it is particularly hard. I believe therefore that before a tournament it is important to decide why you are there: for pleasure or to play the best chess possible. If you want success there are no excuses. You have to keep on fighting the temptations and accept that your skin will still be pale in two weeks' time.

In addition, the following points are important:

1) Be thoroughly rested before each game.

2) Be well prepared for each game.

3) Prepare mentally for each game, but also have energy. Often it is better to take a walk than to go swimming. You should not be tired during the game.

4) Rest between the games, so that your batteries are recharged and you do not become exhausted. It is easy to have too much chess, so I always take a good novel to a tournament.

5) Find a good rhythm during the tournament. Habits save energy, which should be devoted to chess.

6) Turn your nervousness into something positive, so that it becomes a joy and a challenge instead of a burden to play.

Suggestions for Further Reading

Most of the advice in this chapter is based on the book *Bäst När det Gäller* by Willo Railo (SISU, 1992). He gives concrete tips on how to improve your training. I have modified his advice so that it suits chess-players. Railo's book is a classic that I warmly recommend to anyone who wants to go deeper into the subject of mental training. Before Railo's book, *Integrerad Mental Träning* by Lars-Eric Unestähl (SISU) was the one to read. This book was also based on practical experience. Another book is *Psychological Foundations of Sport*, which is a handbook on the psychology of sport.

When it comes to books specializing on chess, the classic is *Psychology in Chess* by Nikolai Krogius (RHM). There is certainly a need for new books on this subject. One recent and ambitious attempt to throw light on this intriguing subject is *The Seven Deadly Chess Sins* by Jonathan Rowson (Gambit, 2000).

13 When the Computer Stands Well, I Pull Out the Plug

On using a computer

You should appreciate that the computer can never replace your own analysis.

Sometimes when I look at *Informator* or I go through some annotated games in magazines I feel exhausted. Who can learn anything from all these variations, variations, and more variations? For the umpteenth time: people cannot utilize this type of information. Instead we look for structures and generalizations that make it possible for us to put things into words. If there are only variations, it is left to the reader to interpret and try to understand them. *Informator* is forgiven because it supplies the latest news in a universal language. Another reason why the language of *Informator* has spread even to magazines is the computer. The machine has created a norm where variations replace words.

Computers do not think like human beings. They have no intuition and cannot make a selective choice of which moves to analyse, so they calculate everything. Computers these days are so strong that they help even the best players to analyse. Answers spill out with symbols and numbers for explanation. It is important to use this information in a constructive way.

First, you should appreciate that the computer can never replace your own analysis. To analyse, to explore deeper into a position, is the most important way to study chess. I therefore analyse my own games without the help of the computer. When I am clear, completely clear, I let the computer check the game. It is mainly in tactical positions that I get help and where I have to reconsider and develop some of the computer's suggestions. Remember that when you play a game your little friend will no longer be there to whisper good moves in your ear.

Second, we risk losing the great annotators. Instructive annotations, explaining the game in human terms, improve the reader's understanding. Therefore it is important that the mere listing of variations is not considered a suitable formula for annotating a game.

Enough complaining. The computer is of great help to me as a chess-player, both as an archive and as a tool for searching for information. I will now describe how I have structured the files in my computer.

My Various Databases

One game database. For example, ChessBase Mega Database 2001 is a large, high-quality database with many annotated games. I update this every couple of weeks via TWIC (The Week in Chess), a website on the Internet where you can download the important games played during the last week.

My own games. A database of my own games, all annotated.

Basic repertoire. A database with the openings that I commonly play.

Surprise database. Opening variations that I do not play regularly, but that I find fun to analyse and where I might find novelties to surprise an opponent.

Under study. A database with variations that I am about to analyse.

Position-types. Here I gather games, combinations, exercises and endings that arise from the same position-type. This database is connected to the openings database and I sometimes move variations between the databases.

Endgame database. Here I collect basic positions for the various endings with my own explanations, and guidelines and positions that illustrate the overall themes.

Grains of gold. The most important database, where I collect the things that make me love the game of chess.

This is my own system. It suits me, but I am also aware that each player has his own method. Therefore, try to find what suits you. The advantage of the computer is that the databases can be updated as you make new discoveries. Not so long ago, players had to make do with folders full of pieces of paper. It is obvious that the computer has its advantages here, especially in saving time.

Playing Against the Computer

With regard to the computer as a player, it is not surprising that it plays quite differently from a human being. The computer is not afraid of anything and has a tendency to go for material. It is dangerous to play a lot against computers because you get used to their style; this can have negative effects in a real game position. If you want to use the computer as an opponent, I think you should do so for the purpose of training. Play it in openings you want to test, position-types that you are investigating, or important endings that you need to practise.

14 Three Schemes for Training

Happy amateur, ambitious aspirant and serious professional

What is more fun than the feeling of making progress?

One Fundamental Rule

Regardless of your level of play, the fundamental rule is to do as well as you can. This means that you should make full use of your ability and make no excuses. This is something that is taken for granted throughout the suggestions below. This in no way contradicts the idea of having fun. On the contrary, they are prerequisites for each other. If we are having fun we are more receptive, and what is more fun than the feeling of making progress and winning against a higher-rated opponent?

The Happy Amateur

Most people seem to suffer from lack of time, both for work and for leisure activities. However, you can do a lot with little time, if you make your training more efficient.

The first thing that I recommend is that you have some chess books on your bedside table. If you solve some combinations every night or go through a game from a book, it will keep your brain in trim. In addition to this, the fundamental things to study are your own games. Remember, as Johan Hellsten said, there you have all that you need to work on. Follow the scheme described in Chapter 2.

When it comes to the weekly visit to the chess club I think it is important not to catch 'blitz chess disease.' However, blitz chess can be good training and I will give you one example. Hellsten, mentioned above, and I have trained together for periods of time. We used to start with five blitz games. We are both competitive and do all we can to win. This means that the intensity is high. We also used to prepare some theory before the training sessions. The blitz games were then a good warm-up for the real training but also a way of stimulating the fighting spirit. What you should try to avoid is a situation where playing becomes routine and you just push wood, not caring about the result.

There are many other ways to run a club. I am an advocate of continuation courses. I believe that everyone, regardless of strength or age, would like to learn new things about chess. If there is no strong player who can act as trainer, then the participants can be in charge of one session each. You can arrange theme tournaments with discussions afterwards, competitions in solving combinations, a training camp one weekend, and so on. To stimulate the members' individual study you can have a library of chess books at the club, have a club computer or put up a weekly chess problem on the notice board. A good way to develop ideas for such activity is to gather for a brainstorming session one evening.

The happy amateur's training contains occasional periods when you can concentrate on chess. Often these may be in connection with a vacation. Here it is important to think about what you need to develop in your play and to study themes that are relevant to strengthening these aspects. Follow a chapter in this book or use one of the other books that I recommend in each area. When the annual tournament comes, I recommend that you read the chapter about mental training. What matters is to focus on chess as much as possible and leave behind the other things that might distract you. If you want a vacation which is partly chess, it is important to give the chess at least some space in your schedule so that you can be focused during the game. Therefore, make room for one hour of mental and chess preparation before the game.

The Ambitious Aspirant

The first thing that I recommend to someone who wants to develop his play is to find a training partner. Important criteria are that the person should live not too far away, have more or less the same playing strength and the same level of ambition. Then you can plan the training together, give each other problems to solve, exchange books, play training games and in all ways stimulate each other to do your best. My book was written mainly for this category. I have tried to give methods for studying various aspects of chess and have recommended literature to complement these methods. If you succeed in following all the suggestions in your everyday life you will not have much time left and therefore you have to be selective.

Do not neglect the basic training, analysing your own games and solving combinations, but try to envisage the other themes as building-blocks that you methodically add to this foundation. To understand which building-blocks you particularly need, it is useful to identify your strong and weak points. Generally, you gain more from working on your weak points, but I have already made it clear how important it is to have fun. Do not waste your time if you notice that you are just not getting the hang of something.

For younger ambitious juniors the mantra is *play, play, play*, as it is important to get as much competition experience as possible. But never forget to analyse these games in order to learn from the mistakes.

The Serious Professional

The serious professional works with all the components that I have discussed in this book, is aware of his own weaknesses, and works methodically to get rid of them. In this context it might be relevant to mention Mark Dvoretsky's division of players into categories: the intuitive and the logical. Intuitive players are creative with a good ability to sense the right move in the position. By contrast they are not so good at calculating long concrete variations. Logical players are not as creative and might miss surprising tactical possibilities, but they are good at calculating long and exact variations.

Naturally most players are not so one-sided that they fit perfectly in either category, but as a starting point for a plan for training, the categorization is useful. The logical player needs to put emphasis on solving exercises with surprising possibilities, like studies, but the intuitive simply must start to work hard on chess. The reason is that an intuitive player has depended too much on his talent for the game. Here the planning is really important. A good idea is to keep a training diary for a couple of months. Every day you write down exactly what you have studied and how much. This makes it easier to draw conclusions on how to improve your training.

Another reflection of mine is that there exist, even among professionals, great differences in ambition. It is important not to be satisfied, but all the time to try to improve. I think that this is connected to the fact that mental training scarcely exists in chess despite the priority that it has in other sports. This is more or less a blank area where more research is needed, and every professional should make an effort to work with the methods that are available. Why not contact a sports psychologist for an individual plan?

There is also the obvious necessity of being in good physical shape. Tough games demand good health.

15　Advice to Trainers

On the role of the trainer

The fundamental basis for becoming a good chess trainer is that you like chess and enjoy teaching.

Two Fundamental Assumptions

That You Want to Be a Trainer

I remember my time at school with mixed feelings. Some subjects were a pain and I dragged my feet walking into the classroom. Others were a joy to study and I did not want to miss a minute of the lessons. With hindsight I can see what a crucial influence specific people have had on what I became interested in. Often it was the teachers, all very different in personality and in their teaching, but with one thing in common: they burned with interest for their subject. They radiated that it was important and fun. If they also devoted their energy to making me understand, then the subject was almost irresistible. I became interested and inspired. Therefore, the fundamental basis for becoming a good chess trainer is that you like chess and enjoy teaching. This is more important than playing strength.

That The Student Wants to Train

My experiences from school also made clear the importance of an interest in learning. Chess is a fantastic world to discover, but without curiosity, the beauty will not appear. Many times I have seen fathers (never mothers) who pressurize their children into training and who also scream at them when they are not interested. I think that this strategy is doomed in the long run. As a trainer, the key is to demonstrate your own love for chess and to try to stimulate the interest of the children, never to force them to like it.

Stimulating Training and Methodical Training

From the two fundamental assumptions, the two concepts of stimulating training and methodical training arise.

In stimulating training the most important thing is to have fun. The development of chess skills is of secondary importance. In methodical training, the focus is on developing knowledge and extending understanding. The two concepts do not stand in opposition to each other but merge together when the training is working well. The key word for this merging together is variety. When you train methodically and, for example, study an ending, it is important to study it in various ways to keep up the interest. You can, for example, start with an instructive game and explain the basics. Then you give the students problems to solve. Let them play a tournament on the theme, give them a quiz about various positions, or put together two teams to analyse an interesting position and then after a while let them play it out, one in each team with White and the other with Black. As a trainer you need to be creative.

It is obvious that the younger the students are, the more variety and stimulus they need, not least because they seldom see the connection between the work they are doing and what they will gain from it in the future. I therefore seldom work on only one theme when I work with very young students.

For the really ambitious there is a higher threshold before they need variety. Here it is the quality of the examples that matters. The stimulus lies in learning something new and achieving new understanding of a theme. However, I believe that it is dangerous to think that good players do not need variety and I am convinced that fun and a spirit of competition are important if you want to keep a high level of concentration.

Two Different Perspectives

IM Rikard Winsnes invented expressions for two methods of training, the 'English' and the 'Russian'. I believe they provide a basis for more advanced study.

The **English method** is based on the assumption that it must always be fun to study chess. Therefore, the training focuses on what the student is already good at. The idea is that the pupil will think that it is so much fun that it becomes important also to work on the weak points, so as to develop further. The method does not put great emphasis on the pupil having a trainer. In Western Europe such a strategy has been necessary, as our culture of training is not so developed. Instead the method is based on the notion that chess is a one-man job, where the lust for training must always be there, because otherwise there would be no training at all.

The **Russian method** is more general and methodical. It is in many ways similar to education in school and stresses the weak aspects of the student's play. The trainer has a more central function and acts more or less like a teacher with both sticks and carrots in the arsenal.

I do not think that the methods differ that much when they work perfectly, but they have different starting-points. Personally, I try to find a good mix of both, in order to exploit the advantages of the two systems. For someone who trains a lot on his own, I think it is wise to go for the English method, but someone with a personal trainer can be inspired by the Russian method.

In Practice

The crucial conclusion that I have drawn is that there is no short-cut. To set up a good training session takes time – at least if it is going to be both instructive and stimulating.

In order to try to weave the methods together, I mainly work with themes. I take an area in chess and go from the general to the specific. I try to find funny names for the training sessions so that people think that they sound exciting. I try to remember anecdotes to tell, but most important is to find good examples that illustrate my theme. I often use the same theme for different groups with varying playing strength. What differs is the level of complexity in the examples and the variety in the training of the themes. I try to make a substantial part of the training similar to a normal game situation and let the pupils solve problems themselves in order to make use of their new knowledge. At the same time, however, it is important when you work with children not to stimulate the competitive spirit in the wrong way such that some drop out. GM Lars Karlsson has a good tip: he lets the children work together in pairs, one of the stronger ones with one of the weaker, so that everyone will be in a winning team once in a while.

I always give homework if I train a group regularly, as my training is mainly intended to show the pupil how to study at home. Regardless of how good the trainer might be, it is not possible to escape independent training. However, I always try to be sensitive to how much the group can take and I never call it homework, as words connected to school tend to make pupils less interested. Often there are problems and combinations from my collection of Grains of Gold with headings like 'the weekly trick' for the pupils to take home. If the pupils are more ambitious, you can give them more normal exercises.

Common Mistakes

- The trainer is not prepared and cannot explain the exercises that he gives out properly.
- The trainer wants to be brilliant and to demonstrate how good he is. However, the point is of course that the student should understand the lesson.

My Teaching Tips

For each training session I put together a leaflet containing the most important points of what we go through. This makes it possible for the pupils to go back and review old sessions. If a task is too hard to solve or they did not really understand it, they also get the chance to look at the position at home. Also, do not forget that repetition is an important technique in learning. I therefore recommend that you start every new training session by briefly summing up the theme of the last session. I sometimes also prepare some small tests on the positions that we have examined, just to see what has stayed in my students' minds.

I always prepare various types of exercise, and always more than we will be able to get through. This makes it possible to adjust to the mood of the pupils and either have in-depth examples or stimulating training if so required.

How I Work with Pupils Individually

The first thing I let a new private student do is to annotate three games, where at least one must be a loss. Use of a computer is not permitted.

With these games as a starting point, I can first of all often see the weak and the strong sides of the pupil and how ambitious he is. Then I try to put together a personal program that includes the things the pupil needs to study, based on playing strength, age and ambition. The foundations of this are the student's own games and the analysis that has been conducted. Often the training sessions start with the student demonstrating a game or an interesting position that has occurred. When I see what mistakes have been made, I give the pupil exercises in that area. This method relates the training to the pupil directly, which often increases the motivation.

This means that the most important aspect of individual training is to encourage the pupils to demonstrate their games. Here I refer to Chapter 2, on how to follow up a game.

Suggestions for Further Reading

It is important for a trainer to have good chess material. I have already mentioned a few good books, including *The Power Chess Program* Volumes 1 and 2 by Nigel Davies (Batsford, 1998 and 1999). Here you find good themes with illustrative games and exercises. A trainer has to add variety and an imaginative way of presenting the material.

Another good training book is *How to Reassess Your Chess* by Jeremy Silman (Siles Press, 1993) for those who have passed the beginner's level. For the more advanced I recommend *The Art of the Middlegame in Chess* by Paul Keres and Alexander Kotov (Penguin, 1964) and especially the books by Mark Dvoretsky and Artur Yusupov, but if you use them in a training session do not use chapters that are too difficult.

These Chapters as a Series of Lectures

I have used Chapters 1-13 in training sessions. I compiled a handout where I summarized the basic thoughts of each chapter for my students. Below this, I listed the most important examples that explain the theme. Be aware of the importance of understanding the themes yourself and varying the presentation of the exercises. It is also important to choose examples that are difficult enough for the group.

I also think that you should use your own experiences as much as possible. Your pupils should find your presence in the lessons, not mine. Therefore, you should expand my chapters by supplementing them with your own games and favourite examples.

Solutions to Exercises

Chapter 1

1)

24 Nxg6+! Kg8

After 24...Nxg6 25 Rxd8+ Qxd8 26 Rxd8+ Rxd8 27 Bxf6+, White either mates (27...Rxf6 28 Qg7#) or wins the rook.

25 Qg7+! Rxg7 26 Nh6# (1-0)

2)

White has played a little strangely in a Sicilian, but it is surprising that the position is already won for Black.

18...dxe5!

Black finds a beautiful win based on trapping the white queen. The point is to flick in moves with the f-pawn at the right moments.

19 Bxe5 f6!

Not letting White play c4 after ...Bd5.

20 Bc3 Bd5 21 Qb6 f5!

To be able to play ...Bc5.

22 Ng5 Bc5 23 Qa5 b6

The net is drawing closer around the white queen as it is forced into Black's position.

24 Qxa6 Nc7 25 Qa7 Ra8 0-1

White's queen is lost.

3)

1 c7 Rd6+

After 1...Rd2 2 c8Q Rb2+ 3 Ka5 Ra2+ 4 Kb4 Rb2+ 5 Ka3 Ra2+ 6 Kb3 Rb2+ 7 Kc3 the white king escapes from the checks.

2 Kb5!

The point is that after 2 Kb7? Rd7 Black can sacrifice his rook for the c-pawn, with a draw. 2 Kc5? Rd1 is also a draw as Black threatens to check on c1.

2...Rd5+ 3 Kb4 Rd4+ 4 Kb3 Rd3+ 5 Kc2 Rd4! 6 c8R!!

6 c8Q?? Rc4+! draws thanks to stalemate.

6...Ra4 7 Kb3

White wins due to the double threat of mating and taking the rook.

4)

1 Bh6+ Kg8 2 g7 Kf7

Or: 2...e5 3 Ke6 e4 4 Kf6 e3 5 Bxe3 h5 6 Bg5 and White wins; 2...e6+ 3 Kd6 Kf7 4 Ke5 Kg8 5 Kf6 e5 6 Ke6 e4 7 Kf6 e3 8 Bxe3 reaches the same position.

3 g8Q+!

This is the main point of the study: Black will be mated in an unusual fashion.

3...Kxg8 4 Ke6 Kh8 5 Kf7 e5 6 Bg7#

5)

1 Kf6 Kh6 2 d6 Ne8+!

This is a strong defensive idea based on stalemate.

3 Bxe8 e3 4 d7!

4 Bb5? e2 5 Bxe2 is stalemate.

4...e2 5 d8N! e1N

The best chance as 5...e1Q 6 Nf7+ Kh5 7 Ne5+ Kh4 8 Nf3+ wins the queen.

6 Nc6 Nd3 7 Ne7 Nf4 8 Ng8#

6)

1 Qb4!

A wonderful move based on the theme of zugzwang. The idea is that White will sacrifice his queen and then promote on b8, skewering the black king and queen. For each of the moves of the black queen, there is a different winning line for White.

1...Qh1

White also wins after 1...Qg2 2 Qa3+ Kb6 3 Qb2+ Qxb2 4 b8Q+ Kc5 5 Qxb2 and 1...♕d5 2 ♕a4+ ♔b6 3 ♕b3+ ♕xb3 4 b8♕+ ♔c5 5 ♕xb3.

2 ♕a3+ ♔b6

2...♔b5 3 ♕b2+ ♔c5 4 ♔a7 ♕h7 5 ♕b6+ ♔d5 6 ♔a6 ♕d3+ 7 ♕b5+ and White wins.

3 ♕b2+ ♔c7 4 ♕h2+!

The real pearl of the study is this skewer on the diagonal.

4...♕xh2 5 b8♕+ ♔c6 6 ♕xh2

White wins.

Chapter 3

1)

This is a classic example: **1 ♗c5! ♗b6 2 ♕f4+!** followed by ♕xd6, winning.

2)

1 ♖c7 ♕xh5 2 ♖e7+ ♔f8 3 ♖xb7+ ♔e8 4 ♖e7+ ♔f8 5 ♖xh7+

Note that 5 ♖xa7+? is a great mistake as 5...♔e8 6 ♖e7+ ♔f8 is only a draw since 7 ♖xh7+? loses to 7...♖xa3.

5...♔e8 6 ♖xh5

White has a won ending.

3)

1...♕d5 2 ♗c4 ♖xf1+ 3 ♕xf1 ♖xf1+ 4 ♔xf1 ♗b5

Black wins.

4)

1 e6 ♗xe6

1...fxe6 loses to 2 ♕xg4.

2 ♗d4 f6

After 2...♗g4 3 h3 c5 4 ♗e5 c4 5 ♗d1 f6 6 ♗xg4 White wins a piece.

3 ♕g4 ♔f7 4 ♖ae1 ♗xb3 5 ♕xd7

White wins.

5)

1 ♕f3

Or:

a) 1...♗xf3 2 ♖xf7#.

b) 1...♘f6 2 ♗xd5 ♕xd5 3 ♕xf6 ♖g8 4 ♖c8#.

1...♗xb3 2 ♖xf7+ ♗xf7 3 ♘e6+ ♔e8 4 ♘xg5+

White has a decisive advantage.

6)

1 ♗f1 ♗b5!

1...♗d7 loses to 2 ♘g5.

2 ♗g2 ♗f1 3 ♗xf1 g2 4 ♘g3!

After 4 ♗xg2 it is stalemate.

4...g1♕

4...♔xg3 5 ♗xg2 ♔xg2 6 f4 and White is winning.

5 ♘f5#

7)

1 ♗b2 ♖h6

Or:

a) 1...♖g6 2 ♖c8+ ♔h7 3 ♖h8#.

b) 1...♖g6 2 ♖c8+ ♔h7 3 ♖h8#.

c) 1...♖f7 2 ♖h3+ ♔g8 3 ♖h8#.

d) 1...♖f8 2 ♖c7+ ♔g8 3 ♖g7+ ♔h8 4 ♔a2 and White wins the rook next move (but not 4 ♔b1?, which allows Black a draw by perpetual check: 4...♖f1+ 5 ♔a2 ♖a1+ 6 ♔b3 ♖a3+).

2 ♖g3+ ♔h7 3 ♖g7+ ♔h8 4 ♔b1!

White wins the rook by moving his own rook next move. Note that after 4 ♔a2? ♖a6+ 5 ♔b1 ♖a1+ 6 ♔c2 ♖c1+ Black has perpetual check.

8)

Here are ten mating positions:

1) e5, exf6, fxg7, ♗h6, exf8♕#.

2) ♗h6, ♗xg7, ♗xf6, ♘d5, ♘xe7#.

3) e5, ♗d3, ♕xg6, exf6, ♕xg7#.

4) ♕d2, ♗h6, e5, exf6, ♕xg7#.

5) ♕d2, ♗h6, ♗g5, ♗xf6, ♕xg7#.

6) ♕d2, ♗h6, ♘h4, ♘f5, ♕xg7#.

7) ♕d2, ♕h6, ♕xg6, ♗h6, ♕xg7#.
8) ♘e5, ♘xf7, ♗c4, ♘d5, ♘xe7#.
9) ♗g5, ♗xf6, ♘g5, ♕h5, ♕xh7#.
10) ♘g5, ♕h5, e5, exf6, ♕xh7#.
Note that there is a mate in four moves!
11) ♘h4, ♘xg6, ♘d5, ♘xe7#.

9)

♖h3, ♖g3, ♖xg6, ♕h5, ♖e6#.

10)

9...♘f3#.

11)

8...♕xe5+ 9 ♘xe5 ♘xc2#.

12)

8...♘e3+ wins the queen.

13)

9...axb5 10 ♕xa8 ♘b6 wins the queen.

14)

6 bxc3 is the best move. After 6 ♕a4+ ♘d7 7 ♕xe4? ♘c5 8 ♕f3?! ♘d3+ 9 ♔d1 c2+ 10 ♔xc2 ♘e1+ the queen is lost. But you have to have seen the move 6 ♕a4+ to get full credit.

15)

Here we have a position where it is easy to go wrong if you do not keep calm at the beginning. I immediately started to analyse 21 ♕xg7+. This resulted in exciting variations that cost me half an hour, but in the end I could not find anything more convincing than a draw. However, there is an easy move to find that wins on the spot. 21 ♗h6 and 21 ♕xg7+ are the two candidates that you should have seen.

21 ♗h6!

21 ♕xg7+ ♔xg7 22 ♗xe7+ ♔h8 (22...♔h6 23 ♘f5+ exf5 24 ♖d4 ♕e4 25 ♘xe4 and

White wins) 23 ♘f5 (with many threats, including both ♘h6 and ♖xd7; instead after 23 ♘db5, 23...f5 disarms the attack) 23...exf5 (23...♖g8? loses to 24 ♖xd7 ♕xg2+ 25 ♔xg2 ♖xg3+ 26 fxg3 ♖xd7 27 ♗f6+ ♔g8 28 ♘d6) 24 ♖xd7 ♕c6 25 ♗xf8 ♖xd7 26 ♗g7+ ♔g8 and White has to go for a draw with 27 ♘d5 ♕xd5 28 ♗h6+ ♔h8 29 ♗g7+ ♔g8 30 ♗h6+.

1-0

Black resigned due to 21...♘xe5 (21...f6 22 ♗xg7+ ♔g8 23 ♗xf6+ ♔f7 24 ♕xe6+ ♔e8 25 ♕xe7#) 22 ♗xg7+ ♔g8 23 ♗xe5+ ♗g5 24 ♖xg5#.

16)

This example was given to me by Mark Dvoretsky in a training session. I immediately chose 1 ♖f8+ as the main variation. I simply could not stop calculating. However, the move has a drawback and when I discovered that, I had to take a step back and start to search for other candidates. To get full credit you should have looked at 1 ♖f8+, 1 ♕c3 and 1 ♕b4.

1 ♕b4!

1 ♖f8+? ♖xf8 2 b8♕ is met by 2...♕f6! (threatening both 3...♖xb8 and 3...♕f2+) 3 ♕xa7 ♗d3, when the mating threat on f1 decides the game. When I had seen this, I started to analyse 1 ♕c3!? and I saw that after 1...♕a5 2 ♕d4 ♕d5 3 ♕xd5 ♖xd5 4 ♖xe4 ♖xb7 White would be better. But is the extra pawn sufficient to win? Black has some pressure against b2. After a while you see that 1 ♕b4 gives a better version of the rook ending.

1...♕b6+ 2 ♕xb6 axb6 3 ♖f4 ♖xb7 4 ♖fxe4 ♖xe4 5 ♖xe4

White has got rid of the pressure against b2 and can now instead put pressure on the black b-pawn with, for example, the rook on b4. White is winning.

Chapter 8

1)

This was Ståhlberg's famous chance to go down in chess history as one of the few players who defeated Capablanca. He starts well with a series of explosive moves.

20 f5! ♘xf5 21 ♘xf7! ♖xf7 22 ♕xe6 ♘ed6 23 g4?

However, he now misses the quiet move 23 ♕e5!, which would have decided the game quickly. For example, after 23...♕xe5 (23...b6 24 ♗xf7+ ♔xf7 25 ♕xa5 bxa5 26 g4 and White wins material) 24 dxe5 ♘e3 25 ♖xd6 ♖xd6 26 exd6 ♘xf1 27 d7 Black cannot prevent the pawn from promoting.

23...♔h8 24 ♕e5

This comes one move too late to be really effective.

24...♕xe5 25 dxe5 ♘e3 26 ♗xf7 ♘xd1 27 exd6 ♖xd6

White still has a small advantage in the ending, but Ståhlberg, shaken by the missed opportunity, settles for a draw.

½-½

2)

1...d4! 2 ♘xe4 ♗xe4

When you look deeply into the position you realize that White has great problems. His pieces are pushed back and his king is weaker than you might think. Note that 2...♕xe4? 3 ♗f3 is bad for Black.

3 f3

Other possibilities are:

a) 3 exd4 ♗xg2 4 ♔xg2 ♕xe2 gives Black a decisive advantage because of White's king and his bad pawn-structure.

b) 3 ♗xa6 ♕g5 4 f3 (4 g3 ♕h5 5 f3 ♖c2 gives Black a mating attack) 4...♖c2 5 ♖f2 dxe3 6 ♖e2 (6 ♖xc2 e2+ 7 ♗e3 ♕xe3+ 8 ♔h1 e1♕+ 9 ♗f1 ♕g1#) and 6...♖d8 decides the game.

c) 3 ♕xa6 ♖c6 4 ♕a3 ♗c5 5 ♕a4 ♖g6 6 f3 ♗c6 7 ♕c4 dxe3 is probably the critical continuation. Although Black is a pawn down, he has great prospects: he has a dangerous attack and the e3-pawn severely restricts White.

3...d3! 4 ♕xe4

Black wins after 4 fxe4 dxe2 5 ♖e1 ♖xc1 6 ♖axc1 ♗xe3+ 7 ♔h1 ♗xc1 8 ♖xc1 ♕c5! 9 ♖b1 ♕f2 with the threats ...e1♕ and ...♕f1+.

4...♕xe4 5 fxe4 dxe2 6 ♖e1 ♖xc1 7 ♖axc1 ♗xe3+ 8 ♔h1 ♗xc1 9 ♖xc1 ♖d8!

Black will win by 10...♖d1.

Training and Playing Diary – Activities

Name				Year		Month		Hours during the month			

Note the sum of hours that you have put into chess during the month.

Day	Date	Normal games	Rapid games	Blitz games	Analy-sis of games	Open-ing analy-sis	Middle game work	End-game work	Play on the Internet	Other activi-ties	Lec-tures	Total for the day
	1											
	2											
	3											
	4											
	5											
	6											
	7											
	8											
	9											
	10											
	11											
	12											
	13											
	14											
	15											
	16											
	17											
	18											
	19											
	20											
	21											
	22											
	23											
	24											
	25											
	26											
	27											
	28											
	29											
	30											
	31											

May be copied for personal use. (From *Chess Training for Budding Champions* by Jesper Hall, published by Gambit Publications Ltd, 2001.)

Training and Playing Diary

Name			Year	Month	Hours during the month

Note for each day what your most important chess activity was.
For example: "Fred Smith – Joe Bloggs, 0-1, Najdorf Variation" or "Have been analysing Spassky-Fischer, Reykjavik Wch (1) 1972."

Day	Date	Hours	The day's main chess activity
	1		
	2		
	3		
	4		
	5		
	6		
	7		
	8		
	9		
	10		
	11		
	12		
	13		
	14		
	15		
	16		
	17		
	18		
	19		
	20		
	21		
	22		
	23		
	24		
	25		
	26		
	27		
	28		
	29		
	30		
	31		

May be copied for personal use. (From *Chess Training for Budding Champions* by Jesper Hall, published by Gambit Publications Ltd, 2001.)

Index of Players

When a player's name appears in **bold**, that player had White. Otherwise the first-named player had White.

Index of Composers

Index of Openings

Numbers refer to pages. Codes are ECO codes.